Sedona
City of the Star People

Christine + Joni
Thank for visiting the
City of the Star People
Namaste,

Mark Ho...

Sedona: City of the Star People

ISBN 978-1-939149-54-1

Printed in the United States of America

Blue Desert by Roger Dean
www.RogerDean.com
Photos by Mark Amaru Pinkham
unless otherwise stated

Cover by Mark Amaru Pinkham

Published by
Adventures Unlimited Press
One Adventure Place
Kempton, Illinois 60946 USA
auphq@frontiernet.net
www.adventuresunlimitedpress.com

Other books by Mark Amaru Pinkham
THE RETURN OF THE SERPENTS OF WISDOM
CONVERSATIONS WITH THE GODDESS
THE TRUTH BEHIND THE CHRIST MYTH
GUARDIANS OF THE HOLY GRAIL
WORLD GNOSIS: THE COMING GNOSTIC CIVILIZATION

Sedona

City of the Star People

by
Mark Amaru Pinkham

Dedicated
to the
King of the World
and his special people,
the Yezidis, Hindus and Hopis

Acknowledgments

A huge thank you goes to the following for their contributions to this book: Larry Welker, Kurt Bagley, Onnie Kahlenberg Gutierrez, Nicholas Mann, Irv Lefberg, David Vatz, Roger Dean, Ani Williams, Enocha "Ranjita" Ryan, Sakina Blue-Star, Jess Kalu, Peter Sterling, Devara ThunderBeat, Shekina Rose, Lane Badger, my beloved teacher Amma, and my wonderful wife, Andrea, the "wind beneath my wings."

Adventures Unlimited Press

wwwAdventuresUnlimitedPress.com

Table of Contents

Introduction

Chapter I: The Land of Oz.. ....pg 1
My Arrival in OZ; The Canyon of the Temples; Keller, Bryant, Albion and the Sedona Vortexes

Chapter 2 The Sedona-Mu Connection...pg 24
A Lemurian Lifetime Revealed; Edgar Cayce, Williamson, et al; Sedona's Crystal City; Psychic Archaeology; James Churchward and the American Southwest; Sedona's Hindu Connection; Sedona's Electromagnetism; The Pentagram and Hexagram of Sedona; Sedona and the Kumaras from Mu

Chapter 3: The Center of the Universe...pg 73
Our Anasazi Snake Clan Guide; Going Home to Hopiland; Tuwanasavi: The "Center of the Universe;" Sip-Oraibi: "Where land first became solid;" The Orion Zone

Chapter 4: The King of the World..pg 96
Real Encounters with Masau'u; A Real Encounter with the Peacock King; The Planetary Logos; The "Fall" and the Trident; Real Encounters with Sanat Kumara; The People of the Peacock Angel; The Royal Road of the King

Chapter 5 The Great Flood...pg 155
Sedona's Flood History; Worlds, Deluges and Temples; Native American Legends of the Underworld

Chapter 6 Palatkwapi: City of the Star People......................pg 168
Who were the Star People?; The Star Nations & Their Missionaries; The Location of Palatkwapi; Building Palatkwapi; The Destruction of Palatkwapi

Chapter 7: Sedona's Court of the King..................................pg 192
The Ancient Of Days; The Knights Templar and The King of the World; The Discovery of Boynton Canyon's Court of the King; The Court of Masau'u, Sanat Kumara, and the Peacock King

Chapter 8: The Sedona Grid...pg 215
The Spine, Chakras & Leylines of Sedona; The White House and The Court of the King; The Sedona Grid and The Tree of Life

Chapter 9: Sedona and the World Grid..............................pg 243
The Etheric Bodies of Earth; Revival of the World Grid; Sedona and the Arizona State Grid; Sedona: Root Chakra of the Earth; Masau'u and his "Twin," Pahana; The Chakras of the Planetary Logos; The Spine of the Sub-Continent of India

Chapter 10: The Redemption of the King and his People...............pg 259
Sanat Kumara also reigns in Sedona as Amitabha; 12-21-2012: Beginning the Fifth World in Sedona; The Hindus identify the Peacock Angel as their Sanat Kumara; When the Hindus and Yezidis were ONE PEOPLE; The Yezidis Come Home to Sedona

Chapter 11: The Return of the Star People & King of the World....pg 279
Hopi, Yezidi, & Tibetan Prophecies of the Return; The Second Coming of Christ?; Interview with Zuni Elder Clifford Mahooty; Interview with Yezidi Faqir Kamal Kaso; The Current Return of the Peacock King

Chapter 12: Interviews and ET Experiences of Sedonians..............pg 303
Ani Williams; Enocha "Ranjita" Ryan; Sakina Blue-Star; Jesse Kalu; Peter Sterling; Lyssa Royal Holt; Devara ThunderBeat; Shekina Rose; Lane Badger; Kurt Bagley

Footnotes: ....pg 347

Author pages:...pg 350

Introduction

Sedona: City of the Star People is a chronology of events that transpired in my life between February 1987 and May 2015. During this period I was led to the discovery that Sedona sits upon the foundations of a very ancient lost city of the Star People. I have learned that this ancient city of extraterrestrials is known in Hopi legend as Palatkwapi, the "Red House," and described as a place where the Hopi Clans settled for a long period of time during their migrations. It was in Palatkwapi that the Star People, the Kachinas, taught the Hopis the mysteries of the cosmos and the rituals they continue to observe today. One of the Star People, Masau'u, the Ruler of the Fourth World, became the special patron of the Hopis, and it is he who still retains his court in one of the canyon vortexes of Sedona. I have discovered that Masau'u is known by many other civilizations worldwide by such divergent names as the "King of the World," the "Planetary Logos," as well as Sanat Kumara (India), Enki (Sumeria), Osiris (Egypt), Dionysus (Greece), King Melchizedek (Middle East) and the Peacock Angel (the Yezidis). Legends state that in a previous Golden Age this monarch united all the worlds' people as one, and it is he who is prophesied to do so again in the future

Only those events that have opened my mind to the existence of Palatkwapi, the Star People, and the King of the World are included in this book. The first part of the text covers my initial discovery of the City of the Star People and our planet's inter-dimensional monarch. The second half covers my discovery of the Court of the King, the Sedona Grid of ley lines and vortexes, and Sedona's status as Root Chakra of planet Earth.

I make no claims regarding the information in this book and its veracity. It is the account of my own personal journey, and the conclusions I have reached came through the experiences I encountered on that journey. Those who are on a similar path will resonate with the book and its conclusions. Please respect that all experiences are valid to the perceiver, even if they don't fit your personal worldview.

Mark Amaru Pinkham

Sedona, Arizona

June, 2015

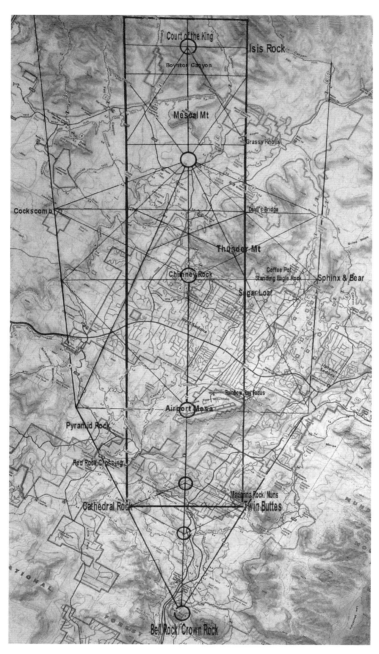

The Sedona Grid
See Chapter 8

The Land of OZ

      Each time I drive down the meandering road that leads from Flagstaff into the heart of Sedona via majestic Oak Creek Canyon I am overcome with powerful feelings of fate and destiny. "What new experiences are waiting for me?" "What will Sedona reveal to me this time?" Then, as the towering red rocks of northern Arizona slowly come into view and engulf me on all sides, those familiar feelings of stepping out of time resurface. I have been given the green light to enter one of Earth's sacred precincts, one of its vortexual time warps. Unseen forces will now usher me through an etheric gateway that leads into another dimension. A broader perspective regarding my present incarnation, as well as further insights into the secrets of the universe, will again be mine for the taking...

In this chapter:
* **My Arrival in OZ**
* **The Canyon of Temples**
* **Keller, Bryant, Albion and the Sedona Vortexes**

My Arrival in OZ

For the past twenty-seven years I have either lived in Sedona or regularly visited the magical city of red rocks. My first introduction to Sedona was in February of 1987, the much hyped year when a "Harmonic Convergence" was supposed to occur and propel us all closer to a heralded Golden Age. Ironically, my first visit to the one of the world's New Age meccas coincided with a belief crisis that had turned me off to nearly everything "New Age." My crisis had been triggered by false hopes and outright lies I received from a contemporary New Age prophet in my home state of Washington. This led to serious feelings of anxiety accompanied by some very debiitating depression. I decided that my best hope for complete healing was to simply get as far away from my everyday life as possible. So, arising from my easychair one bright February morning, I said goodby to my work, wife, car, beautiful log home and faithful dog, and then headed out the door in search of some answers.

In truth, I had no intention of going to Sedona when I left Washington. My destination was Mount Shasta in California, a huge vortex like Sedona where the Earth's energy is intensely concentrated and a seeker can both transform spiritually and find the answers they seek. After arriving at Shasta Mountain and being guided by the locals to the higher elevations of their towering "guru," I immersed myself in a series of daily meditations upon its lower, grass-covered slopes since the upper slopes were still covered with snow. My answer finally arrived via a whirlpool of energy that spiraled around my yogic sitting position and completely engulfed me. Its rapid motion made my inner world spin in synchronization and I soon lost consciousness, falling backwards onto the grass. I remained lifeless on the ground, for how long I can only guess. When I finally returned to normal consciousness I knew I had visited another realm where I had been engaged in a very long and in-depth conversation with another entity, a spiritual being of some sort. Many very high spiritual truths had been communicated; that much I was certain about. Unfortunately, as hard as I tried the only thing I could remember of the dialogue was that the entity would periodically tell me to "Go to Sedona." When I subsequently stood upright and surveyed the expansive California view of

2

mountains in front of me I knew that things were about to change. And they did. From that moment onwards I could get no more answers from the Shasta vortex. For all intents and purposes the mountain had shut itself off from me and I had no choice but to leave.

Two days later I entered Flagstaff, Arizona, aboard a public bus. My timing could not have been worse. The 7000 foot mountain town was in the middle of the worst snow storm in twenty years. And since there was not public transportation to my destination, if I wanted to continue south I was going to have to hitchhike the twenty or so frigid miles down through Oak Creek Canyon that leads to Sedona.

Needless to say I was very relieved when I finally rolled into the 4500 foot high desert town of Sedona. My euphoria was heightened by the sight of towering Cathedral Rock, one of the few red rock formations of Sedona I could distinctly see through the falling snow. My heart missed a beat when the driver of the unheated Jeep I was sitting next to loudly announced "Welcome to Sedona, the Land of OZ!" He might have actually meant "Awes" - I found out later that Sedona's common moniker is the "Land of Awes" - but at the time I could not imagine any place closer to the fabled OZ. And as far as I was concerned, I had just arrived there at the end of a very long Yellow Brick Road.

I was dropped off at the end of town at a small establishment called the White House Inn. My driver informed me that the location of this inn was convenient and within walking distance of most businesses in Sedona, and that the price was closer to my range (i.e., rock bottom) than most of the other hotels. So I with joyous anticipation of getting out of the snow and warming up, I rented a room and quickly disappeared into my heated abode.

The following morning brought the kind of bright sunshine I had associated with Arizona. Thinking that the snow would dissapear quickly, I strapped on my athletic shoes and got directions from the hotel's concierge to the closest "New Age" business, which as it turned out was just a few doors down. Although I never liked to stereotype myself as a "New Ager," I loved the exotic ambiance of New Age bookstores with their humongous crystals, sparkling gems, golden pyramids, billowing incense, and tinkling chimes that split the air with the arrival of every new customer. After entering the store I sauntered directly up to the counter and introduced myself as a "green tourist in search of answers." My spirit began to soar as the store clerk immediately reached under the counter and took out a large map of the four "major" vortexes of Sedona. As he laid the map across the counter the clerk explained that while Sedona is one huge vortex stretching more than twenty-five miles in every direction and currently subdivided into four major vortexes: Bell Rock, Boynton Canyon, Cathedral Rock and Airport Vortex.

When he ended his introduction my new mentor did something I have never seen a store clerk in Sedona do since. He pointed to one of the four major vortexes on the map and fervently instructed "You need to go here first!" The vortex he pointed to was Boynton Canyon, the biggest of the four major vortexes. My download was complete. As I thanked the clerk and walked out the door of the store my mind was already racing about how I was going to make the eight mile journey from my hotel to the canyon the following day. Of course my options were very limited; I would either have to walk or hitchhike.

That night the mercury dipped below freezing and all the snow that had partially melted during the day turned to solid ice. This included Dry Creek Road, the road to Boynton Canyon, which was now one huge sheet of ice. After walking briskly from the inn to the road I waited a few minutes with my thumb out, but to no avail. There were no cars coming my way. So I put on my stoic face and began what I truly believed was going to be a very long and cold eight mile hike.

After about five minutes I turned to see a car. I quickly calculated in my head my chances of getting a ride in the approaching vehicle. They weren't great. I was wrapped up like a plump Charley Brown with my face barely visible, and to make matters worse the driver was a female. So I was more than a little surprised when she slammed on her brakes and came to a sliding stop next to me. "Where are you going" she asked with a welcoming smile as I opened the passenger door. "Boynton Canyon" I stated. She flashed a big grin and announced "Get in, I am going right there!" With a sigh of relief I entered her warm car and together we began our cautious journey along the icy roads leading to Boynton Canyon. I was elated with my good fortune and couldn't help thinking to myself: "Something's up! This has got to be some kind of a sign!"

When we finally arrived at our destination my driver informed me that she worked at a new resort called Enchantment which was right next door to Boynton Canyon and then she left. Glancing around the parking lot I quickly found the trailhead into the canyon, and next to it was a large forest service map that revealed the course and length of the main trail. It was at least two and a half miles from beginning to end. I immediately felt very thankful that I had not consumed all my energy hiking to Boynton Canyon and could now use it on the trail.

Before entering the snow covered trail I paused and requested that my inner guidance "Please direct me to where I need to go." I then began my hike in the athletic shoes and light clothing that I had brought with me from Washington. Fortunately, I had had the sense to pack a down parka and wool hat just in case I needed them. They were to become my saving grace.

The Canyon of Temples

During the first forty five minutes of my hike into the Boynton Canyon vortex the rocky trail moved up and down while hugging the perimeter of what appeared to be a sprawling resort hotel. It wasn't long before my legs were tired and gimpy, so I stopped at regular intervals to ask my inner guidance: "show me where I need to go." Each time my prayer received no response, so I sucked it up and proceeded stoically onwards. Soon I found myself about a mile and a half inside the canyon and fully ensconced within its towering red walls.

As I continued onwards the vortexual power of the canyon began to move within me and I found myself alternately sobbing and laughing. Difficult memories of the past flooded my consciousness and at one point I almost turned around and fled, not knowing if I could handle it if my catharsis became more intense. But something inside drove me onwards.

Soon I spotted an attractive ledge about half way up the canyon wall. As I examined it from afar my inner voice finally awakened from its slumber and firmly instructed: "That is where you need to go." "Oh great, thanks a lot!" was my less that grateful response. A quick scan of the terrain revealed that the ledge could only be reached by bushwhacking through a thick pine forest of ankle deep snow before free climbing one hundred feet upwards on wet red rock.

An expletive-laced struggle dominated my ascent but I finally reached the ledge. After dusting off the newly fallen snow from both the ledge and my en-crusted blue jeans I sat down in front of a makeshift traveling altar that was com-posed of pictures of spiritual masters and deities that had been my constant com-panion and guides during my belief crisis. Closing my eyes I began what had become my familiar prayer: "Give me something to believe in again." Not more than 30 seconds later my inner voice spoke again; clearly and calmly it instructed: "look in front of you." I opened my eyes and there, across from me, appeared be two very commanding and stylish red rock columns projecting towards me from the canyon wall. They were gigantic; I estimated each to be about two hundred feet in height. They also appeared to be unnatural and possibly created with the help of a divine intelligence or even human intervention. An involuntary "Oh my God…" exited my mouth.

Glancing around the canyon I quickly understood why I had been guided to my ledge. From its vantage point I had a bird's eye view of the canyon and I could easily discern a variety of unusual shapes covering it. Punctuating the pan-orama in front of me were what appeared to be temples carved out of red rock. They were of every shape and size, and some appeared to have symbols covering them. Taking out the small pair of binoculars I had had the foresight to bring with me I was able to confirm my vision. My eyes were definitely not paying tricks. The temples were indeed there. Without hesitation I officially dubbed Boynton Can-yon the "Canyon of Temples."

There was no question that the red rock temples looked man made. But if they had been carved by human hands, who could have made them? There was certainly nothing about them or their builders in the tourist guides I had picked up about Sedona. Their design was intriguing, even mesmerizing. Their closest ana-logue were some intricate Hindu temples I had seen during my visits to India. I told myself that if I could only identify their symbols I might be able to determine their architects. But then, on closer examination, I discovered that although their crosses, swastikas, circles, triangles and other geometrical shapes were characteristic of Hindu temples, they were also universal and not limited to any one culture. Then I noticed that situated between some of the temples were tall red statues also carved

The Pillars of Boynton Canyon

Symbol of a Colony of Mu

from the native red rock. "Perhaps they can give me the information I seek," I told myself. These statues were of females with calm, peaceful and joyful faces who carrried baskets full of fruits and vegetables in their arms and upon their heads. I must have risen straight up from my seat when I realized that they also reminded me of India. They were nearly identical to some of the scantily clad tantric statues I had previously beheld in the country. "What are Hindu statues and temples doing in a canyon in the American Southwest?" I pondered out loud.

My eyes then caught sight of a small silver pyramid nestled between the temples and surrounding brush that possessed golden discs on all four sides. It was easy to spot because its color and matrix was incongruous with everything around it. It looked like a metallic temple, but also a spacecraft that at any moment could levitate off the ground and transport itself straight out of the canyon. I decided it must be some kind of ET vehicle and that space aliens had probably played a significant role in the creation and maintenance of the Boynton Canyon temples. Perhaps it would reveal more about itself at a later time.

The last significant image I observed before leaving my perch on that fateful day was a huge rock formation that hugged one of the canyon walls. It appeared to be an important symbol consisting of the large head of a man, perhaps Native American, upon which sat a much smaller head. I paused to analyze this anomaly before I clearly heard from within: "It's a symbol of a Colony of Mu."

This made perfect sense to me, and it also answered some of my mounting questions. It explained why the larger head had the features of a very ancient Native American, the original settlers of North American, and why the smaller head on top of it had a headdress that mirrored those worn by both the Polynesians and Tibetans, two cultures said to have originated on Mu. Having studied the civilization of Mu in depth for many years, I knew that missionaries from the fabled Pacific continent are reputed to have settled in Mexico and Peru, so they could have easily colonized the American Southwest as well. In fact, just before and during its destruction the missionaries of Mu had left their motherland in order to found colonies all over the globe. Legends of their migrations can still be found among the Polynesians, Hindus, Chinese, Peruvians, Mexicans and certain Native American tribes, especially the Hopis of Arizona who currently reside just a couple hundred miles north of Sedona.

It was definitely time a reality check. "This is crazy," I blurted out. "Maybe my inner voice is wrong. Intuition is not always foolproof!" That Mu had existed was certain. But its heyday was tens or hundreds of thousands of years in the past. Was I gullible enough to accept that the nearly perfect temples in front of me had been created by missionaries of a fabled continent that had vanished at least twelve thousand years ago? I decided to give my inner voice the benefit of the doubt, at least for now. So gathering up my belongings I resolved to climb down and give the Temples of Mu some closer inspection. For the rest of the day I was going to be the only kid in a gigantic candy store.

Since the huge pillars were close to me I decided to vist them on my way back down to the canyon floor. In less than fifteen minutes I was encircling them and closely examining their fine craftsmanship. I could not help but exclaim "these rival the pyramids of Egypt! And they are right in our own back yard!"

My euphoria soared as I left the pillars. It was a perfect day and every-thing seemed to be going my way. So I told myself "why not take the fast route to the bottom of the canyon even if it involves a risk or two?" I then began to climb down to the canyon floor via some very tall but thin pine trees. When their upper branches-and my ladder-suddenly ended, I decided to jump the remaining thirty feet and let the accumulated snow break my fall. The snow did indeed break my fall, but the hard ground underneath the snow nearly broke my pelvis and tail bone in two. So I spent the remainder of my day hobbling around with a pronounced limp and a recurring sharp pain at the base of my spine.

I remembered from my time on the ledge the general locations of the temples and traveled directly to them. But it was not long before I realized that either my bearings were completely off or the temples I had spotted were phan-toms. Perhaps I was "seeing things" from the ledge and they had never really existed. Or perhaps they are somehow able to move between dimensions and become invisible. Finally, a large solid temple appeared just a short distance from me. Accelerating my speed, I quickly moved towards it. But when I finally arrived it was gone! The rest of the day unfolded similarly. On numerous occasions I would spot what appeared to be a temple from a distance, but when I arrived at its location I could find nothing but non-descript red rock. My frustration sky-rocketed.

Since it was mid February the hours of daylight were very short. This was especially true in Boynton Canyon, where the sides of the canyon began creating long shadows as early as 3pm. So I was soon forced to make a hard decision. Should I stay and sleep in the canyon or travel back to my hotel knowing that it was potentially an eight mile trek? I was certain that I wanted to examine more of the canyon, so I decided to take my chances and look for shelter.

From my previous perch on the canyon wall ledge I remembered seeing a huge shelf of solid red rock directly across the canyon that was surmounted by a a gigantic monolithic rock with a distinct face. In order to protect myself from whatever might be lurking within the canyon that night I decided to climb to the top of the shelf and look for shelter there.

When I finally arrived, exhuasted, at the summit of the shelf I found the unmistakable monolith. Next to it was another red rock head that sat upon a pedestal as if it was on exhibition. Its distinguishing face and helmeted head made it look like eerily like an ET. I pondered whether the two monoliths might have been some kind of special deities or gods to the ancient natives. But regardless of whether they were or not, I decided that at least for one night they would serve as my own protective idols.

Adjacent to the "deities" was an ancient Anasazi cliff dwelling. I decided that if could scale the sheer twenty foot wall to the cliff dwelling it would serve as a perfect enclosure for the night. With great focus I struggled to reach my prospective lodging for about fifteen minutes, ultimately finding the wall to be a much better slide than a ladder. Finally, defeated and frustrated, I concluded that to get into their homes the ancients must have used ropes or ladders of some kind. Or perhaps they had developed supernatural power that allowed them to levitate up to them? I knew very little about the Anasazi, but I was already in awe of them.

I continued my search until I found a very small cave nearby that was easier to get to but could be only be entered horizontally by rolling into it. Once inside I found the ceiling of the cave to be only about two feet above its floor, so there was very little room for me to maneuver in order to find a comfortable

The idols of Boynton Canyon

position to lie in. There certainly was not enough room to sit up, so I decided to remain horizontal and end my day prematurely by trying to get some much needed rest. As I closed my eyes and laid my head on the sandy floor of the tiny cave I immediately noticed a very strange sound emanating from underneath the cave. A distinct humming noise, something akin to the sound made by a large generator, entered my ears and reverberated within my head. "Could there by a civilization underneath the cave and inside the red rock?" I murmured to myself. In light of the mind-blowing events of the day I was ready to entertain almost any explanation for the strange noise.

Ultimately, the rhythmic noise was overpowered by my own exhaustion and I was soon asleep. But my deep slumber was not to last long, and I was wide awake again within an hour's time. Bitter cold had awakened me. As I lay enshrouded in darkness I wanted to kick myself for not being more prepared. Even if it was Arizona, it was still the month of February! I never imagined that after the Sun disappeared below the horizon the temperature would fall thirty to forty degrees in the canyon. This was going to be a very long night indeed.

During my ensuing fitful night in the cave I would occasionally be awakened by the muscular spasms of shivering. Then in an attempt to get warm I would curl my body into a ball and unsuccessfully try to cover it with my down parka that had been my brother-in-law's and was two sizes too small for me. I would also try to completely envelop my entire head inside my wool cap. When I would finally find an acceptable level of warmth and drift off I wouild soon be re-awakened by more shivering. My yoyo experience continued throughout the night.

At the first sign of light the next morning I was outside my cave trying to quickly warm up by jumping up and down and soaking up the Sun's rays. I rationalized that my excruciating night had been an initiation of sorts; this gave some much needed purpose to my suffering. I told myself that I had been directed to Boynton Canyon to undergo a classic death and spiritual rebirth. I could now check it off my list and move forward into a new chapter of life.

Almost the same moment I began my descent back down to the floor of the canyon it became clearly evident to me that something had changed during the night. I wasn't seeing temples as I had the day before. The temples had been

13

replaced by the outlines of red rock formations that vaguely resembled temples, but they were definitely not temples. As the Sun brought more illumination to my surroundings it seemed as though I was in a new canyon altogether.

Even the brush seemed different. Navigating around it was more difficult and painful than before, and I repeatedly became hopelessly entangled within large clumps of it. As the sharp brush ripped across my bare arms, leaving bright red and inflamed scratches in their wake, I decided that my "honeymoon" with Boynton Canyon was definitely over.

Upon returning to the general area of the temples my disappointment plunged even further. Not only the temples but their corresponding statues were gone. Even the disc-shaped "craft," whose metallic exterior had sparkled so brightly in the sunlight, was nowhere to be found. Of course if it truly was an ET craft it probably had simply flown away during the night.

Dejectedly, I rejoined the main trail and headed towards the parking lot. But just as I was about to leave the canyon and begin my long detour around the hotel, I looked up at one of the walls of the canyon to a rock formation that gave the appearance of a rounded Roman Parthenon. Touching it was the large statue of a young boy with his left arm outstretched. He looked down upon me as if to say: " What you saw yesterday was no mistake, and there is more to see when you return here in the future!"

Keller, Bryant, Albion and the Sedona Vortexes

I spent three more days in Sedona in order to process my experience in Boynton Canyon and learn about the history, people and vortexes of the town. I remained hyper-vigilant of any person, place or thing that could give me some understanding of the temples I had experienced. But no one seemed to have the slightest inkling they even existed. The most affirmative response I received was from a long haired hippy-type guy in a natural food store who commented: "Yeah, sometimes people find red rock formations that look a bit like temples around Sedona." But although I came up short regarding the temples, I did manage to compile a workable data base of information regarding other aspects of the Land of OZ.

First of all I learned that Sedona has always been known as a massive energy center. The Native Americans referred to it as the "Land of Fire"[1] and recognize it as one of the most potent places on Earth. This was according to an article in *Sedona Life* by Heather Hughes entitled "Religion of the Red Mountains" that stated:

"Indian legend tells us that there are four places in the world designated as "power spots" and that these four are broken into two plus two - two positive and two negative or two "light" and two "dark." It is believed that the two "positive" places in the world are Kauai, an island in Hawaii...and Sedona, both red-rock countries. Sedona and Kauai, the Indians say, are vortexes of energy in which the Great Spirit gives birth to rainbows."

"Indians tell us that the towering crimson peaks stimulate sensitivity and that here a man realizes his true dreams and ambitions. They also say that the mountains are like a great magnet and that people are drawn to them because it is the home of the Great Spirit. Amid red-rock country, it is said that man comes face to face with himself and the potentials of his nature."

Sedona's recognition as a major vortex area began in the 1960s with a group of channelers from Phoenix called the Ruby Focus. This group of psychics had received instruction directly from St. Germain to acquire land in Sedona next to one of its power centers. They were told that their property was waiting for them at the base of Airport Mesa and contained a large four bedroom home on it; all they needed to do to was contact a local realtor. This was to be Mary Lou Keller, one of the founders of the metaphysical scene in Sedona and an active realtor who knew the exact location of the future Ruby Ray property from its description. Once the group subsequently secured the property and moved onto it the Ruby Ray group of channelers - led by Evangeline and Carmen Van Pollen - began receiving clear messages regarding the vortexes and mysteries of Sedona from an abundance of entities, including Saint Germain, Sanat Kumara and Sananda Kumara. Later, with the passing of its original founders the place was renamed the Rainbow Ray Focus. You can currently find the entrance to it marked by an unmistakable sign on the right side of Airport Road just before you reach the parking lot for Airport Vortex.

The members of the Ruby Focus had certainly been guided by their knowing spirits to the right realtor. The pioneering Mary Lou Keller, who was at the forefront of all psychic and channeling activity in Sedona, had been in Sedona since 1957 when the town was mostly a collection of uneven, dirt roads, wide open spaces, and home to less than a thousand inhabitants. Keller taught the first yoga and meditation classes in Sedona in the Keller Building, a fixture of the community owned by herself and husband Glenn that is now occupied by the storefronts of Hillside Court on Rt 179. The Keller Building would also become the first location of Sedona's Unity Church and the town's Center for the New Age. Mary Lou Keller was the first to distribute "vortex maps" of Sedona, as well as the first to offer Jeep tours to the power spots. She presented quite a spectacle as she drove her legendary tourqoius Jeep down mainstreet while dressed to the hilt in a tourqoise cowgirl outfit that included sparkling rhinestone boots and a cowboy hat. Through her long years of association with the Hopis, as well as her own explorations into the canyons, Keller came to know of many vortex points in and around the city of the red rocks, yet she was quick to admit that there were hundreds she knew nothing about. In her autobiography published in 1990, *Echoes of Sedona Past,* Keller plainly states: "There are more vortexes than *anyone* knows about in this sacred red rock paradise. And there are a lot of mysteries here yet to be solved."[2]

The current identificaton of Sedona's Four Major Vortexes became official in 1980 following the arrival of the psychic Page Bryant. Bryant was a popular radio and TV personality from the east who had grown tired of telling her audience about Atlantis and wanted some fresh esoteric material to regal them with. So she traveled out to Phoenix and its University of Light Church to speak to minister Alice Bowers about the mysteries of the American Southwest. Bowers sent Bryant to Sedona to talk with her good friend Mary Lou Keller, who in turn directed Bryant to some of the energy spots she had been told about and/or had directly experienced. Bryant made a point of traveling to each of these energetic areas and spending hours studying them as her disincarnate guide, Albion, informed her of their unique, energetic properties. Finally, at the conclusion of many long months of research, Bryant held a special channeling for a small group in November, 1980, during which Albion officially announced the existence of Seven

Major Vortexes in Sedona and their locations. They were Boynton Canyon; Red Rock Crossing; Bell Rock; Indian Gardens, which is located a few miles north of Sedona in Oak Creek Canyon; the hill upon which the Sedona post office is situated; Apache Leap; and the two red rock hills located next to the Airport Mesa.[3] In time, these seven would be consolidated into the four major vortexes recognized today: Boynton Canyon, Bell Rock, Cathedral Rock and Airport Vortex.

Accompanying Albion's revelations regarding Sedona's vortexes was an explanation regarding the special properties each contained. He was explicit that each vortex is either male or female, or "electric" and "magnetic." The male-electric vortexes are physically energizing and can be felt more perceptibly and in less time than the magnetic vortexes. They are better suited for sending magic and prayers into the environment, and stated Albion: "Such vortexes are appropriate for those who seek greater motivation in their lives and greater personal/spiritual empowerment."[4]

Bryant's guide then defined the effect of female-magnetic vortexes, which he described as more peaceful and meditative with a tendency to pull a person's energy inward and downward. They are excellent for connecting with the Earth, as well as moving deep within one's self, and they can open one to interdimensional vision and astral travel.

In Albion's classification of the seven Sedona vortexes only Rock Crossing was identified as a magnetic vortex. Later, when the seven major vortexes were reduced to four, Cathedral Rock was recognized as magnetic and both Bell and Airport vortexes were identified as electric. Boynton Canyon has always been special since it is the only acknowledged electric-magnetic vortex in the area. Its energies are continually moving both upwards and downwards. Albion claimed that Boynton was the largest of Sedona's vortexes, extending out "some twenty-five miles in all directions."[5] He thus implied that it is the center of the huge Sedona vortex, whose radius has been calculated to be twenty-five miles wide.

Albion's classification of the vortexes as electric or magnetic is very relevant to the tourists of Sedona because it is their electro-magnetism that most visitors initially experience. I personally experienced a manifestation of Sedona's

EM power during my first few days in the city while walking along the street. I must have presented quite a spectacle as I kept looking down at my feet to see if they were actually touching the ground! I felt as light as a feather and was sure I had to be walking on air. I also noticed my body straightening up as I walked; any tendency to hunch over was corrected. Apparently all the crystalline matrices of the body, such as the skeleton, slip into their most perfect alignment when influenced by a strong electromagnetic field like one generated by Sedona, and those people who have suffered with chronic health difficulties for many years can be magically relieved of them very quickly.

The source of Sedona's electro-magnetism is its red rock, which is full of iron ore and quartz crystal. When Earth's electro-magnetic field moves through Sedona it is greatly magnified by these substances. When our planet's enhanced EM field interacts with a person's own electro-magnetic sheath it produces many of the results volunteered by Albion.

The iron and quartz of Sedona also amplify the next level of vortex energy that exists just above the area's electro-magnetic field. This is the subtle current of spiraling life force that is generated by the vortexes. As this spiraling life force moves up and down through the red rock it is accelerated by the conductivity of the iron and ampllified by the rock's quartz crystal, thus increasing both its voltage and amperage. When Sedona's intensified vortex power moves through a person hiking or sitting upon the red rock its effect is much quicker and more powerful than that generated by a normal vortex.

Since the subtle life force current of the Sedona vortexes interacts with the subtle body of a person that exists just above their electro-magnetic field. This is a person's etheric body composed of meridians and chakras. When life force enters this body it both increases and moves the energy within it. Blocked toxins in a person can then rise to the surface of the physical body to be expelled, and all parts of the body can begin to operate more efficiently. Blocked emotions, along with the traumatic memories behind them, can also emerge into consciousness to be released.

The emotional "roller coaster" effect that can result from exposure to the vortexual energy was powerfully felt by me in Boynton Canyon, and it was later on display almost every time I walked down a street or hiked a trail in Sedona. I would pass people who seemed to be bursting with joy and skipping merrily along, but following them just a hundred feet away would be another person staring angrily at the ground while audibly railing against some person or thing in their life.

One of the significant effects the subtle power emanating from the vortexes has on a person is through the chakra system that lies along their spine. Since the chakras reside in the subtle body, when the dynamic life force power of the Sedona vortexes moves through the etheric body it can quickly and easily activate or/or further awaken them. This is especially true of two chakras: the Ajna Chakra or Third Eye and the Muladhara or Root Chakra. Activation of the Ajna Chakra endows a person with psychic perception and assists them in connecting to their Higher Self, other dimensions of the universe, and the Great Spirit. Activation of the Root Chakra will make a person feel grounded and more closely connected to the Mother Earth. It can also lead to the awakening of the inner Kundalini or Serpent Power that resides within the Root Chakra, thus initiating a person into a path of alchemical transformation that will eventuall culminate in enlightenment. When this evolutionary force is awakened it works day and night to purify a person, open all their chakras, and lead them to the pinnacle of human evolution. Since the Root Chakra is also continually stimulated by the red color of the rock, Kundalini activation is likely to occur within a person at any time in Sedona. It is because of this potential to activate a person's Serpent Power that Sedona has been called such epithets as the "Holy Grail," the "Land of the Serpent," and the "Land of Initiation." And it is because of this potential of the red rocks that they have, throughout the ages, been so sacred to the Native Americans. For millennia Native Americans have come to the red rocks of Sedona to begin their spiritual path with a vision quest.

Another burning question I sought an answer to during my three days in Sedona was regarding the history of Enchantment Resort I was forced to walk around to enter Boynton Canyon. I was both surprised and confused that those in political office, not to mention the unseen guardian spirits that oversee the area, would allow such a large, imposing resort to be built within national forest land and right on top of a huge vortex. As it turned out Enchantment was a newly opened tennis resort that had been constructed not on public but private land. In 1886, after thousands of years being overseen by Native Americans, the land was purchased by John Boeington, whose name (re-written as "Boynton") lives on as the canyon's appellation. Boeington built a ranch on the property, which was later purchased by a Montana rancher, the literary secretary of Zane Grey, who spent long periods of time in Sedona. The property was then acquired by tennis professional John Gardiner, the original builder of Enchantment.

I did, however, learn that the path to the construction of Enchantment had not been smooth. Boeington had apparently built a huge home on the property and dug up a Native American burial ground in the process. The land was subsequently cursed by a local medicine man and any further construction on the land was henceforth subject to tremendous obstacles and financial hardships. The medicine man's curse was first felt by John Gardiner's Enchantment; even the savings and loan that financed Gardiner's establishment went out of business. At one point Mary Lou Keller and a group of her metaphysical friends came to the rescue. They spent a day on the land while observing intensive rituals to neutralize the curse. But apparently they failed, even though one of them had a flashback of having been the old Native American that had originally summoned the curse. Some years later, in 1990, I discovered that Barbara and Sheldon Breitbart had purchased Enchantment, but they too suffered with their own set of problems and were eventually forced to return the resort to the holding company they had acquired it from. The resort was finally acquired by Enchantment Group, a luxury resort development and management company headquartered in Scottsdale, Arizona, with the stipulation that a local tribe of Native Americans, the Yavapai, be given unobstructed passage into Boynton Canyon so they could observe ceremonies just outside the grounds of the resort. So far, the spirits have been kinder to this group of owners.

One of the many electro-magnetic vortexes in Boynton Canyon.
This vortex sits between Kachina Woman on the left, the female or magnetic pole, and Warrior Rock on the right, the male or electric pole.

The twisted branches of the juniper trees located at the vortexes follow the spiralling path of the vortexes' power.

Mary Lou Keller in her famous tourqoius jeep.

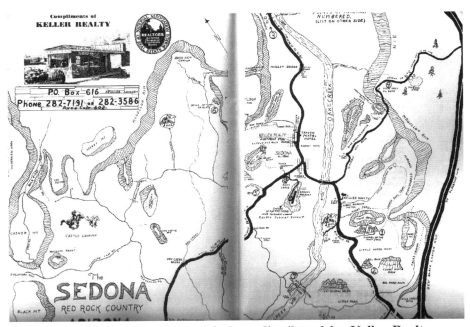

The first "Vortex Map" of Sedona distributed by Keller Realty
Courtesy of *Light Technology Publishing*

The Rainbow Ray Focus

23

The Sedona-Mu Connection

The existence of an ancient continent in the Pacific Ocean named Mu or Lemuria has intrigued me since I was a teenager. From the first time I heard the word "Lemuria" I knew it was my home, although I could not articulate why. I felt strongly that a special sweetness and love existed within the civilization on Lemuria that has not been replicated on the planet since the continent's demise many thousands of years ago. For years I have longed to return "home." But was Mu truly my home in the past or is it just a figment of my day-dreaming mind?

In this chapter:
- *A Lemurian Lifetime Revealed
- * Edgar Cayce, George Hunt Williamson, et al
- * Sedona's Crystal City
- * Psychic Archaeology
- * James Churchward and the American Southwest
- * Sedona's Hindu Connection
- * Sedona's Electromagnetism
- * The Pentagram and Hexagram of Sedona
- * Sedona and the Kumaras from Mu

A Lemurian Lifetime Revealed

When I finally left Sedona at the end of February 1987, I knew that my life's work, at least in part, was going to be dedicated to discovering the origin and purpose of the temples I had seen in Boynton Canyon. In fact, I was already making plans to move to my beloved Land of OZ. Since my life back in Washington had been a financial struggle for some time it was not hard to convince my wife, D.L., to put our log cabin on the market and begin making plans for a move to the American Southwest. I was tired of living hand to mouth as a stealthy acupuncturist who was forced to work "under the table" because I lacked the study credits to procure a state license, and Arizona did not require one at the time. Moreover, my passion was the practice of spiritual acupuncture that utilized a set of Taoist points for consciousness expansion known as *Windows to the Sky,* the points that had assisted Shirley Maclaine in seeing her past lifetimes. Thus, I was sure my work would be more in demand in a spiritual mecca like Sedona.

During my time back in Washington State I also inadvertently began a business selling copper pyramids. I had not set out to get involved in such an enterprise, but I wanted to acquire an all-copper pyramid that included copper corners and there were none on the market. When I approached a local welder with my dilemma he was happy to assist me but only if I ordered at least fifty sets of corners. I could then cut copper pipe myself to fit between the corners. So I decided to suck it up and try my luck in the business world. And, considering I had recently been receiving unusual crown, sceptor, staff and wand designs in my meditations, I decided I could also sell them as a sideline. I called my new mind-expanding enterprise *Journeys Beyond the Mind.*

For inspiration and inner guidance I kept up a schedule of daily meditation and by regularly hiking deep into the surrounding rain forest. Since my log cabin bordered on state forest I could exit the back door and hike for many miles without seeing a soul. I relished the experience of being completely alone and knee deep in ferns growing profusely amid towering evergreens and bowed alders that were completely enshrouded in emerald green moss. The shimmering display of nature in our backyard was both enchanting and transporting. I would sometimes find myself elevated into an interdimensional consciousness state wherein I could

25

see and commune with colored lights that would blink like massive fireflies as they passed in front of me. These, I was told by the locals, were a common form taken by the nature spirits of the rain forest.

On one pivitol day while trudging deep in the forest I suddenly became overcome with the desire to know my past lifetimes, as well as my destiny in the present one. I am not sure where this desire came from. I certainly hadn't waked up with it that day or even left the house with it. Nor had I recently spent an inordinate amount of time contemplating these issues. But I have learned that when such burning questions arise within me they can become obsessive and even destructive if not acknowledged. So I decided to make the day's mantra "Why did I choose this life, and how is my present lifetime connected to my past?"

Although it began quietly, my mantra quickly gathered intensity. A few minutes later I was threatening my informing guides that I was prepared to drown myself in the small stream that ran parallel to my trail unless my questions were answered immediately. In hindsight I can see that this was a rather pitiful threat; the stream was only about eight inches in depth at its deepest point. But at the time I was completely ready to follow through with my threatened demise if need be.

Apparently sensing the gravity of the situation, my guides finally rose to the occasion. A familiar voice emerged inside, speaking slowly and clearly. "Okay," it said. "Calm down. Look ahead of you. See the hill? Climb to the top of it."

Were my questions about to answered? With great anticipation and joy I moved ahead into the sea of ferns and trees covering the small hill and quickly made it to the top. Again came the voice: "See the ferns in front of you? Lie down in the middle of them."

I patted down some of the bigger ferns and layed on top of them. Almost at the exact moment my head hit the ground I felt intense energy at the top of it. My topmost energy center, the Crown Chakra, was suddenly opened wide and energy was rapidly pouring into it.

I was being filled by a bright white light. It entered me while covering my recumbent body in a vibrant white shroud. It appeared that I was being prepped for a very unique experience.

What occurred next defies any rational explantion. To this day I struggle to understand it and very rarely speak about it.

As the white light entered my head it awakened a part of me that had been sleeping for thousands of years. My everyday ego that was Mark Amaru Pinkham, diligent neighborhood acupuncturist, disappeared completely and in its place was re-awakened royalty. An ancient king had suddenly been jolted back to life.

Feeling as though I had just come through the birthing canal for the second time, I struggled to get my bearings. The white shroud was fading but I still felt the electrifying white light pulsing within me from head to toe. As this raw power coursed through every cell it empowered me tremendously. I was sure I could create entire universes if I so desired.

Slowly rising to my feet I surveyed my "new" surroundings. I was anxious to explore this new playground I had just been born into; but, strangely, it did not feel new. My reborn royal persona instantly recognized it as a place it had walked thousands of years before. Powerful feelings of deja vu gripped me and I began shouting and punching at the air while repeating in a new and very strange voice, "It's great to be back! It's great to be back!"

Memories of my former existence then began to flood my consciousness. When I had previously walked those woods Washington State had been part of the great continent of Mu. Apparently I had returned to live in a remaining part of a continent that my "royal" self once called home.

I had been a powerful Lemurian king. Both the cosmic energy now coursing through me, as well as my new expanded awareness, had been my natural state of being. But I also knew that there had been many other empowered kings like me on Mu; I was not alone. I had lived during an era of God Kings descended directly from extraterrestrials.

I recalled reigning when the Pacific Motherland was broken into thousands of islands, each of which was governed by its own king; at least that was true of the larger ones. My island was a tropical paradise just off the coast of Asia. Governing all the island kingdoms and their associated monarchs was the King of Kings, an emperor who was both ruler of Mu as well as the entire Earth. He was the venerable King of the World.

Having been a voracious reader of esotericism for most of my life, I had encountered an ancient figure called "King of the World" many times in my studies. I remembered that this royal personage had been referred to by many names by numerous divergent cultures. The Jews had known him as King Melchizedek, the puzzling ruler who had been born without mother or father. The Hindus remembered him as Sanat Kumara, the royal Son of Shiva and Parvati and an Avatar who had come to Earth to teach the esoteric wisdom regarding alchemy, yoga and the path to human enlightenment. Modern occultists knew Sanat Kumara to be the founder of the Great White Brotherhood, the clandestine organization founded to guard and spread his most secret teachings around the globe.

"Wow..." The word kept trickling from my gaping mouth as I reflected on Mu's king and my ancient lifetime with him .

By this time I felt I had been fully consumed and transformed by the pure white light. It was time to discover how differently my physical, emotional and mental bodies would now function. So, with the enthusiasm of a magical child taking its first steps, I reached down and grasped my homemade staff. Holding it close to me I examined its regal design and, in a flash, clearly understood why I had been receiving the crown, sceptor and staff designs. I was remembering the articles that had once constituted my royal regalia.

As I resumed my march through the rain forest I felt weightless; the pull of gravity seemed less demanding. I stood taller and more erect than normal, and my gate was much more commanding. When I spoke out loud my voice was lower than normal, and it possessed an inflection similar to a thick English accent. But what impressed me most was my confidence level. I possessed a greater amount of both self-confidence and self-esteem than ever before.

Some dirt bikers suddenly appeared ahead of me on the trail. As they approached with their motors blaring loudly I saluted them as if they were my loyal subjects. They barely acknowledged my presence and quickly sped away, no doubt perceiving me as some demented forest wanderer, .

I then began receiving some strong intuitive messages regarding the second part of my question, the purpose of my current incarnation. I intuitively grasped that I was meant to play a role in the government of the new era, although what that role was to be was not made clear. Then I was told I had royal ancestors. I had incarnated into a lineage of rulers because I had contributed to their royal line when I was a Lemurian king and needed its DNA now to effectively serve in my future position. I was certainly not aware of any royal lineage that my family was associated with, nor did I believe I possessed the background or ability to work in a world government, or any government for that matter. So I decided to accept this latter psychic transmission with a huge grain of salt while acknowledging that psychic perception is not always infallible.

I continued hiking through the emerald forest with great exuberance, but soon the excitement of my reborn, regal persona began to wear off. As the afternoon shadows slowly descended over the landscape I found myself beset with both worry and fear. I certainly did not want to return to my former life as an acupuncturist. I was a king and the only thing I wanted to do, or believed I could do, was rule.

A bittersweet but comical dialogue began to occupy my mind. "Now what am I going to do? There are not a lot of help wanted ads for kings these days!"

Moments later my soothing inner voice came to the rescue. I was informed that my awakening experience had not been on the agenda for the day but my zealous determination had called it forth. Now I fully understood why such experiences are commonly withheld from most people. They simply would not want to return to the lessons of the current life which were essential for their soul's growth.

I was told not to worry. Like Dr. Peabody, my guides would bring Simon (me) back from the world he had become trapped in. It would take sometime, but it would happen.

And it did. After three days I was completely back to my normal consciousness and my mundane life as Mark Amaru Pinkham. I knew, however, that memories of the experience would last the rest of my life.

In the weeks that followed the faith in my past life recall began to waver. I decided that moments of denial following a person's first past life remembrance were not uncommon, especially when they become surrounded by "Devil's Advocates" and sceptics. When I first told my wife and friends about the experience their raised eyebrows and strained faces informed me that they were flabber-gasted that a grounded, educated person like myself could have been taken in by such a fantasy. But just when I would dismiss the experience as the fabrication of my very deluded and attention-seeeking ego I wouild relive the feeling of the white light coursing through me. I would vividy recall the unique royal persona I had embodied and the exuberant feeling of being awake on Earth again. And then the entire experience would again become undeniable. In the end, however, I decided I needed legitimate evidence for many of the psychic insights I received before I could fully embrace both them and the experience.

For proof I began by embarking in some intensive study on Mu and soon discovered a map of the continent of Lemuria published by the *Lemurian Fellowship*, an organization in southern California that claims to possess an abundance of information about Mu brought forth directly from the Akashic Records. The map reveals that the ancient eastern border of Mu once encompassed the west coast of the US, so it is certainly possible that thousands of years ago a Lemurian king could have indeed walked through the woods that are now part of Washington State.

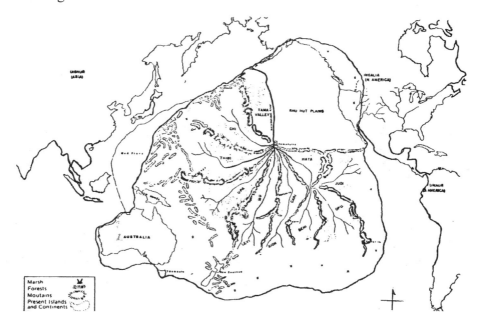

I also investigated my ancestry. I began by asking my father if we had any royal ancestors that he was aware of. All he could tell me was that there was a legend in the Pinkham family that we had descended from the Kings of Judea. That was it. If I wanted to know more I would need to do my own research. Some years later I did just that and discovered that two of my ancestors, John Pinkham and his son, Solomon Pinkham, had both married women from European royal houses that were indeed descended from the monarchs of Judea. John's wife, Martha Otis, was in a line that extended back to Tamra, a Jewish Princess who had escaped from Jerusalem during the time of Nebachadezzer and then married into the line of Irish Kings after reaching Ireland with the Prophet Jeremiah. The wife of Solomon Pinkham, Mary Fields, had been a direct descendant of the French House of Lusignan, which during the time of King Guy de Lusignan counted as its own the crown of the Kingdom of Jerusalem.

When I subsequently traced back the Lusignan to its origin I was amazed to find that it had begun with Melusine, a princess who possessed magical abilities including the power to shape-shift into a dragon. It is she with the lower body of a dragoness and a crown upon her head that is at the heart of the famous Starbuck's logo. Melusine was so dynamically powerful that many of the royal houses of France fabricated their genealogies in order to begin with her, although the only two houses that are currently accepted as her true progeny are the House of Lusignan and the House of De Vere. The Pinkhams are apparently descended from both houses.

After discovering a sorceress princess in my lineage I wanted to know more about her. Where had Melusine gotten her prodigious powers? Had she inherited them from my ancestors further up the genealogical chain? I discovered that before coming to France she had been a Scythian princess living in Scotland, a country her people had settled after migrating from Central Asia as one of the many waves of Scythian hordes that in Europe became the Germans, Slavs, and Gaels, to name a few. The orign of the Scythians in Asia is said to have been the region of Mount Kailash, where legend has it that in a fit of anger the mountain's chief resident, Lord Shiva, banged his matted locks upon the side of the precipice and thereby produced two great warriors. These warriors became the progenitors of the Scythians. This explains why the ancient Scythians had been called Jats, meaning "locks." The Scythians had been born from the locks of Shiva. Could this also mean they were descended from Shiva?

When I realized my lineage originated with Shiva I decided that it must be a metaphor because I did not believe that Shiva was ever physically incarnate. He was a transcendent deity. Then I remembered that in the Hindu pantheon Shiva's Son is Sanat Kumara, the ancient King of the World and another legendary resident of Mount Kailash. Having clearly remembered him as the principal monarch of Mu, I was now convinced that Sanat Kumara once possessed a physical form. So if Shiva had ever incarnated physically it was as his Son. Could this mean I was actually descended from Sanat Kumara, the ancient King of the World? I sincerely doubted it was possible to find corroboration for this notion, and I have yet to find any. I was, however, able to get my geneaology recognized by the House of Lusignan and am now a Knight of the Royal Order of Melusine.

Medal worn by the Knights of the Royal Order of Melusine

Princess Melusine and King Rainfroi de Vere

Melusine in the Starbuck's Logo

When D. L. and I finally returned to my beloved Land of OZ in October of 1988 we went straight to Airport Vortex in order to soak up some of the Sedona power and possibly receive some intuitive guidance about our new life in the American Southwest.

Upon arriving at the vortex we separated to find our individual "power spots." I hiked to a large medicine wheel I remembered from my first visit to Sedona that overlooked the entire southern section of the town, including two of the other principal vortexes, Bell Rock and Cathedral Rock. As soon as I sat down my mind began churning rapidly like a turbine, overflowing with possibilities. I knew that my principal "worldly" focus would need to be my acupuncture practice, but my spiritual agenda, and the one most dear to my heart, was the further investigation of Boynton Canyon and Sedona's link to Lemuria.

Then a very unexpected "AHA" crept into my consciousness that was clearly inconsistent with my other thoughts but certainly merited my attention. I was "told" that it was best for both myself and my wife if we did not live together. This was a bit of a shock, but as I recounted the recent events in our lives it made perfect sense. "But how do I tell her?" I asked myself. "Will she be heartbroken?"

Perhaps I should have expected this directive. I had recently read *Past Lives, Future Loves* by Dick Sutphen wherein the authors comments:

"Couples who move (to Sedona) either develop their relationship far beyond the original unity or they rapidly "come-apart" and go separate ways. There is something about the energy source of the area that no one understands."[1]

Even so, nothing could have prepared me for my wife's reaction once I returned to the car. I looked into her eyes and without saying a word I instinctively knew that she had received a similar revelation regarding our living situation. And the broad smile across her face told me that she was at peace with it. After verbalizing to each other what we both already knew, we climbed back into the car and drove off to find a second home for D.L. to rent.

Since Sedona was already brimming over with acupuncturists I proceeded to open a small acupuncture practice in Cottonwood, a town twenty miles to the southwest of the town. Meanwhile, all my other waking hours were spent exploring Boynton Canyon and researching its possible connection to Mu. I was in my mid-thirties with lots of energy and a foolhardy, intrepid spirit, so no wall or distant rock formation in the canyon was insurmountable for me. I felt invincible, a belief that was daily supported by the extremely dry red rock that grabbed the rubber souls of hiking boots like suction cups and allowed me to easily ascend, spiderman style, to the top of many precipitous canyon walls. Today, when I think back to the risks I took in order to reach the remote caves in Boynton Canyon I can only shake my head in disbelief, but at the time I justified my recklessness as completely necessary. I was on an important mission and truly believed that one or more of caves held some ancient Lemurian artifacts and/or written tablets that were waiting just for me. Even though such caves never materialized, at least I was successful in discovering many intriguing cliff dwellings unknown to most hikers.

I also expanded my investigations to include other parts of Sedona, especially those places where I heard that enigmatic rock formations with well-defined shapes existed. Acting on tips from other hikers, I was able to locate many unique-looking human heads, animals, and vague temple shapes, and soon it became evident that not just Boynton Canyon but all of Sedona had been colonized by a very advanced civilization in the distant past.

At the beginning of every month I made sure to acquire a copy of the monthly guide of events published by the Center for the New Age and then attended many listed events in hopes of finding people who were aware of a Sedona-Mu connection and could give me the benefit of their wisdom and experience. I must admit to hating the label "New Ager," finding it both demeaning and foolish, especially since much of the ideology embraced by so-called New Agers is patently old age and includes Yoga, Buddhism and Taoism. But I decided that if I was going to acquire the information I sought I was going to have to fit the New Ager stereotype....at least for awhile.

It wasn't long after I began attending the daily New Age events in the Sedona calendar that I met teachers and researchers who possessed the kind of information I was searching for. Some of the local visionaries, for example, were able to give me elaborate descriptions of the inhabitants of Lemuria. They informed me that the Lemurians had been highly advanced spiritual beings with the ability to both see and feel subtle energy, which is why they gravitated to those places on Earth where it was most concentrated, like Sedona. Upon arriving at these energetic locations the Lemurians could download psychic blueprints of sacred geometrical temples that would assist them in harnessing, stabilizing, conducting and amplifying the power of the vortexes they discovered. In some cases, like the Gods of the Dreamtime alluded to in the history of the Aborigines of Australia (a country that was once part of Mu), these enlightened missionaries could even artificially create ley lines and additional high powered vortexes at will.

Most of the pertinent information I found regarding Sedona and Lemuria was principally channeled by the town's resident psychics, mediums and clairvoyants. I was told that that is the nature of obscure Atlantis-Lemurian history; one must depend on channels and psychics to tap the Akashic Records and fill in details that are missing from historical references and scientific inquiry. But since I was not willing to be completely taken in by potentially dubious information from unreliable psychics, I decided to supplement my intake of the local "brew" by revisiting some of the reputable psychics of the past century that had spoken extensively about Mu.

Edgar Cayce, George Hunt Williamson, et al

Edgar Cayce was one of those "reputable" psychics. The "Sleeping Prophet" will always be regarded as a "pure" channel because he brought through his other worldly information while his conscious mind was asleep. He was also a fundamentalist Christian, which precluded him from having access to any of the esoteric and "heretical" information that colors his readings.

One of Cayce's earliest readings alluded to the size and shape of North America circa ten million years ago. At that time, states Cayce:

"What is now the central portion of this country, or the Mississippi basin, was then all in the ocean; only the plateau was existent, or the regions that are now Nevada, Utah, and Arizona formed the greater part of what we know as the United States."[2]

Cayce was explicit that Arizona had existed since the dawn of human civilization and could have thus accommodated human settlements millions of years before the other states. Another of Cayce's readings referred specifically to an ancient Arizona-Mu colonization. In this reading Cayce mentioned a woman named A-mel-elia who was a priestess in the "Temple of Life" and facilitated communications between different parts of the Earth, including Mu and the American Southwest. During her time, states Cayce, "Arizona and Nevada (were) a portion of the Brotherhood of those people from Mu." [3]

Another famous channel and author with a reliable pedigree I revisited was the late George Hunt Williamson from nearby Prescott, Arizona. Until his death in 1986, Williamson was well known in esoteric circles both for having accompanied UFO contactee George Adamski to a pre-arranged location in the Arizona desert for a rendezvous with a Venusian spacecraft, as well as for having located a secret Lemurian monastery in the Peruvian Andes that had anciently been built by missionaries of a Venusian brotherhood from Mu. In his book *Secret Places of the Lion* Williamson includes information about ancient Arizona that he claimed some Venusians directly downloaded into his consciousness. His download included information about Venusians who anciently visited a large Lemurian colony known as "Telos" in what is now the northern part of the Grand Canyon State. Arriving aboard "Light Ships" and led by "Merk," the Venusians were met by "Sun Lady," who served as a special liaison between the earthlings and the visiting ETs. Working together, Merk and Sun Lady created a set of records called the "Telonium Tablets" that both recounted the Venusians' sojourn on Earth as well as the history of Venus and other parts of the galaxy. [4] A memorial was subsequently erected over the place where the Light Ships from Venus had landed, but unfortunately time has not been kind to it. Both the memorial and the Telonium Tablets are currently believed to be buried under tons of Arizona sand.

Merk remained on Earth until the final days of Mu, when cataclysmic waves and floods sank the last vestiges of the once great Pacific continent. Telos was the only part of Mu to survive the destruction. According to Williamson, many thousands of years later when the Spanish explorer Coronado came looking for gold in the American Southwest he was actually following up leads he had received regarding Telos, which was then identified as one of the Seven Golden Cities of Cibola.. He kept going when he arrived in the Sedona-Verde Valley area because the real Telos did not look anything like the golden metropolis he was searching for. In truth, Telos's "gold" was the hidden Telionium Tablets.

I found that both Cayce and Williamson were popular among the esoteric historians of Sedona in the 1980s, so it was easy to find like-minded individuals to discuss the area's occult past. When I eventually concluded that there were enough of them in the area to warrant the creation of a regular group, I founded "The Ancient Mysteries of Sedona." I chose my own home as the venue for the first meeting of the group, and to insure it was a success I invited as our premier guest speaker a new friend of mine, local psychic and ET expert Tom Dongo.

Having previously taken a hike with Tom in nearby Fay Canyon and being acquainted with some of his extraterrestrial experiences and visions of Sedona, I knew he would be a crowd pleaser. Tom was the first person I had met in the area who had, like myself, encountered etheric temples dotting the landscape and similarly identified them as part of an ancient Lemurian city. I placed Tom in the category of credible psychics I had met in Sedona, probably because he had inadvertently and hesitantly accepted his psychic abilities. Not more than a couple years before he had been living a mainstream life in Reno, Nevada, with absolutely no "New Age" predilections whatsoever. The psychic world was, in a way, suddenly thrust upon him, and he seemed very grounded and matter-of-fact about his new calling.

At the lightly attended premier meeting of our group Tom shared information and anecdotes from his recently published book, *THE MYSTERIES OF SEDONA: THE NEW AGE FRONTIER*, that was a compilation of both his and other people's interdimensional and ET experiences in the Land of Oz. Like myself, he felt a strong pull to Boynton Canyon and had spent an inordinate amount of time investigating its mysteries. Being able to see energy, Tom had discovered a portal in the canyon through which ETs and other interdimensional beings were able to come and go at will. This included the "Rock People," which he learned were known about by the local Native Americans as the "Wapeka." I was particularly amused by Tom's description of a race of three-foot tall, green-colored ETs he occasionally saw dancing in front of unsuspecting hikers while making the kind of comical faces typically exhibited by pre-pubescent children. Thinking that Tom was no more able to see them than the other hikers, they would also make their crude faces while looking directly at him. But then Tom would turn the tables and make the same faces right back at the little tricksters. Startled, they would jump away and quickly disperse into the safety of the surrounding brush.

Tom also gave us a preview of his next two books that were to be sequels of his first one and go into much more detail regarding the ET encounters reported in Sedona. Entitled *THE MYSTERIES OF SEDONA PART II & PART III,* these later books recount Tom's personal experiences of UFOs as well as those of the locals. Tom told us of flying silver saucers having been sighted by a group of men hiking in the back of Boynton Canyon thereby ostensibly confirming my own initial UFO sighting in the canyon. He continued to keep us spellbound when he next recounted the amazing Boynton Canyon experience of Sharon Forrest, an energy healer from Montreal, who was teaching a seminar in Sedona for forty-six students. During one day when the group visited Boynton Canyon Sharon found herself and a student below Kachina Woman, a tall red rock formation near the beginning of the canyon's trail, while she shared her desire to stand at the top of the eighty foot tall edifice. In the next moment they were both there! Then, after enjoying the view at the summit for a few moments, they began to deliberate on how to get down. In an instant they were transported back to their original place below Kachina Woman. There they were met by one of the other students who having witnessed the event excitedly began inquiring what special ability had allowed them to dematerialize and then rematerialize on top of Kachina Woman. While he questioned them the two women were again teleported. This time when they opened their eyes they were back in the parking lot!

In his popular books Tom delineates three kinds of UFOs that are most consistently encountered in Sedona and the outlying areas. The first type manifests as a "large ball of white light with a much smaller red ball of light attached to it." The smaller sphere is often seen to separate from the white ball and fly around while the larger sphere remains in one place. A second kind of UFOs manifests as a triangular-shaped craft. These crafts are not to be played with as they are typically associated with the "most sinister" of encounters. And the third kind is a huge disc-shaped craft, more than 100 yards in diameter, that suddenly appears above the observer.[5]

Sedona's Crystal City

Tom's enlightening presentation gave me fresh inspiration to resume my esoteric research into the mysteries of Sedona. With abandon, I opened myself to another wave of psychic information regarding a crystal city located directly beneath the Land of OZ. I first found mention of this city and its crystals through studying the transcripts of Dick Sutphen's Seminars which were held annually at one of the local resort hotels. During his seminars Sutphen, who eventually came to believe that Sedona is "situated over an ancient Lemurian city,"[6] would hypnotize the participants in order to extract from them psychic information regarding the Red Rock Country. I was particularly intrigued by these transcripts because they referred to an abundance of crystals, both physical and etheric, in Boynton Canyon. An example of Sutphen's extracts is from a woman named Helen C. Fredericks, who received the following download while in Boynton Canyon:

"Boynton Canyon is the center of the Inner City. Here is the purification center...This will be the center of the coming age. Once again the people of Mu will switch frequency and lead the populace to peace, harmony and a high spirituality. ..The Inner City is now used as a monitoring center of earth. The large crystal controls all activity. The red earth carries the healing energies of the crystal to all who seek it. Each is drawn to the spot of frequency closest to their own....The maze of tunnels covers the whole area...."[7]

The psychic insights of Fredericks and other attendees of the Sutphen Seminars were later confirmed by a couple of Sedona's internationally known and reputable psychics. The first was Robert Shapiro, whose spirit guide Zoosh announced to a local audience:

"Under that area (Boynton Canyon) there are crystal streams, so it is like the ultimate antenna. Anything that is going on energetically nearby may be affected or amplified... Underneath this enchanted area there is a spider web of crystal veins that run deep, creating a "dish antennae"...It can both radiate and receive...Much of the crystal web is etheric, so one might have occasional feelings of what could be misinterpreted as ghost energy."[8]

Zoosh's pronouncement was echoed by Vywamus, the spirit channeled by another famous psychic, Janet McClure. Vywamus borrowed McClure's body to tell a small gathering that a "Crystal City lies under Sedona." According to him, this city had anciently been "carved out" by ETs using alien technology and later provided sanctuary for those escaping some threatening events on the surface of Earth.

The garrulous Vywamus also stated that Sedona had been the site of a very ancient city, ostensibly Lemurian, that served as a "forerunner of what would occur in the Atlantean era." The city was "spiritual in nature and quite lovely, (and) endured for approximately four hundred thousand years." Added Vywamus: "One reason the energies are so strong (in Sedona) is because of many spiritual events that happened (there)."[9]

Thus, a plethora of psychics all confirmed the existence of Sedona's "Crystal City." I was hooked on its existence. But I also decided I would need confirmation from credible, scientific sources, if I was going to completely "buy into it."

Some scientific confirmation would soon come my way in the form of a report prepared for the Department of the Interior by the United States Geological Survey. While testing the geological strata of the area's vortexes, or as the team called them, "electromagnetic "anomalies," a group of experts not only determined the existence of a huge layer of crystals underneath Sedona, they also theorized that this layer might even be the principal source of Sedona's electromagnetic power. The conclusion of their report states:

"A Precambrian crystalline basement is the most likely source of the broad magnetic high in the Sedona area. The long-wavelength nature of the magnetic high indicates that the [crystal] source of the anomaly is buried [underground]."

Although I was excited by this news, my exhuberance was tempered by the fact that if the Crystal City was indeed solely underground I doubted whether I or anyone else would ever discover it. So its existence would forever remain dubious. But then my perspective broadened when I attended a full moon meditation in Boynton Canyon that was led by Sakina Blue-Star, a middle-aged Native American woman of Lakota-Cherokee descent and a long time resident of Sedona. Before beginning a guided meditations for a small group of myself and about twenty-five other participants, Sakina shared that Sedona was anciently known as

"Nawanda" and visited by native clans and tribes from all over the Americas. According to her, during the time of Mu Sedona was an island surrounded by water and known as the "Crystal City of Light," a moniker that apparently referred to its abundance of quartz crystal-infused sandstone. And then, as if she were speaking directly to me, she added: "The Red Rocks of Sedona were the sacred Temples of the Ancients." I was so impressed by Sakina's insights that a few days later I visited her at her small home in Sedona. When I told her of my visions of the red rock temples she flashed a knowing smile and congratulated me for having been blessed by the Kachinas. As we parted she encouraged me to remain open for future revelations (see my interview with Sakina in Chapter 12).

Sakina's insights answered questions I had regarding both the red rock temples as well as Sedona's Crystal City. I now acknowledged that my quest for the Crystal City did not need to be limited to Sedona's subterannean foundations, but could also include its above-ground structures. With this new-found perspective I began scanning Boynton Canyon for large crystals. My gaze naturally gravitated upwards, where the towering white sandstone took the shape of striated columns and finger-like projections that resembled gigantic crystals. And then it finally hit me. I knew from seeing the glittering sand and rocks in Boynton Canyon that its sandstone possessed a very high concentration of quartz, so what appeared to be crystals really were. Feeling a bit embarrassed I now realized that the Crystal City had always been right in front of me and I did not even know it!

Psychic Archaeology

Soon after my "discovery" of the Crystal City I found a book that spoke to my current approach in uncovering the mysteries of Sedona and even gave it a name. Entitled *Psychic Archaeology,* the book was authored by a man in Arizona who had been able to form a reliable bridge between psychic information and scientific evidence. He had achieved great success through the same approach as myself, and I hoped to be able to follow in his formidable footsteps.

The author of the book was Jeffrey Goodman, a credible scientist with advanced degrees in archaeology, anthropology and geology, who like myself was led by psychic clues to discoveries that were later confirmed scientifically.

"The Red Rocks of Sedona were the sacred Temples of the Ancients."

Photo by Lynn Seivwright Koch

The Crystal City of Sedona

The Crystal Mountain

While a student of archaeology at Northern Arizona University during the early 1970s Goodman befriended a psychic who assisted him in his quest of finding remains of the oldest civilizations in the American Southwest. The psychic, Aron Abrahamsen from Oregon, possessed both intuitive and scientific credentials that included aerospace engineer for one of the principal contractors involved in the first moon landing. Under Abrahamsen's intuitive guidance, Goodman was led to a plot of land near Flagstaff where he dug a pit twenty feet deep before discovering some very ancient, manmade stone tools. The recovered tools were dated to 100,000 years in age just as Abrahamsen had predicted. In his very next communication Abrahamsen told Goodman to "rejoice." He had discovered the remains of a Lemurian civilization that was from 50,000 – 500,000 years old!

In the years that followed Jeffrey Goodman contacted and worked with other renowned psychics with equally efficacious results. One psychic led Goodman to a site in the nearby San Francisco Peaks where local Hopis informed him their ancestors had once lived. Goodman's ensuing excavation uncovered a chipped blade that has since been dated to 125,000 years by Dr. Thor Karlstrom, a senior geologist.

Then in 1979, as icing on Goodman's expanding cake, the excavation near Flagstaff produced yet another priceless artifact through the assistance of Dr. Alan Bryan of the University of Alberta. Working alongside Goodman, Dr. Bryan and his team found an engraved stone 23 feet below the surface. Now called the "Flagstaff Stone," this artifact has been dated 100,000 years in age and according to Goodman is "one of the most important artifacts ever found in the whole world."

In *Psychic Archaeology* Goodman confesses to being over the moon with the results of his excavations in northern Arizona, but at the same time he admits that they were not altogether unforeseen. He had previously worked with Dr. Louis Leakey, the famous archaeologist who had traveled to the American Southwest in the 1960s with a mission to find signs of human habitation earlier than the accepted 30,000 years. Leaky found what he was looking for at the Calico Hills in California's Mohave Desert, where excavations exposed manmade stone tools estimated to be 100,000 - 250,000 years old. Goodman assisted Leakey in his excavation and then made the controversial claim that the tools were actually 500,000 years old. His assertion has, however, not held up well within the archaeological community.

Goodman was also aware of other anomalous archaeology discoveries in the American Southwest. One made during the 1960s in Northern Arizona pushed human occupation in North America back millions of years earlier than even Leakey's Calico Hills discovery. When plane trouble forced amateur archaeologist Eryl Cummings out of the sky, the author of *Noah's Ark: Fable or Fact* made an emergency landing on a dirt road along the Moenkopi Wash near Tuba City in Northern Arizona and discovered archaeological "gold." Cummings had located some fossil tracks which appeared to be that of a barefoot human child, and next to them were dinosaur tracks. He recognized the strata of the tracks as belonging to the Kayenta period, which occurred 190 million years ago. Cummings find was later corroborated in 1984 when archaeologist Paul Rosnau visited the area and discovered 60 human footprints, dinosaur tracks, and the print of a child that had apparently slipped and put his hand down to catch himself. Rosnau later published his findings in the September and December 1989 issues of *Creation Research Society Quarterly.*

The fossilized footprints of Cummings and Rosnau have been controversial and judged questionable in their likeness to human footprints, but a later discovery made in the American Southwest was more conclusive. A fossilized footprint was discovered in a wilderness area of New Mexico by a hunter in the 1990s that is a nearly perfect anatomical match to a modern homo sapien footprint. Known as the "Zapata Track," the footprint was studied and photographed soon after its discovery by an investigative team that included archeaologists Dr. Don Patton and Dr. Carl Baugh and determined to be as old as the Permian rock it was embedded in, or approximately 250 million years old. Unfortunately, the footprint was discovered on private property and its examination was cut short by the inhospitable land owner bearing a very large shotgun.

Recognition within the academic community for such anomalous finds as Cummings' fossil tracks and the New Mexico footprint are rare to non-existent simply because they do not fit the accepted scientific model of when humans are supposed to have occupied the Americas. A large tome full of discarded anomalous discoveries of this nature was published in the early 1990s by amateur archeologists Michael A. Cremo and Richard L. Thompson. Entitled *Forbidden Archaeology,* the book reveals an abundance of extremely ancient human fossils that have been discovered all around the world but later dismissed, ridiculed, hidden and/or convienently lost because they did not fit the current academic paradigm. Some of the discarded fossils found in the American Southwest include a fossilized shoe sole discovered in Nevada that was embedded in Triassic rock 213-248 million years old, as well as a fossilized shoe print discovered in 1968 by William J. Meister near Antelope Spring, Utah, that dates to the Cambrian period, 505-590 million years ago.

James Churchward and the American Southwest

I was more than a little delighted to find so much scientific evidence supporting pre-historic human settlements in the American Southwest. This evidence corroborated Cayce and Williamson's assertions. It also echoed the history promulgated by author Col. James Churchward of the British Army, the author of a series of popular books on Mu. Having been an avid fan of Churchward's books since my teenage years when I inherited a few of them from my grandfather, I decided to revisit the explorer who has, over the past one hundred years, done more than any other author to put Mu on the ancient world map.

Churchward's Mu books, which include *The Lost Continent of Mu,* and its sequels, *The Children of Mu* and *The Sacred Symbols of Mu,* were penned in the mid 1800s and quickly became required reading for all esoteric researchers. Churchward's books both recounted the history of Mu as well as the location of colonies founded by Lemurian missionaries in the American Southwest and other parts of the globe. Churchward maintained that most of his information was derived from stone tablets he had discovered in a monastery in northern India that possessed the inscriptions of Naacal (Serpent) missionaries from Mu. The discovery and translation of these tablets told the story of Mu and later inspired Churchward to embark on missions to many Pacific islands and pan-Pacific countries to corroborate them. After a few years of such expeditions he had compiled a data base of corroborating first-hand experience as well as authoritative texts

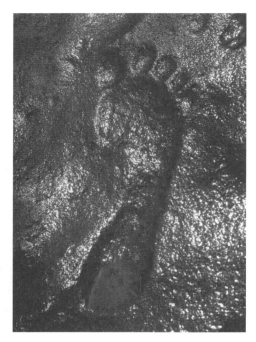

**Fosslized Human Footprint from New Mexico.
Discovered in Permian rock 250 million years old.**

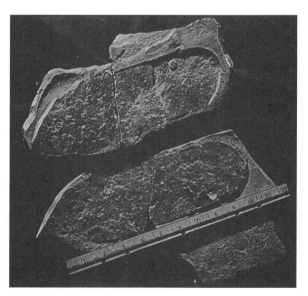

**Fossilized Human Shoe Print found in Utah
505-590 Million Years Old**

that included the ancient *Lhasa Record* that had been discovered in a Buddhist temple in Lhasa, Valmiki's *Ramayana*, the *Troano* and *Cortesianus Codices* of the Maya, the Easter Island Rongo Rongo tablet, 2,500 stone tablets discovered by William Niven in Mexico, and a historical record of the Nootka Tribe of British Columbia.

Churchward's revelations were a shock to the esoteric community, especially his assertion that Mu was the original Garden of Eden and at one time home to 64,000,000 inhabitants. He described the Eden of Mu as "...a beautiful tropical country with vast plains...No mountains or mountain ranges stretched themselves through this earthly paradise, for mountains had not yet been forced up from the bowels of the earth."[10] Perhaps most shocking was Churchward's contention that most of Mu's 64,000,000 inhabitants perished when much of the continent suddenly descended to the bottom of the Pacific Ocean.

According to Churchward many of the citizens of Mu that survived the destruction of their Motherland were able to establish colonies around the globe. Churchward personally visited many of these colonies which were located in such disparate countries as Burma, India, Egypt, Babylonia, Mexico and North America. Of these diverse colonies, Churchward states:

"...North America and eastern Asia were the two countries where (Lemurian) man made his first settlements away from the Motherland."[11]

Churchward arrived at this assertion through studying the Naacal Tablets and other texts, as well as by extensively searching for Lemurian remnants in the parched deserts, lofty cliff dwellings and pueblos scattered throughout the American Southwest. Eventually having discovered so many links between the symbols and legends of Mu and those of the Navajos, Hopis and Zunis he felt confident enought to proclaim:

"Various Pueblo traditions, their language, their sacred symbols and other evidences prove that the Pueblo Indians originally came to America from Mu."[12]

As to when the Lemurians may have initially reached North America, Churchward contended that their first migrations from Mu began 70,000 years ago, at a time that preceded the manifestation of the towering mountains that now punctuate the American Southwest.

In the last fifty years modern authors following in Churchward's footsteps have corroborated his findings. They have also revealed additional evidence for Mu and its colonies. One such author is the studious Stephen Oppenheimer, a British medical doctor who practiced his trade in the Far East while spending hundreds of off hours researching what was once an ancient corner of Mu in the region of Malaysia. In *Eden of the East*, Oppenheimer discusses this region, which he calls Sundaland because it sits upon the Sunda Shelf, and the civilization it once harbored. Oppenheimer contends that Sundaland was a huge land mass "twice the size of India" that united Malaysia and Indonesia and served as the Garden of Eden for the cultures of Southeast Asia. His research revealed that the flood waters that sunk Sundaland were the result of glacial melting during the last Ice Age. During the period that the flood waters inundated their land 18,000 – 7500 years ago, states Oppenheimer, the people of Sundaland left their doomed corner of Mu and as missionaries spread their culture, traditions, history and language throughout eastern Asia and those parts of Lemuria that are now Australia, Polynesia and Micronesia.[13]

In 1986 more corroboration of Churchward's sunken Pacific continent was discovered off the coast of Yonaguni, which is part of Japan's Ryukyu Islands. Next to the island and at the bottom of the Pacific Ocean is a group of columns, pillars and platforms that are so expertly cut that many archaeologists contend only human hands could have created. Dating back thousands of years and now known as the Yonaguni Monument, many divers, including author Graham Hancock, have studied these blocks and uniformly confirmed them as being artificially cut and the remnants of a very ancient civilization. Many experts on Mu currently tout these blocks as a "smoking gun" for the existence of a Pacific continent that anciently slipped below the ocean waves.

Churchward's work is also corroborated by the Hopis. In *The Book of the Hopi*, Frank Waters presents Hopi legends that positively confirm Churchward's assertion that "the Pueblo Indians originally came to America from Mu." Waters' legends maintains that the ancestors of the Hopis arrived on North American after "island hopping" across the Pacific Ocean. After reaching the shore of North America they looked back from whence they had come and watched in terror as cataclysmic waves consumed many of their island stepping stones. Their arrival in the Americas apparently corresponded with one of the many disasters that sunk Mu and began a cycle of time that the Hopis refer to as a "World." The arrival of the Hopis in North America corresponded to the end of the Third World and beginning of the Fourth World. Waters' legends also maintain that the Hopis took many generations to complete their journey across the Pacific, so even if they began their journey on continental Asia by the time they arrived in the Americas their culture had become Lemurian.

Sedona's "Hindu" Connection

Churchward's work also sheds some light on the Boynton Canyon temples. It is possible that they could have been built by the Naacals. According to Churchward, the Naacals settled in India after leaving their homeland of Mu, the continent that is today remembered in many Hindu scriptures as Kumari Kandam, Kumari Nadu, or Rutas, and referred to as the homeland of some very ancient misisonaries and colonists that arrived on the sub-continent. In corroboration of this truth, one ancient Tamil tradition of South India has published a map of India that shows both India and Sri Lanka united to Lemuria circa 30,000 BCE.

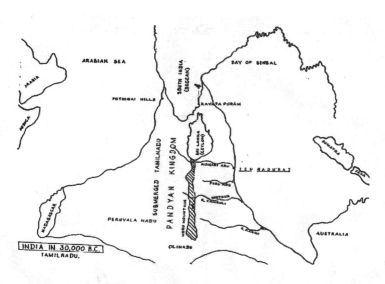

Map taken from *Ancient World* by N. Mahalingam

51

If the same Naacal missionaries of Mu also migrated to the American Southwest as Churchward asserts, they would have brought with the same building skills and symbols that they took with them to India. This would explain why some of the temples and columns I envisioned in Boynton Canyon possessed a salient Hindu motif. Such temples could have been designed and built by the same Naacal missionaries who built similar temples in India.

A popular symbol in Sedona that may reveal the city's ancient colonization by the Naacals and/or missionaries from India or Lemuria, is a pictograph attached to a wall in the Hopi-Sinagua ruins of the National Monument of Palatki, a sacred place once inhabited by the ancestors of the modern Hopis. Among the assortment of pictographs and petroglyphs covering the walls of Palatki, some of which have been dated back 15,000 years or more, is one that looks very much like the Sanskrit OM symbol of the Hindus.

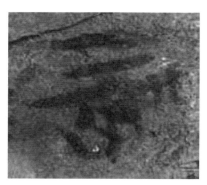

Pictograph at Palatki resembling the Hindu OM

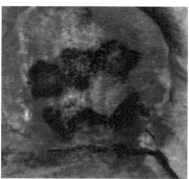

Symbol at Palatki reputed to be 15,000 years old

52

The very ancient and sacred site of Palatki

A Hindu style pillar stands at the entrance of Boynton Canyon

Sedona's Electromagnetism

My scientific research into the mysteries of the Sedona continued when I began asking rational questions regarding the area's strong electromagnetic force. Scientists have long contended that the electromagnetism of the Earth is created by its rotating iron core, and that vortexes or electromagnetic anomalies on the surface are directly or indirectly connected to this molten core. For this reason I was not completely content with the explanation for Sedona's magnetism in the report prepared by the US Geological Survey and decided to look further.

My new search brought me in contact with a book written by local author Richard Dannelly entitled *SEDONA, POWER SPOT, VORTEX, AND MEDI-CINE WHEEL GUIDE.* According to Dannelly the Sedona vortexes are directly linked to the center of our planet via the Oak Creek Fault, a seam of volcanic, basalt rock that rose from the center of the Earth to the surface. The seam begins in the volcanic region around Flagstaff, Arizona and then moves east as far as New Mexico.

In his own words, Dannelly explains this electromagnetic phenomenon:

"The Vortex activity in the Sedona area seems to indicate that the Oak Creek Fault allows an abnormal amount of electromagnetic Earth Energy to emerge from deep in the Earth.

"This energy is conducted by iron-bearing veins of basalt (lava), which were formed long ago during an age of volcanic activity.

"Oak Creek Fault gave birth to the most powerful mountains in Arizona – the San Francisco Peaks. These ancient volcanoes are located at the north end of the Oak Creek fault, some thirty miles north of Sedona near Flagstaff."

And in reference to the massive size of the Oak Creek Fault, Dannelly states:

"Oak Creek Fault runs right through the Sedona area at a right angle to the transition zone. This fault is a forty-mile-long "crack" on the stable land mass of the Colorado Plateau."

"According to geologists, Sedona is in the transition zone between the Desert Basin and the Colorado Plateau. The transition zone is a large region that runs East to West, across the state of Arizona and on into New Mexico."[14]

54

The San Francisco Peaks in Flagstaff, Arizona

Fields of volcanic rock spread out below Sunset Crater in Flagstaff

The Pentagram & Hexagram of Sedona

My education regarding a Sedona-Mu link resumed in the Fall of 1988 when I was introduced to a new branch of psychic research that I have since named "Psychic Geomancy." My teacher in this area of study was Nicholas Mann, who with his partner, Ani Williams, moved into the large home I was renting in Sedona and for some time helped share the expenses of living there. Ani, a long-time resident of Sedona, was an accomplished harpist, a talent she acquired under the guidance of angelic beings from other dimensions (see my interview with Ani in Chapter 12). Nicholas was a Brit and a geomancer who had spent many years studying the vortexes, ley lines and stone circles of his native England. He had acquired an eye for ley line alignments and could easily discern geometrical alignments in the Earth's landscape. During the months that we lived together Nicholas used his innate skill in Psychic Geomancy to discover some important "Landscape Temples" that provided some much needed understanding regarding the Sedona Grid and the city's esoteric history.

On the Winter Solstice of 1988 Nicholas felt the intuitive call to climb to the top of an elevated vantage point in Sedona. Then, with his psychic powers fully operational, he was able to discern two massive geometrical shapes in the Sedona landscape, the corners of which were marked by massive red rock formations. These geometrical shapes divided Sedona into two distinct sections: a southern section composed of five red rock formations united as a five-pointed pentagram and a northern section comprised of six equidistant formations joined together in the form of a six-pointed hexagram. The two landscape stars were tied together by the "bridge" of Airport Vortex, which also separates Sedona into its two distinct parts.

The Sedona pentagram, which Nicholas referred to as "The Temple of the Law of Human Life" and which many of the locals have come to know as the "Temple of the Goddess," is built around the definitive symbol of the Universal Goddess. The five pointed star, which neatly holds within it the human form, represents the Goddess as pure energy (the Golden Mean Spiral is the foundation of the pentagram) that during the process of creation condenses to become the five elements. The Sedona pentagram has near its center two matching red rock formations, the Twin Buttes, which because of their location I have named the "Breasts of the Goddess." And in the exact center of the pentagram is a rock formation in the shape of a Madonna, which in many parts of the globe is venerated as an anthropomorphic image of the universal Goddess. Next to the Madonna is more Goddess symbology in the form of two monolithic figures known as the "Nuns."

By contrast, the hexagram shaped landscape temple is denominated the Temple of the Son and contains within it an abundance of male symbology. The hexagram, with its upward and downward pointing triangles, denotes the union of the God and Goddess as the Son. In the center of Sedona's six pointed star is the city's tallest mountain known as Capital Peak or Thunder Mountain, which as a towering, phallic, yang peak represents the male theme of the Sedona hexagram.

There are many implications underlying the existence of the pentagram and hexagram landscape temples in Sedona, one of which is that the rock formations situated at their points and centers were strategically placed there by "Gods" of the Dreamtime who arrived from Mu or perhaps another dimension or star system. The overseeing role of an alien or indigenous intellegence in their placement seems probable in light of the fact that diameters of both the pentagram and hexagram are an exact fraction of the Earth's circumference. On the book he eventually wrote on the Landscape Temples entitled *SEDONA: SACRED EARTH*, Mann states:

"The diameter of the pentagram is 101.376 feet x 220 = 22,302.7 feet, or 1 part in 5,890 of the earth's circumference. The diameter of the hexagram is 101.376 feet x 311 = 31,527.9 feet or 1 part in 4,167 of the earth's circumference. The distance of the two figures combined is 101.376 feet x 531 = 53,830.7 feet, or 1 part in 2,440 of the earth's meridian circumference. In other words, exactly 2,440 Sedona Landscape Temples laid end to end would go completely around the world."[15]

Since the base measurements of many of the ancient monuments worldwide constructed by the legendary "Gods" of the past were similarly based upon the Earth's radius and its circumference, including the temple compounds of Tiahuanaco and Zimbabwe, it seems more than likely that the Sedona Landscape Temples could have been constructed by the ancient Dreamtime Gods or ETs,

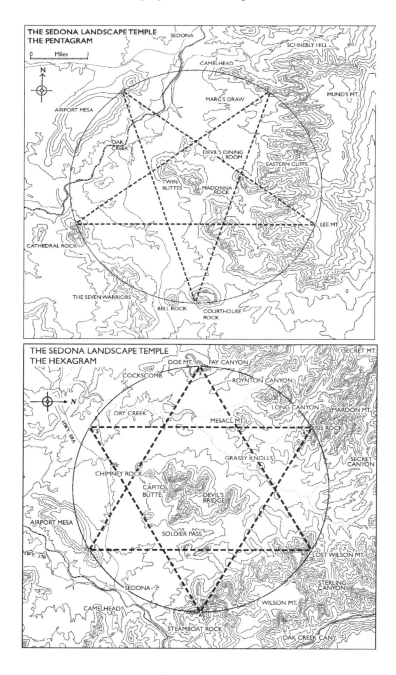

Drawings from: *SEDONA: SACRED EARTH*
Courtesy of Nicholas R. Mann

Sedona's Pentagram. The "Goddess" Landscape Temple

Madonna Rock at the center of the Sedona Pentagram

whom the Hopis refer to as the Kachinas. Perhaps the Kachinas worked their magic in the Sedona landscape after arriving from another star system via the Motherland of Mu.

The next logical question is why the landscape temples were formed as an adjoining pentagram and hexagram.? Did these shapes have a special significance to the Dreamtime Gods and/or the Lemurians? Ostensibly they did, at least according to the records of the Pacific islanders and the ancient Hindus who originated on Mu. Their legends of both reveal that the Goddess and Her Son were the principal deities of the Motherland of Mu. Hawaiian legends refer to the Goddess as Rua and her continent of Mu as the Land of Rua, while the Hindus refer to the ancient Pacific continent as both Rutas (an obvious link to Rua) as well as as Kumari Kandam, the "Land of the Kumari," with Kumari being a name for the Universal Goddess. And in regards to Her Son, the Hindus maintain that the ancient king of Lemuria was the Son of the Goddess named Sanat Kumara.

From another perspective, Mu was a Neolithic civilization and therefore most likely championed the ubiquitous legend of the Neolithic Goddess culture. According to this global myth, the Goddess annually gave birth to a Son, the Green Man, who as vegetation sprouted in the spring, flourished in the summer and then died in the fall. During his short life the Green Man served as King of the World, which he goverened under the authority and power of his mother. Knowing this, many of the earliest cultures always anointed their kings as incarnations of the Son or Green Man. A good example is the civilizations of Sumeria and Babylonia, where the monarchs were touted as incarnations of the Green Man Dammuzi or Tammuz, and Son of the Goddess Inanna or Ishtar. Another example is Egypt, where the pharaohs of Egypt were venerated as the incarnations of Horus, the Son of Goddess Isis (for more examples see James Frazer's *The Golden Bough*).

The Yavapai, the indigenous Native Americans of Arizona, would agree that the Sedona pentagram and hexagram represent the Goddess and Her Son, whom they remember in their legends as their matriarch and patriarch, Kamalapukwia and Sakarakaamche. The legends of the Yavapai maintain that they were once inner Earth people when a deluge threatened to destroy their underworld civilization. So a young girl named Kamalapukwia was placed in canoe in order to save her and the Yavapai race from complete obliteration. Kamalapukwia floated up to the surface of the Earth through what is today Montezuma Well, and then continued floating for many miles since the upper world was also covered with flood waters. She eventually arrived at Boynton Canyon, which then became the birthing place and Garden of Eden for the Yavapai on the surface of the Earth. In order to begin producing a terrestrial Yavapai race, Kamalapukwia traveled first to Mingus Mountain, where she was impregnated by the rays of the Sun, and then returned to Boynton Canyon where she gave birth to a baby girl. When her daughter came of age she followed the same practice as her mother and gave birth to a boy, Sakarakaamche, although she died soon afterwards and did not get to see her son grow to manhood.

Today, Kamalapukwia and Sakarakaamche are recognized as the First Woman and First Man, the matriarch and patriarch of the Yavapai tribe on the surface of Earth. Kamalapukwia's Goddess presence can still be felt in Boynton Canyon, and in the form of a woman holding a bird high on one of the high ridges she can be seen overseeing the canyon today. Her spirit also fully pervades the Sedona pentagram. Sakarakaamche's presence can be detected strongly both within Boynton Canyon as well as within the terrestrial hexagram. The ancient legend of Kamalapukwia and Sakarakaamche will continue to live on in Sedona, as well as through the area encompassing the Sacred Triangle of ley lines that unites the vortexes of Boynton Canyon, Montezuma Well and Mingus Mountain. This Sacred Triangle delineates the path taken by Kamalapukwia to propagate the Yavapai tribe on the surface of the Earth.

Since Mann discovered them, Sedona's landscape temples have been compared to another part of the world where the pentagram and hexagram are similarly united in the sacred landscape. In *GENISIS: The First Book of Revelations,* surveyor David Wood reveals his work in discovering a united pentagram and hexagram in the landscape of the Langueduc near Rennes le Chateau.[16] It is interesting to note that the ancient history of the Langueduc exactly mirrors that of Sedona by virtue of also featuring the Goddess and Her Son. The Goddess of the Languedoc has been associated with both Isis and Mary Magdalene, the Beloved Disciple who is said to have been joined there by Jesus, the "Son," some years

The cave where Kamalapukwia began the Yavapai race on Earth

Montezuma Well

The Goddess of Boynton Canyon, Kamalapukwia, sits high upon a ridge in Boynton Canyon. She holds a bird. In front of her is her loyal dog.

Yavapai Ceremony in Boynton Canyon
Every February the Yavapai sadly remember the time they were forced off their native land in Sedona and relocated on reservations in southern Arizona.

after his crucifixion and then raised a family with him. Among some Gnostic sects that colonized the Langueduc Mary Magdalene was venerated as an incarnation of the universal Goddess Sophia, and Jesus was an incarnation of Her Son, whom she had anciently sent into the Garden of Eden as the Serpent of Wisdom to enlighten humanity. Both Mary Magdalene and Isis have been associated with the Black Madonnas of southern France, which are representations of the Universal Goddess holding Her Son.

Sedona and the Kumaras from Mu

During my last few months in Sedona I received additional revelations regarding the Goddess and Her Son, especially in his manifestation of Sanat Kumara. As I studied many Gnostic, Hindu, and esoteric traditions, I came to know Sanat Kumara as not only the King of the World, but the orignal Son of the Goddess who had been sent to Earth by his mother for the purpose of awakening humanity to its divinity. According to most legends, his arrival corresponded to the Garden of Eden. One estimate has him arriving on the "Eden" of Mu six million years ago with an entourage of enlightened extraterrestrials. At that time he became the Planetary Logos or Planetary Will by projecting his spirit inside the Earth; but as an omni-present deity he also retained a physical or semi-physical form that resided in numerous courts around the globe. Today, one of Sanat Kumara's vestigial courts exists on Kauai, the oldest Hawaiian Island said to have been created approximately six million years ago. Sanat's spirit inhabits the tropical island and his seven chakras are marked physically by the seven primitive rock temples that sequentially ascend Kauai's dormant volcano. Sanat Kumara is also said to inhabit Mount Kurama in Japan, which similar legends claim became home to his spirit six million years ago. Mt. Kurama is popularly known as the place where Dr. Usui intuitively received the healing system that would eventually become known to the world as Reiki. Additional places inhabited by the spirit of Sanat Kumara include legendary Shambhala, Mount Shasta in California, Sri Lanka and Sedona. When I first moved to Sedona I heard rumors over the psychic hotline that Sanat Kumara had officially moved his principal headquarters from Shambhala to Sedona. Although there might actually have been some truth to this pronoucement, I accepted it with a huge grain of salt knowing that any supportive, physical or scientific evidence would most likely be out of the question.

During my first months living in Sedona in 1988 I learned that a woman I had met in Mount Shasta the previous year during my first trip to Arizona had recently moved to town. This was Sister Thedra, the head of *The Association of Sananda and Sanat Kumara* or *ASSK*. Thedra was residing in a small house located just off Dry Creek Road, the road leading to Boynton Canyon, that she and her attendants referred to as the "Gate House." Curiously, this is the same name she called her home in Mount Shasta that was located on the road up the mountain. Thedra's Sedona Gate House thus led directly to the source of the power just as her Shasta Gate House once did.

I had initially visited Sister Thedra in California because I thought she could help me with my belief crisis. While in Washington I had read that this remarkable woman experienced an instantaneous recovery from terminal cancer in her 50s, and that she was still resilient in her late 80s. Her story stated that while on her death bed during a visit to the Yucatan she would daily pray "Take me now, Oh Lord, or heal me and I will forever be in your service." One day Jesus spontaneously appeared physically in front of Thedra and proceeded to lay his hands upon her. A complete healing ensued. Jesus then instructed Thedra to call him by his true name, Sananda Kumara, and to get ready to serve him. She would soon become his prophetess, and through her he would alert humans about the coming Earth changes. Soon after this event Sananda's photo on the following page was taken at nearby Chichen Itza.

Before assuming her spiritual name and status, Sister Thedra had been Dorothy Martin, an esotericist and Theosophist living in Chicago in close proximity to another famous esoteric native of the Windy City, George Hunt Williamson. When Sananda determined that Sister Thedra was in need of special training he sent her to Peru as part of an expedition that was led by Williamson. This expedition, which was dedicated to finding the Monastery of the Seven Rays, never actually reached the abbey, but according to each of their later testimonies both Sister Thedra and Williamson discovered the abbey on their own. Under the pen name of Brother Philip, Williamson would later write about the Monastery in arguably his best known book, *Secret of the Andes.*

Sister Thedra maintained that she continuously lived in and/or was intimately connected to the Monastery of the Seven Rays for five years, during which she learned many of the mysteries of the Brotherhood of the Seven Rays. These timeless mysteries had been brought to the Andes from Mu by the Lemurian sage Aramu or Amaru ("Serpent") Muru along with ancient power objects like the great Solar Disc. This renowned disc had been manufactured and brought from the planet Venus and then hung in one of the principal temples on Mu. The Brotherhood of the Seven Rays is simply another name for the Kumara Brotherhood that was anciently founded on Lemuria by missionaries from Venus. Another, more universal name for it, is the Great White Brotherhood. At the highest tier of this Brotherhood are Sananda and Sanat Kumara, the "Twins" who used Venus as a way-station between the Earth and other parts of the galaxy. Once established on Earth the Kumaras took charge of the spiritual evolution of humanity.

When her five years in the Andes were complete, Sananda guided Sister Thedra first to Arizona and then to her new home in the small town of Mount Shasta. She was told that Mount Shasta was a powerful vortex and its energy would assist her in receiving clear messages from Sananda. She also learned that the mountain was once part of Mu and contained a vestigial community of Lemurians who were living within and/or under the towering edifice.

An actual photo of Sananda taken in 1961 at Chichen Itza by Dr. Steinbeck, an Austrian archaeologist working at the temple site. Sananda instructed Steinbeck to give the photo to Sister Thedra.

I reflected on my previous interaction with Thedra as I knocked on the door of her Sedona Gate House. It was she who had advised me to daily ascend Shasta Mountain and mediate upon its slopes in order to get my answers. She had greatly helped me once and I sincerely hoped she could do so again.

An attendant answered and led me through the immaculately clean home into the living room where Thedra sat upon a well-padded chair. I humbly took my seat on the rug in front of her and we briefly reminisced about our first meeting in Shasta. Then she asked about the purpose of my current visit. Did I still have a belief crisis, she thoughtfully inquired?

Our conversation eventually touched upon Peru, which I took it as a cue to ask Thedra the location of the Monastery of the Seven Rays. For much of my life I had felt a deep connection to ancient Lemuria and these feelings had been significantly heightened by my recent experiences in Boynton Canyon. I felt an inner pull to travel to the Andean monastery in order to connect (or re-connect) with my brother and sister Lemurians who were living there as well as to learn the true history and teachings of Mu. Thedra was sensitive to my inner longing but cautioned me that even if she were to give me exact directions to the monastery I could stand right in front of it and never see it unless it was my destiny to find it. I took this to mean that either the monastery was cloaked with invisibility or that it actually moved between dimensions. When Thedra then asked if I was ready to make the journey south and possessed the necessary funds, I sheepishly informed her that I did not but was planning on taking another waiter job (which I did) in order to quickly save the money I needed. She smiled at my determination, and as we parted company she left me with one final instruction: "Let me know when you are ready to go." As fate would have it that would be many years later and Thedra would have transitioned by then. After a very productive life, she passed away in 1992.

One of the major catalysts of my initial Peruvian adventure of 1993 was a woman who in April of that year entered the alternative bookstore that I owned and operated with my second wife, Andrea, in Washington State. This lady had recently been to Peru and met a man named Anton Ponce de Leon Paiva, a Peruvian authority on UFO encounters she had read about in Shirley Maclaine's book *Out on a Limb*. This woman was able to arrange a meeting with Anton in Cuzco and then made a strong connection with him, ultimately promising him to send him a pair of high-powered binoculars. When she heard of my potential journey to Peru she thought she may have found a courier for her gift.

When Andrea and I arrived in Cuzco the following September Anton met us in a tea shop of the main square. A short, stocky man with large black and very bushy eyebrows, he could have easily passed for a spry leprechaun. After regaling us with some personal stories of alien encounters and the Men in Black who had pursued him, Anton invited us to his ancestral land in the Urubamba Valley which he had transformed into the headquarters of the Intic Churincuna, the "Brother-hood of the Sun." This was an esoteric society Anton was the head of and an organzation that was closely linked to Aramu Muru and the Brotherhood of the Seven Rays. Anton had been initiated into the Intic Churincuna years before in a ceremony that first required him to be blindfolded and led on horseback for three days to a secret village deep within the Andes Mountains that was inhabited by Incan initiates of the Brotherhood of the Sun. Over the course of the following seven days, while living among enlightened Elders who looked to be in their 60s (they were actually in their 90s), Anton received a download of pure Lemurian teachings that culminated in his formal initiation into the Intic Churincuna.

On the morning of our second day in Cuzco Anton met us at the main square and then whisked us away to the headquarters of the Brotherhood of the Sun to attend a ceremony in honor of the Four Elements that I was told had its origin on Mu. After the rite we took a tour of the grounds, stopping in front of a rose garden which displayed some stones arranged in the shape of the symbol of the Brotherhood of the Sun. When I commented to my guide how beautifully the stones had been laid out, his reply literally made my heart stop. Under the stones were the ashes of Sister Thedra!

Apparently Sister Thedra had been great friends with Anton, and he had even visited her at her Gate House in Mount Shasta. Both were initiates of orders that could be traced back to Aramu Muru and Lemuria. I was elated with this discovery and immediately began making plans to return the following year to receive initiation into the Brotherhood of the Sun.

Sister Thedra and Anton Ponce de Leon Paiva

My association with the Brotherhood of the Sun lasted for the next five years. During this time I met Jorge Luis Delgado, a member of the Brotherhood and head of a travel business located in Puno, a city on the shores of Lake Titicaca. Jorge shared an equally intense interest in finding the Monastery of the Seven Rays as myself, and since he was responsible for having scattered a second portion of Thedra's ashes over the surface of Lake Titicaca I viewed him as another beacon on my path. Jorge's claim to fame was the discovery of Amaru Muru's Doorway, which he was led to after a series of dreams revealed a red rock path leading to the Monastery of the Seven Rays. When he finally discovered the same red rock path in his waking state it was just a short distance from his home and did indeed lead to the Monastery, albeit via the Doorway. According to the locals, the Doorway is an interdimensional portal that many people have walked through and never returned. Demons have even used it as entrance into the third dimension, which is why many of the locals have named it the "Devil's Doorway." When Jorge first meditated at the Doorway he had a vision of Aramu Muru disappearing through it while carrying the great Solar Disc he had brought to the Andes from Lemuria. Apparently, the Lemurian sage was using the Doorway to transport him and his power object back to the Monastery at the time of the Spanish invasion. Thus, even though Jorge's path did not lead directly to the Monastery of the Seven Rays, it did so indirectly through Aramu Muru's Doorway.

Aramu Muru's Doorway

Jorge and I eventually organized a small expedition to find the Monastery of the Seven Rays. Five of us met at his lakeside hotel and then charted a path to the Monastery in accordance with some esoteric clues at our disposal. Then, with an entourage of food preparers and pack horses, we hiked for three days along Andean trails as giant condors the size of gliders swooped down and flew right above our heads. At each village on our path we inquired if any of the natives had heard of Sister Thedra or the Monastery. Our persistence paid off. The natives in one village informed us that although the location of the monastery was not known to them, it was probably in the vicinity of a huge mountain that looked like a man with his arms outstretched in welcoming. And even though the name Sister Thedra did not ring a bell, a man by the name of Philip would often stay in their town while making continual excursions into the mountains in search of something "precious." We decided that this was most likely a reference to George Hunt Williamson, who apparently used his pen name of Brother Philip during his excursions to find the "precious" Monastery of the Seven Rays.

On the fourth day of our journey we were crossing a ridge when I noticed directly across from of us a very unusual mountain. I knew instantly it was the mountain referred to by the natives, and it did indeed appear to be in the shape of a man with his arms outstretched in welcoming, albeit with a "head" that looked like a pyramid. A scintillating white light emerged from the mountain man's heart and flooded the canyon below, sending rays in our direction. We all quickly sat down and soaked up as much of the light as possible, and soon each of us was having a powerful heart chakra opening and activation. I am sure I must have sighed loudly in relief when we then received a an intuitive directive from the mountain man. We were told that he had adminstered the same initiation that we would have been given at the monastery, so we did not need to go any further. Up until this point in our Andean journey I had been painfully walking with a wooden cane, the result of an accident sustained on our first night when I slipped on a wet rock and completely wrenched my back out of place.

Jorge would return two or three more times in search of the Monastery of the Seven Rays with groups from the Netherlands. And he and I would return one more time a few years later in the springtime, only to find our path blocked by small avalanches and massive flooding that were the result of a particularly brutal rainy season. Today, when I reflect on the figure of the huge mountain man deep within the Andes I can not help but think that it is another dominating edifice inhabited by the spirit of Sanat Kumara. The energy radiating from the mountain was nearly identical to the power I would later feel when in proximity to other places and landmarks recognized to be habitations of the King of the World.

**The "Mountain Man" deep in the Andes.
A manifestation of Sanat Kumara?**

The Center of the Universe

I once had a transcendental experience on the slopes of Mt. Shasta in California during which my waking consciousness moved inside my heart and merged with my indwelling Spirit. The result of this alchemy was that I suddenly knew my true identity as the one Infinite Spirit that has existed for eternity. I knew that I eternally dwell in the Center of the Universe as its Creator and I also exist in everyone's heart as their inner Spirit. But I also knew that my revelation applies to all of us. You are also the Creator of the Universe and exist in my heart as my inner Spirit. So the next time you pass someone on the street remember that you dwell within them as their Spirit, and vice-versa. It might change how you feel about them. We are ALL ONE.

In this chapter:
* Our Anasazi Snake Clan Guide
* Going Home to Hopiland
* Tuwanasavi: The "Center of the Universe"
* Sip-Oraibi: "Where land first became solid"
* The Orion Zone

In August of 1989 I returned to Washington after getting suddenly fired from my waiter job at a local Sedona hotel. I was very distraught at first, knowing that this would consitutute a major setback in my plans to travel to South America. But then I decided it was a sign for me to take a different course and surrendered to it.

The previous February I had driven my wife back to our log cabin after a lease-option-to-buy agreement fell through on our log cabin. We continued to write and phone each other occasionally over the coming months, and eventually began a dialogue about the possibility of living together again in the fall. So, given my new circumstances, I decided to surprise her by returning home earlier than expected. I definitely succeeded...but certainly not in the way I had imagined or hoped for. Instead of the long heartfelt embrace that I had fantasized about during my long 1500 mile drive north, I was met with disdain and awkwardness. After perfunctory greetings the first words out of her mouth were: "I guess you did not get my last letter..."

I had arrived at a very inopportune time. D.L. was in the midst of a hot and heavy affair and I was the last person she wanted around. When I informed her I had no place else to go, she proceeded to make life as miserable as possible for me until I found one. So, after a couple of weeks of continually licking and bandaging my deep wounds of rejection, I gathered up my stuff and left.

I decided to remain in Washington and attend night school in Seattle until I had accumulated the requirements needed to acquire an acupuncture license. In order to create an environment supportive of my education I tried to find some people in Olympia interested in a live-in healing center. Fortunately Andrea, a friend I had previously known in Washington when she was the publisher of the local alternative newspaper, was looking for the same thing. In the aftermath of a divorce Andrea had left Olympia about the same time as me and had recently returned. We soon found a house and waited as long as we could for some other roommates to show up; and we then moved in together.

Just before we reconnected Andrea had been holding Holotropic Breathing workshops in the area. These healing seminars utilized loud music and rapid breathing techniques to help all the participants move stagnant, emotional blockages in their energy fields. Since I had been doing similar work with acupuncture we decided to team up. While the evocative music played I would administer acupressure to strategic points in order to better facilitate the release of emotions. Some of the pressure points I chose to use were part of *Windows to the Sky* acupressure and involved stimulation of certain points on the neck, head and upper body of a person to assist in opening their spiritual faculties. Legend has it that these points were some of the most ancient used in China, and that acupuncture and acupressure were first utilized among Taoist monks to facilitate and expedite each other's spiritual awakening and evolution.

Our Anasazi Snake Clan Guide

We then set about contacting disembodied teachers that could help guide us in our new joint mission. We wanted to help the world in the best way possible. As a vehicle for our interdimensional communication Andrea and I began experimenting with psychic tools, including automatic writing and the Ouija Board. Of the two we decided the Ouija Board was by far the most reliable and instantaneous in achieving results.

Once our new Ouija Board entered our home we quickly ripped off its cellphane wrapper and immediately sat down to test it. We began by invoking deceased relatives and then asking them questions that only they and not some random spirit would know the answers to. Andrea and I were both very impressed when one after the other our summoned ancestors arrived on the board and duly passed our test. We then progressed to invoking teachers and masters we had known either physically and/or on spiritual planes. Once they arrived we then plied them with questions we had previously only asked in silent prayer but had still not received answers to. When we summoned Sananda Kumara the energy in our room increased palpably. Love and compassion surrounded and filled us. By contrast, when Sanat Kumara arrived shortly afterwards his energy was commanding and akin to what I would expect a king or celestial father to feel like. I was even able to summon my recently deceased spiritual teacher from India in order to ask him why he had tarnished his reputation with sexual liasons with his students while alive. His answer was simple and to the point: "My karma is my own." In other words, take heed of your own karma not mine, especially if it does not directly effect you!

Next, we summoned any common guides who worked with both of us. Almost immediately an ancient Chinese acupuncturist who had been a teacher of Andrea's and mine in another life showed up with some very radical and highly spiritual information regarding Chinese diagnosis and treatment. As the cursor rapidly flew across the board I took copious notes regarding the "higher" spiritual influences of the inner organs and the acupuncture points that could activate a person's spiritual body. This continued for a few days and I nearly had enough information for a small book when other entities began showing up and demanding equal time on the board. One of them, Melwa, introduced himself as a nature spirit who resided principally in Boynton Canyon. When we inquired how long he had been there he stated "from the beginning." Then we asked who the builders of the temples were. His quick reply was: "Gods like me." His answer caught me by surprise since I was fully expecting him to say Lemurian colonists. I did, however, remember a psychic friend in Sedona telling me that the Lemurians *were* the ancient Gods. Many of them possessed special abilities that allowed them to co-create the Earth's flora and fauna. Finally, an entity from the Pleiades showed up, followed closely by a Native American spirit whose aggressive communication nearly made the cursor fly off the board. When the smoke cleared our new guest had spelled out his first message: "I am Thunder Eagle!"

Thunder Eagle introduced himself as the spirit of a Anasazi medicine man. During his last lifetime on Earth he had been a Hopi Snake Clan member living on what is now the Hopi Reservation. Andrea had been with him as his wife and I had been his son. This was about 1200 CE. At some point during that lifetime Thunder Eagle had initiated both of us into the Snake Clan.

As the Ouija cursor heated up Thunder Eagle rapidly communicated to us that at some time, perhaps in another dimension, Andrea and I had made a contract with him. This "contract" stated that duirng the present incarnation Andrea would channel his voice and I would bring forth his spiritual power into the third dimension. We glanced at each other with expressions that suggested: "Do we really want to get so involved with a discarnate spirit we just met?" After some quick deliberation we decided what Thunder Eagle had proposed was credible and had merit. If he had been a member of any clan other than the Snake Clan, however, we probably would have declined any further relationship with him. We were both consumate "snake" people. For most of my life I had felt like a member of a universal Snake Clan, and Andrea had recently completed a vision quest on Garden Island in Lake Michigan during which she had directly discovered her personal totem was the snake. This came as a great surprise to her Ojibwa teacher since it was very uncommon for a member of her tribe to be aligned with the Snake Clan. So, given our mutual snake affiliations we decided to adopt a "wait and see" attitude after saying our good-byes that night to Thunder Eagle . If there was indeed such a contract as he claimed then our destinies would naturally unfold and we would soon be inspired to embody our new friend. We just hoped that doing so would not turn our lives upside down.

When I first met Thunder Eagle I was in the midst of researching my book *The Return of the Serpents of Wisdom,* so any information regarding snakes and dragons naturally piqued my interest. Waves of excitement washed over me as I contemplated the prospect of gaining some secret wisdom from Thunder Eagle that I could use in the book. My research up to that point had revealed in ancient times humans associated with snakes and dragons, such as Thunder Eagle, had once served communities around the globe as dynamic spiritual masters. They had been teachers, initiators, and ceremonial adepts of the most profound and secret mysteries, including those related to the activation of the inner Serpent Power or Kundalini. Most of these serpent masters were in lineages that stretched back to Mu, which had been the original home of Peru's Aramu or Amaru Muru, the "Serpent" Muru, as well as Churchward's Serpents of Mu, the Naacals. Thunder Eagle's serpent wisdom could have arrived in North America via Serpent missionaries from Lemuria, or it could have reached the Americas via Atlantis. The founder of the Hopi Snake Clan was initiated at one of the headquarters established by the Atlantean Serpents on a Caribbean island. This was a young Hopi boy, who after inadvertently floating on a raft all the way down the Colorado River and into the Caribbean Sea, bumped directly into the island of the Snake People. The boy was met there by Spider Woman who escorted him through a secret passageway to the subterranean temple of the Snake People. Then, in the "House of Snakes," the Hopi lad was fully initiated and indoctrinated into the rites and mysteries of the Serpent Masters. He was then given a serpent wife and instructed to return home and teach the rites to his people.

My understanding of the Serpent Masters and the power they wielded was about to be experiential. Two weeks after our introduction to Thunder Eagle I was moving energy up the spine of a client in my healing room when a huge jolt of electricity suddenly shot up my spine and then moved to all parts of my body. The experience must have been similar to a full blown electrocution, although there was no pain. Instead, my consciousness fully expanded and my body shook in pure ecstasy. The entire room filled with a bright silvery light and I was at the very center of it.

My client also felt a surge of power moving within her body, and together we began to gyrate in a clockwise motion. I decided that Andrea should also have the benefit of receiving the power, so I called for her to come quickly into the room. A few seconds later she was on her knees next to me and I had my hands directly over her heart. Together we shook with the ecstasy of divine love.

After a few minutes, when the electrical intensity subsided, I took Andrea's hand in mine and ran to the kitchen table. I said thank you out loud to Thunder Eagle and then waited as we spelled out his reply on the Ouija Board. He also said "Thank You." This told me that I had succeeded in moving his prodigious power through my body and was beginning to meet the terms of our "contract" with Thunder Eagle. And what volcanic power it was! Although I was aware that the Serpent Masters and members of the Snake Clan possessed special "snake" power, I never expected there to be such an explosive intensity behind it. This was the kind of power I had associated solely with the Kundalini Masters of India. Now I knew that the adepts of the Native American Snake Clan were just as powerful. I certainly reached a new level of respect for both Thunder Eagle and the Hopi Snake Clan that afternoon, and it continues to this day.

Soon after my initial transmission Andrea and I traveled to Orcas Island to visit my brother Sahar and his wife Mocha who had recently bought a house on the island. Orcas Island is one of Washington's San Juan Islands and the home of a very powerful vortex. It had the reputation of being very sacred to the Native Americans and a portal to other dimensions. Now it was Andrea's turn to fulfill her end of the contract and channel Thunder Eagle.

One night, as we four sat in front of the fireplace, Sahar and Mocha joined me in trying to convince Andrea that she would never be in a more supportive environment to begin channeling the voice of Thunder Eagle. She had been feeling severe anxiety since our first encounter with Thunder Eagle and really did not know what might happen if she opened herself up to a powerful spirit that was still very foreign to us. So the three of us tried to make her feel as secure as we could by assuring her that we were there for her if anything threatening should occur.

Our gentle cajoling paid off. Soon Andrea sat in front of us with her eyes shut while silently repeating a prayer to receive only "those of the Light." Moments later I noticed above her an etheric head slowly drop from the ceiling. As it descended I could clearly perceive the features of a man in his mid 70s. There were deep wrinkles, a large nose, and a partially bald head. The phantom head continued downwards until it had completely superimposed itself over Andrea's. At that very moment Andrea opened her eyes wide and looked directly at me. With great joy and exhilaration she - or the spirit now inside her - loudly exclaimed: "My son, it is so good to see you again!" Thus began my post Ouija Board relationship with Thunder Eagle.

In the days that followed Andrea channeled Thunder Eagle many times in order to become fully accustomed to his energy. This was requested by my new "Dad," who also took it as an apportunity to learn what it felt like to inhabit a physical body again. Since Andrea was not required to completely leave her body during the channeling and could simply share it, she was soon able to relaxe with the new arrangement. But even though she never completely "checked out," she could not remember what was said during a session. So, with me as the fortunate questioner and recipient of Thunder Eagle's profound words, we began recording the channeling sessions. Besides answering many of my serpent-related questions he also taught me some Snake Clan history that had occurred "many moons ago."

When Andrea felt ready we began incorporating Thunder Eagle into our workshops. In the new format Andrea first channeled his wisdom, which covered the changes humanity was experiencing as a whole from a Native American perspective and how we all had a great opportunity to heal and transform. I would then channel his energy with the intention of awakening each person's Kundalini and catalyzing a healing process that would unfold during the workshop. As soon as I placed my hands on the participants the immense energy of Thunder Eagle would shoot through me and into them. Depending on the person and what they needed, the energy could be soft or intensely strong. Many of our students responded with classical Kundalini activations that manifested as intense body shaking (kriyas) accompanied by both heat and pressure at the base of their spines. Visions and deep meditative states were also common occurances. At times weeping, shouting, or laughter would pierce the relative stillness of the workshop as someone released some old blocked emotions.

Our workshops continued with Thunder Eagle for about a year. Then Andrea decided she had fulfilled her contract and was not willing to channel our Anasazi mentor anymore. I was crestfallen, both because I had become addicted to feeling the dynamic energy of Thunder Eagle, and also because I knew I was going to lose a dear friend. I finally agreed to her resolve with the condition that Andrea continue to channel Thunder Eagle until the end of a journey to the southwest we were planning for the coming April. I was going to undergo a vision quest in Boynton Canyon at that time and wanted Thunder Eagle's instruction both before and after the rite. We also planned to visit the Hopi Reservation, which meant that we three were going home.

Going Home to Hopiland

Traveling in the American Southwest with Thunder Eagle added another dimension to my experience there. I got to "see" the high desert through the eyes of a Native American spirit who had once lived there and intimately knew everything there was to know it.

The night before my vision quest was to begin my Anasazi "Dad" gave me final instructions regarding the ancient initiatory rite and its sacredness. He coached me on what I should do during the vision quest, as well as what to look for during my three days and nights alone in Boynton Canyon. He assured me that his spirit would be with me the entire time and he would later speak to me through Andrea when it was over.

As the area for my "fasting lodge" I chose to return to the elevated shelf with the huge monolith I had found shelter during my frigid night in February, 1987. With two gallons of fasting tea in tow, I watched the Sun rise to its zenith point in the sky as I climbed up to the summit of the familiar shelf and then began looking for a suitable cave for my "fasting lodge." My intuition guided me to a small Anasazi dwelling at the base of the towering monolith that I had failed to find before. It was certainly much larger and more comfortable than what I had settled for back in '87.

After rolling out my sleeping bag and erecting a small altar, I took the new shaman drum Andrea had gifted me with and began to chant the native songs and prayers that she and Thunder Eagle had taught me. Almost immediately they began to expand my consciousness while simultaneously enclosing me within an aura of peace and protection. Once I had completely drifted into a euphoric state of wellbeing my lodge suddenly became electric. A surge of energy moved through me. It was the calling card of an old friend. I could not see Thunder Eagle, but I definitely felt his dynamic "snake" presence move in and around me like an etheric wind. He had kept his word. His spirit arrived on cue and would remain with me throughout my vision quest.

When I next lit my chnoupa (ceremonial pipe) and began to send my prayers to the Great Spirit the energy of my questing lodge increased even more. I was soon transported into the deep, meditative state that would become my most consistent state of awareness during the following three days. Although my fearful lower self would occasionally alert me to any aberrant noises, especially during the darkest hours of the night, for the most part I was able to keep my inner chatter to a minimum and simply witness its fluctuations. This allowed me to re-main in a timeless, intuitive state of gnostic awareness within which many of the questions I had brought with me could be answered by the Great Spirit.

Throughout the ensuing three days I would occasionally observe walking meditation upon the high canyon shelf while closely examining its unique red rock formations. My intuition seemed to consistently guide me to formations that were

My Vision Quest Lodge at base of the towering monolith in Boynton Canyon

symbolically unique and poignant to my vision quest. At night I would spend the quiet hours meditating on the starry heavens in anticipation of an ET craft sighting. My attention would typically be drawn to a shooting star or enigmatic ball of light. A sparkling orb would first appear stationary but then dart rapidly and erratically across the heavens. Sometimes it would roll across the sky like a dynamic ball of fire while shooting out multi-colored streams of light in all directions. After such sightings I always said prayers thanks to the Great Spirit.

Other than an occasional bird or rapidly moving lizard, I did not encounter any wild animals during my vision quest. Perhaps this was because I already knew that my animal totem was the snake and did not need confirmation. I did, however, hear faint voices of other people in the canyon in the dead of night that were accompanied by the soft sounds of drums and flutes. I could not be sure if I was hearing humans camping illegally below me or the etheric sounds produced by phantom Anasazis. Perhaps it was the latter. Years later I would lead a ceremony in Boynton Canyon during which one of the participants distinctly heard natives dancing while playing instruments and chanting. When she rushed me to the place she had heard the sounds there was nothing there but a huge field of brush.

When Andrea finally came to get me at the end of my three day quest I had just completed a very long chnoupa ceremony during which I had resolved to dedicate the rest of my life to serving the Earth and all its inhabitants. This was a significant resolution for me since I was known to regularly complain about the hardships of living on planet Earth. Sometimes I even threatened to "check out" unless things got easier. Now, I felt I had a purpose that would keep me rooted on Earth until my pre-destined time of transition arrived.

Andrea took me to the sweat lodge she and I had previously erected out of willow branches on the property of some friends. The structure was ready for me to enter once we had cooked a pile of rocks on top of a roaring fire until they were nearly molten. After entering the womb-like structure and crawling over the moist earthen floor to a centrally located seat in my dark hut, I watched as the rocks were brought in, one by one, and placed in a hole next to me. The door was then closed and I sat anxiously in complete darkness and silence. As Andrea began to bang a drum outside the heat of the rocks elevated the temperature of my lodge to such a degree that I could hardly breathe. Copious waves of sweat rolled down my naked body. In an act of self preservation I instinctually moved as far away from the rocks as possible and buried my face in the moist earth with the hope of getting cooler and breathing easier. Fear began to mount within me as I contemplated remaining in this lodge for the recommended three hours.

Almost exactly one hour later Andrea opened the door and I was momentarily relieved by the cool air that entered the lodge from outside. Round one was complete and it was time to bring in more rocks. As Andrea transported the flaming rocks into the central hole she noticed that I had not been pouring water onto the stones as required and motioned to the four big jugs that had been set next to the hole. Her instructions were to immediately drain one gallon jug onto the rocks as soon as soon as the door was shut again. When the hatch subsequently closed shut I completely froze. I knew what was about to occur if I did as instructed, but I also wanted to follow the rules of the sweat lodge and experience its full benefit. So I hesitantly complied. The temperature instantly shot up an additional twenty degrees as expected and my lodge became a dense steam bath, thick with mist. This made it much harder for me to breathe. With mounting trepidation I decided that I had transformed my environment into one that was not only unbearable, but physically dangerous. It was common knowledge that if a person can withstand the intense heat of a sweat lodge they were likely to receive the blessing of a visionary experience from the Great Spirit. But at that moment I truly believed that if I was visited by such a visionary experience it could be permanent; i.e., I could travel out of my body to another dimension and not return. A conflict began to rage inside of me. On the one hand I did not want to be disrespectful and not complete the sweat lodge ritual, but I also needed to respect the vow I had made at the end of my vision quest. How was I going to serve the planet if I was dead! So, with gasping breaths I crawled to the doorway and stuck my sweaty, red head out of the lodge. One glimpse of my terror stricken demeanor was enough for Andrea. She knew it would be pointless to try and talk me back into the lodge. But, amazingly, she was okay with ending the ritual prematurely. Just moments before my episode she had broken her drumstick and took it as a sign that the sweat lodge was complete!

Tuwanasavi: the "Center of the Universe."

Our highly anticipated visit to Hopi Mesas was the last leg of our southwest journey. It was exciting to think that we would revisit the place the three of us had lived together nearly a thousand years ago, but at the same time it would also mark the loss of a friend and mentor. This might be the last time I would be able to hang out on the physical plane with Thunder Eagle.

Driving through the Hopi Mesas is a bit like visiting a communist country. The homes are mostly nondescript, photos are discouraged, and the natives tend to keep exclusively to themselves. So it helps if you know someone, or at least arrive with a specific agenda and destination. Neither applied to Andrea and I. We had no idea what Thunder Eagle's agenda might be.

Our first stop was the Hopi Cultural Center for a small lunch and to get directions. The Cultural Center is one of the only places tourists are encouraged to stop on the Hopi Reservation. Inside is a restaurant, small museum, souvenir shop and plenty of information about Hopi customs and history.

When we sat down at our table in the restaurant the first thing I noticed was my placemat. Upon it was was written in bold letters "Hopi: The Center of the Universe." I had seen this kind of unsolicited pretentiousness before. Every culture likes to advertise that it is the first and greatest civilization that the world has ever seen, and that it exists at the very center of the world. It's certainly a good marketing tool. But to call your homeland the "Center of the Universe" definitely seemed over the top to me.

After a lunch of Navaho Tacos we got some directions from a Hopi lady manning the cash register. We learned that Cultural Center was located on the second of the three mesas comprising Hopiland. Since we were in the middle of the reservation we decided there was no need to drive any further and pointed our vehicle to a town just a few minutes away.

A we pulled into the small town of Shungopavi we spotted a group of buildings where big gathering of some kind was in progress. Long lines of cars dotted both sides of the road leading up to the buildings. We decided that this was definitely a place to check out.

We parked our vehicle and walked into one of the the buildings to take a

A Kachina Dance at Shungopavi

look. Throngs of spectators blocked our view, but we could still discern a sea of dancers wearing vibrant costumes ahead of us. We asked one of the more congenial-looking Hopi men for an explanation of what was happening and were told it was a sacred Kachina dance. Such dances, stated the man, are the foundation of Hopi spiritual life. Each dancer goes into a trance and fully embodies the spirit of one of the venerated Kachinas, which collectively live half the year on the reservation and the other half on top of the San Francisco Peaks in Flagstaff. Since most Kachina dances are private and by invitation only, we were fortunate to arrive during one open to the public.

When the dance had finally concluded Andrea and I decided to walk to a nearby bluff that overlooked the surrounding desert. Once there, we sat down upon a flat rock and surveyed the panorama in front of us. Andrea quickly descended into a trance state and when she re-opened her eyes Thunder Eagle was sitting right next to me, staring straight head into the desert..

I could tell that my ancient Hopi "Father" was emotionally shaken by what he was seeing. With deep feeling spread across his normally placid face, he pointed straight ahead while announcing in a quivering voice: "That is where we used to live together." He then began to sob as the memories of our life together resurfaced.

Even though Thunder Eagle seemed deeply connected to the distant spot in front of us, I had to admit that I was initially very sceptical that he had located the exact plot that our ancient home once sat upon. But as I would later learn, Shungopavi is the most ancient of the Hopi villages and much or most of it has been swallowed up by the desert. So, Thunder Eagle's recollections could have indeed been accurate.

When Andrea returned to normal consciousness Thunder Eagle's tears were still streaming down her cheeks. Her vague memory of our Anasazi guide's cathartic recollection was so profound that she soon added some of her own tears to the gathering sheet of liquid. I embraced her and then stood up with the intention of walking along the bluff to in search of another lookout point where I could process my own grief of loosing Thunder Eagle.

I strolled along aimlessly for a few minutes until I sensed I had "arrived" at the place I needed to be. I scanned the desert in front of me for a few moments and then realized some new and very bizarre sensations were emerging within me. I felt that I was standing in the exact center of something. I was, of course, in the center of the Hopi Mesas. But this was different. It was greater and grander than any reservation. Then I realized, as strange as it must seem to the reader, that I was standing in the exact center of the entire universe! My sandstone bluff suddenly became the stage I stood upon while countless spectators (the stars, planets of the cosmos, ETs, etc.) directly focused upon me. I then remembered our lunch at the Cultural Center and how I had ridiculed the pretentious moniker on my placemat. I could now say, without any reservation whatsoever, that the Hopi Mesas were indeed in the "Center of the Universe."

Sip-Oraibi: "Where land first became solid"

As I basked in this new expansive sensation mild feelings of shame momentarily hung over me. The experience of being in the Center of the Universe showed me that I had been much too hasty in judging the Hopis. The "People of Peace" are recognized around the globe as being some of the most unpretentious and honest people on the planet, and they certainly are not in the business of attracting any undue attention to themselves. I resolved from that day onwards to accept any claim made by the Hopis as worthy of investigation, no matter how unreasonable they at first appeared. These people had opened my eyes to something I had never dreamed possible.

The sensation of being in the Center of the Universe remained with me as we drove out of the Hopi Reservation and began our long trek back to Washington. I contemplated how the Hopis could have known about the center of the cosmos. How could such a simple, unpretentious people know something that the rest of the world, including the so-called "educated" scientific community of advanced scholars, did not?

Upon our arrival home I immediately acquired all the available books on Hopi history I could find. None of them was forthcoming about how the Hopis located the Center of the Universe in North America other than they were guided there by Masau'u, their patron deity and King of the World. Masau'u had led

88

them there following their arrival on the continent at the start of the Fourth World.

Apparently, when the Hopis arrived in the American Southwest Masau'u had already located the Center of the Universe and was living there himself. His personal home later became the site of one of the first Hopi towns, Oraibi, which is short for "Sip-Oraibi," meaning "the Center of Earth where land first became solid." This instructive name points to Masau'u's home having been at the Center of the Earth, and it may indicate that his arrival on our planet occurred at a very remote time when Earth was still molten and "soft." Perhaps as an ET he had knowingly landed on the spot on Earth that was destined to first become hard; or perhaps he had been one of the early creator "Gods" on our planet that helped precpitate its crystallization. As to how Earth became known as the "Center of the Universe" - perhaps our planet merited that moniker because of its special destiny and function in the galaxy. It was obviously destined to be very special to Masau'u, the ET who would eventually become its king.

One of the reasons that Masau'u led the Hopis to their home in the "center" of both the Earth and the cosmos involves their special function as a people. Masau'u informed the Hopis that their service was to help keep a balance of the various fields surrounding the Earth, including the biosphere, the electromagnetic field and our planet's subtle grid of ley lines. By keeping the Earth in balance and in a proper rotation they would be helping it and its people live in balance while also contributing to the greater universal harmony. The Hopis would best be able to perform their service by residing in the Center of both the World and Universe where they could perform their Kachina Dances, thereby sending powerfully balancing spiritual energy through both the terrestrial and cosmic grid of ley lines that connected them to all points of our planet and the outer cosmos.

Today, there are not one but two places in the American Southwest that have been accorded the Hopi name of Tuwanasavi, meaning "Center of the Universe." Both were once part of Hopiland, which over time has shrunk considerably as the US government have apportioned large chunks of it to its neighboring Navajos. The second Tuwanasavi is identified as as the Four Corners, which is the point where the states of Arizona, New Mexico, Utah and Colorado come together. The Hopis contend that the huge cross at the Four Corners is not simply the creation of geo-political boundaries but represents a huge vortex that has existed in the area since the beginning of time. Some Hopis believe that this is the true magnetic center of the world and that the Four Corners mark the beginning and end of all their migrations.

The Orion Zone

In the last ten years author Gary David has written a series of books, beginning with *The Orion Zone,* that add fuel to the Hopis' assertion that their homeland lies at the center of both the world and the universe. After studying author Robert Bauval's *The Orion Mystery* regarding the three pyramids in Giza, Egypt, and how they had been built in the same spatial relationship as the three stars of Orion's Belt, David was inspired to see if the same "as above, so below" relationship held true in Tuwanasavi. Following in Bauval's footsteps, David superimposed Orion's trinity of belt stars over the three Hopi Mesas and saw that they did indeed line up. And just as Bauval had discovered that other pyramids and temples of Egypt aligned up with the other stars in the Orion constellation, David was similarly able to find terrestrial reflections to Orion among the villages and sacred sites on or near the Hopi Reservation. It is interesting to note that the land the Giza pyramids sit upon has also merited the sobriquet "Center of the Earth."

Gary David's discovery inspired me to ask some new questions, such as why two very different civilizations on opposite sides of our planet would pinpoint the center of Earth and then build upon it towns, temples and other terrestrial landmarks that are aligned with the stars of Orion. A little research revealed that the Celestial Hunter had great significance in both civilizations. In an "as above so below" relationship he represented the terrestrial King of the World in the starry heavens. The ancient Egyptians identified the constellation of Orion with Osiris, the archetypal pharaoh, Green Man, and King of the World, whose terrestrial body was synonymous with the entire landmass of Egypt. Similarly, the early Hopis identified Orion with Masau'u, the King of the World, and ostensibly recognized Tuwanasavi as his terrestrial body.

In *The Orion Zone* David reveals that the link between Masau'u and

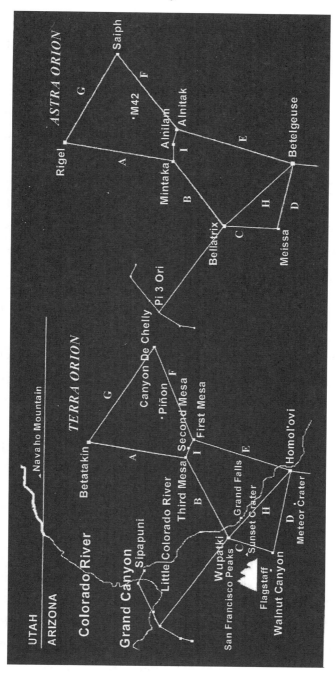

From *The Orion Zone* by Gary A. David

Orion is clear and unmistakable. Masau'u is portrayed by the Hopis as a club-wielding hunter just like the celestial Orion, and he is often invoked by the tribe for success in hunting. David also mentions Matsop, a Hopi Kachina that appears to be the counterpart of Masau'u, as being traditionally covered with stars that "might signify Orion's "belt" in both the rising and setting positions."[1] David also taps the Kachina Sohu as another ostensible twin of Masau'u because he wears three stars in his headress symbolizing the three stars of Orion's belt. Interestingly, Sohu's name echos that of the Egyptian name of Orion, Sahu or Sah.

My study led I me to other cultures around the globe who had made similar associations between Orion and the King of the World. The Persian Magi, for example, venerated Orion as Mithra, their warrior savior and King of the World. After being set free from their Babylonian captivity by the Persian conqueror Cyrus the Great, the Jews renamed Mithras St. Michael and made Orion his constellation. And since Michael's alternate epithet is Melchizedek, King of the World, it simultaneously became his starry abode as well. In the Near East, the Hindus conceived of Orion as the celestial home of their trident-wielding deity Shiva-Rudra, whose tangible form on Earth is his Son, Sanat Kumara, the King of the World and counterpart of both Mithras and St. Michael. And in both Asia and Europe it was once commonplace to underline the royal nature of Orion by referring to his belt as the "Three Kings." As author Ralph Ellis points out, even the Egyptian name of Orion, Sah, became associated with terrestrial monarchs worldwide. He states:

"...the name Sah has become a royal appellation, not just in Egypt, but all over the world. It has been transliterated into nearly every language in the western world and used as the title of nearly all our kings. Sah was seen as a sacred title by the Magi and used in Persia, where it became the royal title Shah. Further eastwards, in India, it became Sahib. In the greatest of all ancient empires, Rome, the kings chose the appellation Caesar. In the frozen wastes of the north, Russia, they inherited the same tradition and the title became Tsar. Word of the power of such a sacred name spread far and wide, so in the damp north-west of Europe, Britain, the royal appellation became Sire. For less nobles here, the title became Sir, but in the military world the tradition remains and this is always pronounced "Sar"!"[2]

Kachina Matsop
Courtesy of Museum of Northern Arizona

Kachina Sohu

It is also true that the legends worldwide ascribed to the celestial Orion mirror the myths associated with his terrestrial counterpart, the King of the World and Green Man. Echoing the legends of the terrestrial Green Man who was both Son/Lover of the Goddess and King of the World, one of Orion's cosmic legends state that he was born from the celestial Goddess, the Pleiades, and then grew rapidly to become the passionate hunter and lover who is ever in pursuit of his mother-lover. With the support of his mother, the Universal Goddess, Orion became ruler of the entire universe. In the Hindu version of his legend, Orion is born from the Pleiades (Sanskrit: Krittika) as Karttikeya ("Son of Krittika") and then becomes the commander-in-chief of the celestial army. On Earth, Karttikeya, who is also known as Sanat Kumara, became the King of the World.

Thus, my research had revealed that the King of the World resides in a couple places on Earth that reflect his celestial constellation of Orion. But knowing that the presence of the King of the World is everywhere on our planet, I decided there had to be much more to that story. I resolved to commit some needed research to this entity or consciousness I now knew as the King of the World.

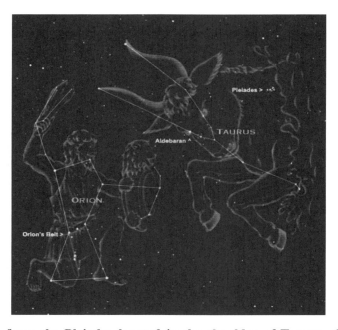

Orion faces the Pleiades located in the shoulder of Taurus, the Bull

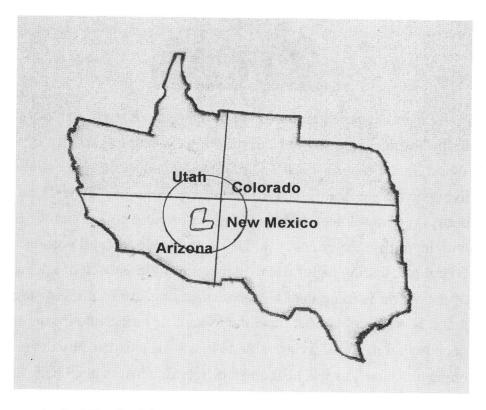

Ancient Hopiland included the Four Corners and much of Arizona

The King of the World

I first began to embrace the concept of a King of the World in my twenties and did not question his existence. The idea of a World Soul directing the affairs of all two and four-legged entities living on the surface of the Earth made perfect sense to me. It still does, only now I seek to balance my esoteric theories and ideas with legitimate experience and factual evidence, if at all possible. Of course, finding legitimate evidence for the existence of a King of the World is more than a little challenging. And I am not sure that it is possible without traveling to another part of the Earth, or deep within it. But if we are able to know his existence by developing the faculty to see, hear and feel interdimensionally, I believe many of us are very close to having an intimate encounter with the world's immortal monarch.

In this chapter:
- * **Real Encounters with Masau'u**
- * **A Real Encounter with the Peacock King**
- * **The Planetary Logos**
- * **The "Fall" and the Trident**
- * **Real Encounters with Sanat Kumara**
- * **The People of the Peacock Angel**
- * **The Royal Road of the King**

I soon dove into my new area of research, the truth behind a "King of the World." I decided that compiling legends and factual information about this enigmatic monarch would be the perfect way to spend my rainy days in Washington State. At least the days would go by faster.

Over the years I had heard the term "King of the World" associated with many ancient civilizations worldwide. In some of his legends the planetary monarch was definitely more fable than fact, but I would occasionally come across an historical reference that portrayed him as being an alive and conscious entity. In fact, in the Far East he had been consistently acknowledged by many Buddhist sects to be a living and breathing monarch who had existed for many thousands and possibly millions of years. Since information regarding this eastern version of the King of the World was the most abundant and credible, I decided to begin my new exploratory research with him.

I first read about the oriental King of the World many years previously in the writings of the *Theosophical Society,* whose original headquarters were in Adyar, India. He was identified as an immortal man-god who had lived hundreds and thousands of years. He was typically referred to as an ET who had come to Earth from a distant star, planet or dimension (usually Venus or the Pleiades) millions of years ago, and after arriving on our planet had assumed the mantle of a priest-king who was both the ruler and Savior of Humanity. As the Savior of Humanity he was reputed to be the first to teach fledgling humanity the mysteries of the alchemical path that leads to union with God.

The head of the *Theosophical Society,* Madam Blavatsky, made a good case for the existence of the King of the World. She qouted numerous ancient Hindu scriptures and supplemented them with firsthand accounts of the monarch disclosed to her by an elite group of secret adepts that helped found her organization. She called them "Ascended Masters." Blavatsky's information later became even more convincing when much of it was confirmed by some early 20th century adventurers who heard first-hand accounts of the monarch while traveling in the Far East. This included the Russian painter Nicholas Roerich, the Polish-born Russian explorer Ferdinand Ossendowski, and the intrepid German adventurer Theodore Illion.

In the diary of his travels Ossendowski quotes some very authoritative eastern sources regarding the King of the World that includes the supreme rulers of Mongolia as well as many of the country's renowned Buddhist Lamas. In *Beasts, Men and Gods*, Ossendowski claims to have been repeatedly informed that under Mongolia the Earth is honeycombed with caves and tunnels that are part of a subterranean realm known as Aghartha that is ruled by the "King of the World." Aghartha, he was told, was created sixty thousand years ago by the Earth's monarch as a place of refuge leading up to a terrible cataclysm that destroyed much of the continent of Lemuria.

Apparently, over the centuries an assortment of famous spiritual leaders have traveled to Aghartha to meet with the King of the World, including Lord Buddha and the Avatar Rama, as well as certain groups seeking refuge from fascist and despotic rulers on the surface of Earth. When Ossendowski visited the Buddhist monastery in Narabanchi the Hutuktu, the highest ranking monk of the abbey, told him that the king of Aghartha had on numerous occasions visited his abbey, as well as Mongolia's famous Sakkai Monastery. During one of his visits to Narabanchi in 1890, the King of the World sat before the resident monks and made a forecast of future events that were destined to occur soon upon the Earth. Ossendowski was shown the throne-seat the ruler sat upon as when he made prophecies, which included fifty years of strife and misery, followed by seventy-one years of happiness, and then an eighteen year war. The completion of these series of events would occur in the year 2029, when the existence of the Kingdom of Aghartha would be finally revealed to humans around the globe and many of the subterannean kingdom's inhabitants would then return to the surface of the Earth. When Ossendowski inquired whether there were other times the King of the World had made a public appearance on the surface of Earth, the Lama recalled five recorded appearances that he had made in Thailand and India. During one of those appearances, recalled the Hutuktu:

"He rode in a splendid car drawn by white elephants and ornamented with gold, precious stones and finest fabrics; he was robed in a white mantle and red tiara with strings of diamonds masking his face. He blessed the people with a golden apple with the figure of a lamb above it. The blind received their sight, the dumb spoke, the deaf heard, the crippled freely moved and the dead arose, wherever the eyes of the King of the World rested."[1]

In contrast to Ossendowski, the German Theodore Illion claimed to have had a direct, personal experience of the King of the World. Leading up to his exploration of Tibet in the 1930s, Illion spent years studying the Tibetan language and achieving the summit of physical conditioning by walking the entire distance of his native Germany. Illion was able to avoid detection by the Tibetan authorities by darkening his fair German skin with brown shoe polish and then traveling clandestinely to the capital city of Lhasa. In the Holy City he located a contact who gave him directions to a placed called the "Valley of Mystery" located approximately fifty miles from Lhasa. There he discovered a secret doorway that led him into an underground kingdom governed by the King of the World. In *Darkness Over Tibet* Illion recounts the days he spent in the subterranean "City of the Initiates" that was comprised of a multitude of tunnels and large cavernous rooms. The largest of these caverns comprised an entire underground palace and court occupied by the King of the World. Here the "Prince of Light" and "Exalted Jewel" sat upon a jewel encrusted throne. Illion found the the Prince and "Holy Ruler" to be a very tall man with long white beard and flowing gown who served as both ruler and guru of the City of Initiates. His supernatural powers to govern the world were prodigious and legendary:

"They [the Initiates] even seemed to feel that the Holy Ruler could actually influence the destinies of the world by hastening the outbreak of wars, the evolution of new types of epidemics and the disappearance of older kinds of disease, as well as the action of other scourges of humanity, including the various catastrophes of nature. They seemed to consider the Holy Jewel as a kind of supreme judge dispersing Divine Justice…"[2]

When the Holy Ruler met Illion in his palace he began to teach the German how to manipulate and control matter through embodying the power of Divine Will. By mastering the Force, Illion was informed he could alter world events by serving as another pair of eyes and arms for the Prince. This meeting with the Exalted Jewel completely spooked Illion, who as a devoted Christian concluded that the supernatural powers wielded by the Prince of Light proved him to be none

The King of Aghartha, monarch of the world. This image was published in *Amazing Stories*, May 1946. The accompanying article states:

"He came here ages ago from the planet Venus to be the instructor and guide of our then just dawning humanity. Though he is thousands of years old, his appearance is that of an exceptionally well developed and handsome youth of about sixteen. When mankind is ready for the benefits he can bring, he will emerge and establish a new civlizatiion of peace and plenty."

100

other than the evil Prince of Darkness. He fled the underground city soon afterwards and never returned.

Roerich's final opinion of the King of the World after two years of traveling throughout the Far East was the antithesis of Illion's. In fact, when the Russian painter left the East he was convinced that the King of the World was an infinitely compassionate being whose principal agenda was to rid the world of evil. Roerich's writings reveal that he was aware of an Aghartha-Shambala link. He apparently believed that Aghartha is and underground part of Shambhala. Certainly Roerich's belief in an underground civilization of spiritual adepts is unquestionable. He states:

"Great is the belief in the Kingdom of the subterranean people. Through all Asia, through the spaces of all deserts, from the Pacific to the Urals, you can hear the same wondrous tale of the vanished holy people [who went there]."[3]

Roerich was shown some of the entrances to Aghartha and his Tibetan caravan would occasionally come to a sudden stop in order to listen to the sounds ricocheting within the tunnel system below. He may have even entered one of more tunnel entrances in search of the Earth's monarch. One of his reasons for being in the Far East was to return to the King of the World a piece of the Chintamani Stone – a magical stone reputed to have been anciently brought to Earth by missionaries from Sirius – that had been in the possession of the League of Nations before its sudden demise. Many of the paintings Roerich produced during his journey features this stone, which he is either holding or transporting by horse through the Himalayas. Supposedly the stone had been sent to the League of Nations by the Panchen Lama of Tibet and Roerich was returning it to the Lama's headquarters in the city of Shigatse.

Roerich would eventually discover that many Ascended Masters had traveled to Shambhala from Shigatse, the headquarters of the Panchen Lama who had written a guide book with specific overland directions to Shambhala. The Panchen Lama knew the route because he was an incarnation of Amitabha, the Dhyani Buddha who rides upon a peacock and is the Tibetan Buddhist version of Sanat Kumara. Amitabha also incarnates in the line of mortal kings who sit on the throne of Shambhala as King of the World. So Roerich's final revelation was that there had been many world monarchs incarnating the spirit of Sanat Kumara - Amitabha.

Treasure of the World. N. Roerich's depiction of the Chintamani Stone

Self Portrait with Sacred Casket. N. Roerich holds the Chintamani Stone

Command of Rigden Djapo. **Roerich's version of the King of the World**

Roerich would eventually become a student of Master Morya, one of Shigatse's Ascended Masters, and learn from him the practices of Agni Yoga, a form of Kundalini Yoga. Along with Kuthumi and Saint Germain, Master Morya was a founder of the *Theosophical Society,* and together the three Ascended Masters transmitted their psychic instructions to Madam Blavatsky for the organization's evolution and maintainence. They also transmitted secrets of the Great White Brotherhood and its founder, King of the World Sanat Kumara, to Blavatsky which she later wove into her elaborate, esoteric tomes entitled *The Secret Doctrine* and *Isis Unveiled.* Another medium who began her psychic career as a ranking member of the *Theosophical Society*, Alice Bailey, also achieved fame for receiving messages from a Shigatse Ascended Master. Her mentor was Djwhal Khul, "the Tibetan." Like Blavatsky, Bailey referred to Earth's ruler, Sanat Kumara, as the Lord of the World and "Planetary Logos," whose residence is Shambhala. In *Ponder on This* Bailey states definitively:

"The Lord of the World, the One Initiator, He who is called in the Bible "The Ancient of Days," and in the Hindu Scriptures the First Kumara, He, Sanat Kumara it is, Who from His throne at Shambhala…holds in His hands all reins of government…"[4]

When it arrived, the notion of a King of the World promulgated by Blavatsky, Bailey, Roerich and others was not entirely new to the West. Notions of a world monarch had entered Europe between the 12th-17th centuries when a ruler proclaiming himself "Prester John" sent a series of letters to the Catholic Pope and many other European dignitaries, including the Holy Roman Emperor Frederick II, within which he described his paradisiacal kingdom in the East and vowed to send an army to rid Christendom of its Moslem infidels. While identifying himself as the King of the World, Prester John proclaimed:

"I Johannes the Presbyter, Lord of Lords, am superior in virtue, riches and power to all who walk under heaven. Seventy-two kings pay tribute to us. Our might prevails in the three Indies, and our lands extend all the way to the farthest Indies where the body of Saint Thomas the Apostle lies."

Seventy-two is a universal number that is often used when alluding to the sum total of the world's tribes, kingdoms, monarchs, etc. Prester John's pretentious claim that seventy-two kings payed tribute to him thus indicates all the world's kings were subject to him. This puts him in the same class as those eastern monarchs encountered by Ossendowski, Roerich and Illion who similarly proclaimed themselves King of the World. But did Prester John actually exist, or was he a fabricated ruler and his letters plagiarized?

Both his name and legend could identify Prester John as a fictionalized version of Sanat Kumara. The name of "John" links him directly to Sanat Kumara, whose epithets include the Sanscrit Jnana and English John. And the title ascribed to Prester John of "Fisher King" by Wolfram von Eschenbach in *Parzival* is another important link since esoterically Sanat Kumara is known to be the first and definitive Fisher King of the East. Prester John's identity as Sanat Kumara is further revealed in *A Hundred and One Nights*, wherein the Arabic author apparently locates Prester John's throne on Sri Lanka, the ancient home of Sanat Kumara. When Sinbad arrives on Sri Lanka and meets with its king the monarch gives Sinbad instructions to deliver a special note to Caliph Harun al-Rashid, of which the introduction reads: "Peace be with thee from the King of Al-Hind (India)." The title "King of Al-Hind" identifies the Sri Lankan king as Prester John, who often used the epithet in his correspondences to western rulers.

Real Encounters with Masau'u

Once I was satisfied with the testimonials I had compiled regarding the existence of a King of the World in the East, I turned my attention to the West and the legitimacy of the Hopis' King of the World, Masau'u. Could I also find legitimate evidence of his existence? The Hopis assert that their patron does indeed possess a physical form and they have numerous encounters with him on record to prove it, beginning with their initial emergence into this Fourth World. Throughout the years Masau'u has appeared to the Hopis as a very handsome man with long black hair and numerous turquoise necklaces dangling from his neck, as well as a giant skeleton clad in a torn woman's dress, and a hideous monster that walks the earth at night carrying a big torch. In this latter manifestation Masau'u is reputed to possess a bald head covered with burns, sores and dried blood, and it has even been reported that he once sported a long reptilian tail that he dragged behind him through the desert sand. This fact has not been lost on Christians who have used it as proof that Masau'u is their malevolent Devil. But no matter how bad or evil he may have appeared to an observer, Masau'u has always been benevolent to his own people, the Hopis, who venerate him as their foremost patron and protector. An example of his compassion and desire to please the Hopis is evident in a legend wherein Masau'u cuts off his own tail. At one point the King of the Fourth World realized that his tail was eliciting fear and trepidation among the young Hopi children so he severed it from his body, cut it into numerous pieces and flung them into the sea. Each piece then magically transformed into a fish and swam away.

Unfortunately, there are very few contemporary physical encounters with Masau'u on record. But this is to be expected considering that most Hopis avoid contact with him at all costs since the sight and/or touch of the Lord of Death is reputed to cause death. In this regard, one of Masau'us's epithets is "the one whose touch destroys." The only Hopis allowed to gaze upon or touch Masau'u without fatal consequences are members of the Kwan or One-Horned Society, a clan directly patronized by the Lord of Death that directly summon the world of the dead. However, legend has it that during one ceremony of the One-Horned Society a person who was not even a Hopi had a direct encounter with Masau'u and survived. This was Jesse Walter Fewkes, a Harvard-trained anthropologist and archaeologist who spent many years in the American Southwest studying the Hopis and other indigenous tribes. This unexpected meeting between Masau'u and Dr. Fewkes occurred when the anthropologist visited the Hopi Mesas during the month of November, when the Kwan Society was administering the forbidden rites of Wuwuchim. During this all night ceremony the spirits of the dead are summoned and allowed to reside in the land of the Hopis for exactly one night.

As the story goes, when it was time to start of the Wuwuchim ceremonies Dr. Fewkes was just finishing a day taking notes in one of the Hopi kivas. Fearing that the anthropologist might have a fatal encounter with Masau'u once the evening rites got underway, the Hopi Elders instructed him to return to the house he was staying in on the reservation and lock himself tightly within it. He was warned to keep the shades drawn and not attempt to look outside no matter how strong the temptation. By not following these orders the doctor risked certain death.

Within minutes of returning to the supposed safety of his house, Dr. Fewkes was suddenly overwhelmed by the feeling that someone or something had also entered his room. Looking up, he saw in the dim light of his room the outline of a tall man standing before him. Shaken, Fewkes questioned the intruder:

"What do you want and how did you get in here?"

"I have come to entertain you," came the quick reply.

"Go away, I am busy and I do not wish to be entertained," countered the frightened Fewkes.[5]

The tall man suddenly disappeared, but then Fewkes heard his voice coming from another part of the room.

"Turn your head a moment," instructed the visitor. The doctor turned around and could plainly make out a different phantasmagoric figure, only this one possessed very grotesque features.

"How did you get in?", questioned Fewkes, to which the hideous-looking man replied:

"I go where I please, locked doors cannot keep me out! See, I will show you how I entered."

As Dr. Fewkes watched the demonic figure "became like a single straw in a Hopi hair whisk and he vanished through the key hole."

Now Dr. Fewkes was frantic with fear. With the intruder's formidable magic there seemed to be no way to keep him away. Two minutes passed and the stranger was back again and standing directly in front of him. Fewkes demanded to know his visitor's intentions a second time and again came the response "I have come to entertain you."

With no other option in sight, the Doctor surrendered to the inevitable and became hospitable to his guest. He offered the stranger a cigarette and a match to light it, but the man laughed, saying:

"Keep your match, I do not need it."

The visitor then blew a stream of fire from his mouth and lit the cigarette. This was enough for Dr. Fewkes. He now knew for certain who his formidable guest was and the potential danger he was in. It was Masau'u, the Lord of Fire and Death, the Kachina who can kill with just a look.

It took awhile, but Dr. Fewkes eventually began to feel safe in the presence Masau'u. The Lord of Fire and Death talked to the Doctor for many hours that night, eventually convincing him to become a Hopi. Masau'u then used his magic to transform both of them into little children, and they laughed and played games through the remainder of the night.

The grotesque face of Masau'u

Jesse Walter Fewkes

A Real Encounter with the Peacock King of the World

Like Dr. Fewkes, I also unexpectedly encountered a manifestation of the King of the World. This event occurred high in the Andes during the mid-1990s, when Andrea and I ran a travel company called *Soluna Tours* that offered annual visits to Peru and the headquarters of the Brotherhood of the Sun. Although I loved what I learned within the Brotherhood during those years, most of it was academic and I longed for a deeper, more mystical experience. So my attention was piqued one day during lunch at the compound when I overheard a member of the Brotherhood from Lima sharing his visions and interdimensional experiences after drinking the juice of a native cactus known as San Pedro or Wachuma. We spoke separately for a few minutes, and after feeling my intense desire for a similar mystical experience as his my new friend invited me to an upcoming entheogen ceremony.

I met my friend's Wachuma shaman two weeks later and was immediately impressed by his unassuming and unpretentious nature. He, A.C., only requested a donation for his shamanic services, the amount of which would be of my choosing. As we sat over tea in a small Lima café he told me that he was a Wachuma shaman descended from the Moche, a coastal tribe that had once covered much of northern Peru and used the Wachuma sacrament regularly for consciousness expansion. A.C. shared some of the eye-popping experiences he had had under the influence of the cactus, including being taken aboard a Venusian spacecraft, but he also assured me that the spirit of the plant, the Universal Goddess, would make any experience safe and peaceful. His own gnostic revelations had revealed that the plant had originally come to the Andes from Venus via Mu, the primeval Land of the Goddess, and the symbol of its migration to the Andes, a dragoness carrying the plant, can be found molded into the side of a circular temple built exclusively for Wachuma ceremonies at Chavin de Hauntar. Chavin is the cradle of the Wachuma tradition in the Andes and a place where adepts of the past have achieved complete enlightenment solely through imbibing the Wachuma. Someone could have knocked me over with a feather if they had told me then that years later A.C. and I would travel to Chavin twice for Wachuma ceremonies.

Dragon carrying San Pedro. Motif from Chavin de Huantar

109

Beginning with my initial ceremony with A.C. each of my Wachuma adventures took place on multiple dimensions and were very eventful. My first ceremony occurred at one of the most sacred of shamanic sites in the Andes known as Marca Wasi, a plateau 13,000 feet in elevation that is regarded by many as an ancient colony of Mu. Like Sedona, Marca Wasi is covered with many unique and enigmatic rock formations that appear as though they must have been carved by human hands. The most captivating of Marca Wasi's formations, the "Faces of Humanity," has incorporated into it the profiles of the five races of humanity, the White Race, the Yellow Race, the Red Race, the Black Race, and the Brown Race. It has been suggested that the Faces of Humanity and the other distinctive formations of Marca Wasi were magically formed either by Lemurian colonists or ETs. The latter conjecture is the result of Marca Wasi having more UFO sightings than anywhere else in Peru. All its trail guides and many of its visitors have had direct encounters with extraterrestrials. The guide named "Omar" told me that while on the Marca Wasi plateau he once experienced a large group of ETs with grossly deformed human faces and wearing classical silver seamless garments.

Our ceremony in Marca Wasi was held in an ancient "Water Temple" that my new shaman explained was originally at sea level during the time of Mu and had its floor completely covered with water. The temple is now a natural amphitheatre with one wall featuring a vestigial, gigantic fish sprawled across it.

Marca Wasi was very special to A.C. because it was there that he had undergone a classical death and rebirth experience that transformed him into a shaman. He had been sent there alone by his Wachuma teacher many years earlier with instructions to imbibe the sacred liquid once darkness had fallen and then to witness the events that unfolded. As soon as A.C. was under its influence had a powerful vision of the seven-rayed Goddess that inhabited the plant. She first took the form of a young Andean girl and then manifested as seven rainbow rays that completely filled the Water Temple. A.C. was then confronted by a live, ferocious condor that landed directly in front of him and proceeded to rip his body to shreds with its razor sharp talons. A.C. fainted from the loss of blood and moments later found himself flying as a bird high above his own mangled body. In the form of a huge condor he continued to soar with a new found freedom through the

The Faces of Humanity. White Race profile is on right, Red Race on left.

Profiles of the Black Race (left) and Yellow Race.

The giant fish of Marca Wasi's "Water Temple"

gown was sitting next to him and completing the healing work on his battered body. Assuring A.C. that "all will be well now," the old man walked across the Water Temple and directly into the rock wall that formed one of its sides. Noticing that not even a scratch remained on his body, A.C. stood up and began to triumphantly jog around the temple. He had experienced death and survived. From that moment onwards his shamanic name would be "Kuntur," the Quechuan word for Condor. He had fully received the power of the condor and was now destined to live as its human embodiment.

The first time I ingested the frothy green liquid handed to me by A.C. I transformed into a puma and spent most of an afternoon and evening crawling on the ground while snarling, spitting and hissing at anyone foolish enough to come near me. An explosive energy surged within me and if there had been any trees close by I am sure I could have easily scampered up to their highest branches. Instead, I spent much of my time rolling like a playful cat on the grassy ground, completely covering my new white woolen poncho with both dirt and blades of grass. Later, when the effects of the Wachuma had worn off A.C. informed me that I had been "visited" by the Spirit of the Puma. I was not, however, aware of the extent of the visit until Andrea later met A.C. and another member of our ceremony at a tea shop and requested a critique of the ceremony. According to them not only did I assume the temperament of a snarling puma, at one point I had shape-shifted and by body was completely covered with cat fur!

I apprenticed with A.C. over the next three years. During that time I had many life-changing experiences on Wachuma in sacred Andean locations that included Marca Wasi, Machu Picchu, Chavin de Hauntar and Cuzco. But the most pivotal experience of all was my I encounter with the King of the World. This occurred at 11,000 feet in a lush green Andean valley fed by glaciers where I attended a private ceremony with only A.C. and his translator.

On the morning of our special ceremony we arose well before sunrise and walked briskly through the darkness of Churin, a shamanic retreat where for the previous three days we had soaked in the purifying medicinal waters of the area's hot springs. After climbing into a battered old public van that was waiting to take us to our destination, we soon found ourselves swaying violently back and forth as our vehicle bounced upon large boulders that peppered the dirt road leading into the high mountains. I commended myself for having followed a strict fasting regime of fruit in preparation for our ceremony, the effects of which were already paying great dividends. Finally, an hour later we reached our destination. Although we all felt thoroughly beaten up, after stepping off the bus and into a heavy white mist that partially cloaked towering snow-capped peaks bathed in the pinkish glow of sunrise, our pains quickly dissipated.

We walked briskly past a couple of slow moving villagers of the sleepy mountain town of Huanca Wasi before entering a gate leading onto private property. A.C warmly greeted the native landlady who stood outside on her doorstep to greet us, and he then knowingly led myself and his translator down a descending path behind her house.

I had been informed by A.C. that we would be performing our ceremony near or within a hot spring, so in my mind I pictured a rustic pool, possibly bordered by a ring of jagged, arbitrarily placed rocks. I was, therefore, quite pleasantly surprised when the trail led to a small, beautifully constructed pool made of polished blue tile and nestled comfortably among the tall grass and surrounding peaks. The entire scene was as close to paradise as I could imagine.

At A.C.'s command the three of us set about making our new environment "Wachuma friendly." We placed our drinking water and shamanic instruments, such as drums and rattles, at strategic locations around the perimeter of the pool. Then we each found a private location for changing into our swimsuits before meeting at the side of the pool to begin our ceremony.

When A.C. finally handed me the familiar clay mug full of slimey green liquid I instantly knew that this batch of Wachuma was different than the rest. It was much thicker and heavier. Feeling a bit anxious, I hesitated, knowing that thicker usually meant stronger. But then A.C.'s resonant command split the mountain silence. The stern voice of the presiding shaman instructed me to "drink it all right down." And it was gone, in two big gulps.

Moments later we all entered the warm pool and the three of us quietly moved to our own private corner of it. I proceeded to play a cd of Sanskrit mantras while A.C.'s translator, who was also another apprentice of his, shook rattles and danced in the center of the pool. Then, for the following hour we either sang along with the mantra, played our instruments to hypnotic rhythms, or meditated on our surroundings, all depending on how the Wachuma inspired us.

After an intense episode of projectile vomiting, I quickly descended into that familiar place that I had come to know as "Wachuma Land." Since we all reached that space of heightened awareness together, A.C. asked us to converge on one side of the pool so he could begin his shamanic teaching. The three of us then fixed our gaze on one of the tall peaks surrounding our little oasis while trying to surrender to whatever visions or communication the spirit of the mountain (or Wachuma) had to give us. Andean shamans do not consider the mountains as simply colossal mounds of lifeless, inanimate rock, but as the embodiments of Apus, fully conscious beings. As we opened ourselves to this particular Apu I did indeed feel as though I was communing with a live, animate being. I could "see" the pulse of its respiration, and felt its eyes upon us. Then, almost in unison, we three spotted the form of a temple just below the mountain's summit. This wasn't just any dilapidated temple ruin, but a glowing, magical temple from a storybook world of fantasy. And even though it was in pristine condition, it gave the impression of being older than any megalithic temple I had ever seen. I decided I was seeing an interdimensional stucture similar to the temples of Sedona and estimated that it had probably been made thousands or millions of years ago by some masters from another world, perhaps missionaries from Atlantis or Lemuria.

Staring at the mountain made me dizzy, and I was soon helplessly vomiting with an intensity and amount I was not accustomed to. I knew that my retching was the result of having consumed an inordinately strong dose of San Pedro, but A.C. had trained me not to be too concerned by it. Vomiting the cactus is considered auspicious by the Peruvian shamans; it is cleansing to the digestive system and ultimately allows one to enter into more profound depths of "Wachuma Land." Apparently I was getting prepped to go deeper than ever before!

Hoping that my "cleansing" episodes had finally ceased, I sunk back into the warm water in order to heal my exhausted, stomach muscles and internal organs. Then, while slouching against the side of the pool, I looked glassy-eyed at my surroundings as they magically transformed into the surreal terrain of another dimension. I didn't completely lose touch with the physical world; this new dimension co-existed with the one I was accustomed to. Within my new hybrid realm every plant and animal magically glowed with consciousness, and I was suddenly surrounded by a host of new friends.

My environment continued to transform. Soon all the surrounding rocks and plants acquired large, expressive eyes. It seemed as though all the forms of nature had awakened at once from a long slumber and were now opening their sleepy eyes in unison. I calmly accepted the myriad eyes until I realized that they were all staring directly at me! I witnessed my mind begin to spin out of control as I contemplated whether the eyes were those of one omnipotent being or that of thousands of individual entities. And what could they possibly want from me, anyway? Taking a few deep breaths I looked closer and realized that these eyes were not entirely human but appeared surreal and otherworldly. Then I knew. They were the "eyes" one finds adorning peacock feathers! And just as I was beginning to let this process this vision I discovered that each one was, indeed, part of a graceful, sweeping, peacock feather. I chuckled in delight as I realized I had been transported into a higher dimensional realm comprised of a sea of peacock feathers!

More eyes and feathers appeared in the terrain surrounding our pool until they were all I could perceive in any direction. And then, magically, the peacock feathers joined together as peacocks of various sizes, some of which moved freely around me. Wherever I looked I now beheld both feathers and complete peacocks either standing in place or prancing around.

One of the larger peacock eyes directly in front of me suddenly changed into a luminescent form of the Flower of Life, which is a sacred geometrical figure comprised of numerous vesica pisces "eyes." I had seen the Flower of Life engraved upon temple pillars in Abydos, Egypt, and even through I knew it to be a form of the "many-eyed" Osiris I was not entirely sure of its meaning. But now, having witnessed this interchange between the peacock eye and Flower of Life I knew that they were intimately related. I intutiively sensed that all forms merge out of the Eye of God, which in its dreamy, primeval state, appears first as a peacock eye followed by the precise geometries of the Flower of Life. I knew unequivocally that the peacock eye and Flower of life are manifestations of the Creator and the parents of all physical form.

A couple hours passed in my new peacock realm before A.C. instructed his translator and I to gather up our belongings so each of us could find our own individual, private location for meditation. I was still seeing peacocks everywhere and found it very difficult to walk without trampling some of them; but I was excited about visiting a new location and communing with new peacock friends.

Setting off alone, I soon found myself wandering along a stonewall and then into a large field. I sat down in the tall grass to admire the vibrant green meadow around me and the towering mountains surrounding it. One lofty mountain directly in front of me appeared particularly interesting, so I studied its contours and ridges closely from beginning to end. To my amazement I discovered that one of the longer ridges resembled the features of a peacock's back in both color and shape. As I followed this ridge further it seemed to slope down before tapering into what appeared to be a huge tail covered with peacock feathers. Scanning the ridges on the neighboring ountains for more peacock shapes, I found I could distinctly make out not only tails but complete peacock bodies. And each of these giants was completely alive. Each mountain was a living, breathing peacock. Then I noticed where two mountains joined together a larger peacock was formed, and when they were joined with another mountain an even larger bird emerged. I could only speculate that if peacocks were joined together in a never-ending succession of increasingly larger shapes the entire Earth itself would eventually become a peacock, followed by the Solar System, the Milky Way, and, ultimately, the entire universe. Such a revelation was almost too much for my limited mind to grasp, and I didn't know where to go with it. "Who would believe me anyway?" I blurted out while playfully throwing up my hands in resignation. So, with the polar opposite feelings of enlightenment and confusion quickly growing within me, I slowly ambled back to the company of A.C..

After returning home to the US I doggedly searched for answers regarding my visions of the peacock eyes and strutting peacocks. Having been deeply involved with the yoga path of India I naturally associated peacock feathers with Murugan or Sanat Kumara, the Son of Shiva and Parvati, who was typically portrayed as riding upon a peacock. So I first reviewed some Hindu texts regarding him but none of them said anything about an interdimensional realm where everything becomes peacocks and peacock plumes. I also reviewed some of the legends of Osiris since I had come to regard the Flower of Life as a symbol of the many-eyed Egyptian deity. But although Osiris was sometimes pictured as green and associated with the Green Man, other uniting references were lacking.

After many days of concerted effort my investigation finally bore fruit. I discovered some images online that resembled my peacock visions in the Andes. The source of these images was a people known as the Yezidis, a greatly maligned religious sect of Kurdistan in northern Iraq who venerated a deity known as Tawsi Melek, a term that translates into English as "Peacock Angel" or "Peacock King." As I studied the images and legends of the Peacock Angel it quickly became clear that the realm I had visited in the Andes was indeed his. According to Yezidi history, his realm was first created when solid land rose up above the surface of the vast ocean that once covered Earth. The emerging landmasses were barren, hot and shaking with continual earthquakes. Then God, the Supreme Being, sent the greatest of angels to Earth to bring our planet into balance while endowing it with both life and color. As the angel descended from the heavens it assumed the form of a huge peacock whose body and plumes contained all the seven colors of the rainbow. After landing in Lalish, which today is located in the center of Kurdistan and identified by the Yezidis as the most sacred spot on Earth, the Peacock Angel spread his plumes all around the Earth, completely covering our planet with vibrant color. The etheric plumes then crystallized into the multi-colored physical flora that then covered our planet even though they continued to retain an etheric manifestation on another dimension. That is the realm I had been transported to.

It now made sense to me why I experienced all the forms of nature simultaneously opening their eyes. The Peacock Angel *is* all the forms of nature. I had, therefore, beheld one spirit with thousands of eyes, not thousands of individual entities. It now became clear to me that the Peacock Angel is that deity who since ancient times has been known worldwide as both the Great Watcher with millions of eyes, as well as the Green Man. This revelation helped me understand my vision of the Flower of Life. The vesica pisces "eyes" of the Flower of Life are the eyes of the Peacock Angel, whose counterpart is Osiris, the Egyptian Green Man.

I would eventually discover many salient links uniting Osiris and the Peacock Angel, the most important of which is that the Egyptian pharaoh of legend wears a white crown with peacock feathers attached to each side of it! Moreover, as Ptah-Sokar-Osiris, Osiris is the Creator of the Universe, just as the Peacock Angel is ascribed that function among the Yezidis. And just as the image of Osiris is the microcosmic form of his macrocosmic body, the body of a live peacock is a model of the Cosmic Peacock whose peacock eyes are hundreds of spinning galaxies.

I next felt compelled to study and compare the names, titles, and legends of the Peacock Angel with the Hopis' Masau'u. To say that I was astounded by all the similarities would be a huge understatement. Besides their mutual status as King of the World, both deities are associated with feathers ("masa," the root of Masau'u, is a Hopi word meaning "wing" or "feather") and each is recognized within its respective culture as a manifestation of the Green Man. Green Man Masau'u taught the Hopis agriculture; he also supplies his people with the seeds to plant each year and even brings fertility to their land. One Hopi belief asserts a dream of Masau'u, who is often portrayed as carrying a huge club full of seeds, is

The Flower of Life

Osiris wearing his "Peacock Crown"

The body of a live peacock is the microcosmic form of the Cosmic Peacock Creator. The "eyes" on its feathers, which are set into multiple Golden Mean Spirals emerging from the central body of the peacock, reflect the multitude of galaxies that form upon the body of the Cosmic Peacock.

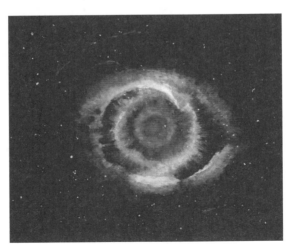

Galaxies do indeed take the form of "eyes."

120

The Peacock Angel. Painting by Larry Welker

The above image of the Cosmic Peacock Creator reveals his creation of the universe, as well as his eventual landing on Earth. From the central body of the peacock emanates seven feathers representing the Seven Great Angels that worked under the Peacock Angel to create the universe, as well as the seven colors and sounds that characterize all manifest form. Behind them are twelve more feathers symbolizing the twelve signs of the Zodiac that the Cosmic Peacock becomes as it expands into the fledgling universe. The Peacock Angel stands upon Earth, the fortunate planet he eventually chose to make his home.

believed to herald a good harvest. At the beginning of each planting season the Hopis celebrate the Green Man Masau'u with a dramatic reenactment of the life cycle of a corn plant, which they identify as a manifestation of Masau'u just as the ancient Egyptians and Greeks once associated corn with their Green Men, Osiris and Dionysus.[8] Another outstanding link between Masau'u and the Peacock Angel are their names. In the language of the Yezidis the name of the Peacock Angel is Taus Malak or Tawsi Melek, meaning Peacock Angel or Peacock King. Sometimes the name is reversed as Melek or Malak Taus. When said rapidly the latter sounds very close to "Masau'u."

But of all links between Tawsi Melek and Masau'u the most confirming is the Luciferian "fall" each is reputed to have undergone. According to Yezid legend, the Peacock Angel's fall occurred in the Garden of Eden when he disobeyed God after being instructed to bow down to Adam. While the other six Great Angels quickly obeyed the Creator and lowered their heads to the first man, the Peacock Angel stubbornly demurred because of his pride. He was the greatest of angels so he was certainly not about to bow down to a creature made out of the clay of the Earth. Following his transgression the Peacock Angel existed on Earth for many years as a rebellious outlaw. Some say he was exposed to the fires of Hell at this time but completely extinguished them with his own tears. Then God forgave Tawsi Melek and returned him to his former power and glory. Masau'u's legend is nearly identical. When the Hopis' Green Man was made the ruler of the Third World he became full of pride regarding his exalted status and his glaring ego interfered with the proper performance of his duties. During his subsequent fall he lost his position when God sentenced him to live in the fiery underworld as its ruler. He was violently tossed into the fiery abyss and nearly consumed, the result of which can be seen today as the red blotches of blood that now cover his burned and hairless head. As Lord of the Dead Masau'u sebsequently acquired (and still retains) the alternate form of a human skeleton. But like the Peacock King, Masau'u was finally forgiven and returned to his throne in the upper world as King of the World. This was at the start of the Fourth World. Even today Masau'u retains his title of Lord of the Dead, and during the darkest period of the night it is said that Masau'u still walks the Earth as a giant skeleton with his signature, fiery torch lighting his path.

Thus, Tawsi Melek and Masau'u are united through their Luciferian "heritage." But it should be noted that even with their respective Lucierian falls from grace neither Tawsi Melek or Masau'u *are* Lucifer, who is a synthesized entity invented entirely by the Catholic Church. Even the casual observer will not fail to recognize the glaring difference that separates the two deities from Lucifer. Tawsi Melek and Masau'u were both forgiven by God for their transgressions and REDEEMED; Lucifer was not. For his crimes, Lucifer remains relegated to the bottomless pit.

The Planetary Logos

Since Masau'u and the Peacock Angel are both manifestations of the King of the World and Green Man, by extension they also share the epithet of Planetary Logos. This moniker became popular by Blavatsky's Ascended Masters as a name for Sanat Kumara, thereby making the King of the World synonymous with the inner spirit, mind and will of Earth. It is, perhaps, the most all-encompassing title wielded by the King of the World, who as the Green Man has made the Earth his physical body, and whose mind and will controls the actions of all life forms that move upon its surface.

Another name of the Planetary Logos as it applies to the human race is the Collective Consciousness of Humanity. Just as the name implies, each one of us is a spark of the planetary consciousness of the King of the World. He is us, and we are him. The evolutionary changes that occur in the Collective Consciousness of Humanity reflect the ongoing evolution of the Planetary Logos.

Therefore, the "fall" and redemption of the Planetary Logos in its persona of Masau'u or Tawsi Melek is synonymous with the fall and redemption of the Collective Consciousness of humanity. From this perspective, the "fall" of Masau'u and Tawsi Melek corresponds to the "fall" of humanity, i.e., when humans developed an ego and intellect and then "fell" away from their previous intuitive connection with God. And the redemption of the Planetary Logos corresponds to the period when more humans begin to re-awaken to their divinity and then initiate their journey back to oneness with God.

According to esoteric history, the "Fall" of the Planetary Logos occurred during the Atlantean Age and Third World of the Hopis. This was when humans achieved staggering heights of technological mastery but also a rabid egotism determined to employ a technology of mass destruction to enslave and conquer the world. In *Genesis,* this era of human development is portrayed as a latter stage of the Garden of Eden, when Adam and Eve consumed the apple from the Tree of the Knowledge of Good and Evil and immediately developed a strong egoic sense of self, as well as a discerning intellect that naturally perceives and categorizes the differences that separates themselves from each other and all life forms.

It is said that the "Redemption" of both the Planetary Logos and all humanity has now begun and will gain momentum when humans move into the next major cycle of time known by the Hopis as the Fifth World. At that time both humans and the King of the World will become fully redeemed and realize their collective true nature as the Christed King.

Once I understood Masau'u and the Peacock Angel as the Collective Consciousness of Humanity I could truly begin to understand Lucifer in a completely different light. I had previously believed that Lucifer's legend was based on an older myth of the "Light Bearer" who was the Savior of Humanity and was continuously inquring how could he have become the maligned evil demon of western religion. Obviously the catalyst of his gruesome transformation was his "Fall," but when understood from the earlier perspective Lucifer's Fall was a sacrifice. As the Planetary Logos Lucifer chained his spirit to the material Earth so that all humans could achieve salvation. And it is because of him that souls could afterwards incarnate on Earth and undergo the "Luciferian Program," which involves a "Fall" followed by a Redemption. Only by incarnating physically and developing a limited sense of self or ego, as well as a discriminating intellect, does a soul have the wisdom and desire to embark on a journey to realize its true nature. Therefore, far from being "bad," the so-called "Fall" and eviction from the Garden of Eden, when humanity developed a sense of self and intellect, was a necessary event in human evolution. Humans needed to sever their intutive link to God (leave the Garden) in order to acquire a limited sense of self. Only then could they attain true Self-Knowledge. This, states the Mystery School Traditions of the

Left Hand Path (the gnostic-alchemical path), is the goal of human existence.

With my new understanding of Lucifer came revelations regarding the crucifix and its original meaning. Lucifer was the original Savior nailed to the Cross of Matter (the Cross *is* the symbol of matter) for the redemption of all humans. He "nailed" himself to matter by taking a material body, i.e., the solid Earth, within which he could catalyze and oversee the evolutionary unfoldment of humanity. Without his sacrifice humans would not be able to achieve Self-Knowledge and complete their spiritual evolution upon our planet.

The Gnostics and Yogis of the Left Hand Path have helped me develop my new understanding. According to them, the Garden of Eden scenario has been completely mis-construed by dogmatic theologians. It was, in fact, an opportunity taken by Sanat Kumara or the Peacock Angel (or Lucifer) to uplift humanity; and this is why he assumed his form of the wily Serpent on the Tree. The Serpent, they assert, was a form of the Divine Son sent to Earth by his mother, Sophia, the Universal Goddess who dwells in the Pleiades (the Seven Pillars of Sophia), in order to save Adam and Eve and all humans on Earth by teaching them the Path to Self-knowledge. As the snake, the symbol of energy and wisdom, the Divine Son spiraled down to Earth from the Seven Sisters along the universal Tree of Life and became the Planetary Logos. Then as part of his mission to enlighten humanity he also took his seat at the base of the human spine, the inner "Tree of Life." There, as the Kundalini Serpent, he waits for his host to cultivate the desire for Self-Knowledge before being stirred into action and rising up the spine to activate the chakra centers of gnostic awareness alongside it. Thus, the Savior Son bestows gnosis both by teaching humans the practices to awaken the Serpent Power, as well as manifesting within them as the evolutionary force to fully awaken their centers of gnostic awareness.

Real Encounters with Sanat Kumara

After positively identifying Masau'u, Sanat Kumara, and the Peacock Angel as multiple versions of the same King of the World, I began to refer to the world's monarch as Sanat Kumara-Masau'u-Tawsi Melek. I also decided it was time to travel to one of Sanat Kumara's world headquarters, Sri Lanka, in order to test if he, like his counterparts Masau'u and Tawsi Melek, was a real living and breathing entity. If nothing else, by going to Sri Lanka I would be fulfilling my duty as a devotee of the Hindu Savior. For many years I had heard that all devotees of Sanat Kumara needed to take at least one pilgrimage to Sri Lanka during their lifetimes, so this was to be mine.

On my way to Kataragama I stopped off at nearby Adam's Peak, the first place on Earth that legends contend Adam was placed by God. One legend asserts that the first man descended the mountain and then traveled to Kataragama, where the Garden of Eden scenario played out. There is, therefore, an important historical link between Adam's Peak and Kataragama. Having heard that a footprint of Adam still remains where he was placed on the summit of Adam's Peak, I decided that the opportunity to pay homage to it should not be missed.

After checking into my hotel room at the base of Adam's Peak and catching a little sleep, I arose at the darkest part of the night and then began my ascent up the mountain at 2 am. This was a traditonal time to climb Adam's Peak so the path was well lit. As I ambled up the never-ending stone stairs I rejoiced in the cool, damp morning air and the surrounding dense jungle foliage. I knew that by mid-day these same stairs would be a tropical steam bath.

When I finally arrived at the 7,000 foot summit I found it very cold, windswept and pelted by rain. I was tired, and my legs were screaming with pain, but I decided it was a small price to pay to see Adam's Footprint. The time was about 6 am and the sole temple at the summit, the Temple of Sri Pada, the "Sacred Footprint," was about to open. When my chance finally arrived to enter the temple I strolled in victoriously, ready to claim my prize. But when I glanced around all I could see were multi-colored prayer shawls. My heart sank as I realized that they were completely covering Adam's Footprint. What I had labored so hard to see was now completely hidden from me. Fortunately, I had been in situations like this before.Having visited many third world countries over the years, I knew that where there's money, there's a way. So, after taking a couple deep breaths I counted out the Sri Lankan currency I had with me and offered the attending Buddhist priest some sizable baksheesh. He then lifted the prayer cloths and what was revealed to me was certainly worth the price. I had expected a naturally formed depression in a large rock that could vaguely pass for a human footprint, but what I got instead was a fully detailed human foot print, nearly six feet in length. "If this is really Adam's footprint," I told myself, "he was one big guy!" I stood frozen, with my mouth agape, until the priest quickly re-covered my prize. In the stunned silence that followed I realized that I had been so in awe of Adam's Footprint I had completely forgotten to take a photo of it!

After seeing Sri Pada for myself I retraced the trail Adam might have taken while hiking down Adam's Peak on his way east to the Garden of Eden of Kataragama (Kataragama = "Place of Karttikeya"). Unlike Adam, however, I decided not to to walk to Kataragama. A hired car suited me just fine.

When I finally arrived at the Sri Lankan Garden of Eden that night, with tongue-in-cheek I congratulated myself for being one of the few humans who had been able to "return" to the fabled Garden. Then, following a good night's rest, I gave myself a walking tour of Kataragama's temples, shrines, gigantic trees and large patches of grass to see what noticable changes had been made in the Garden since Adam and Eve left. The Serpent on the Tree was still there, of course. He was a manifestation of Sanat Kumara.

The first sign that the wily Serpent had achieved redemption following his legendary transgression against God was the presence of three separate world religions all venerating him at Kataragama. Each religion had erected a shrine for the worship of the Savior Son, although they invoke him by their own special name. The principal shrine in the compound is the Hindu temple dedicated to Sanat Kumara in his form of the six-headed Karttikeya. In back of the Hindu temple is a huge stupa where Buddhists venerate Sanat Kumara as Kataragama Deviyo, the "Kataragama Deity," and to the right of the Hindu Temple is a mosque adorned with green streamers and flags where Muslims venerate Sanat Kumara as al-Khadir. When I first heard the name "al-Khadir," meaning Green Man, I was particularly excited since it conclusively proved to me that the Hindu King of the World was indeed the Green Man.

I spent the next three days at Kataragama meditating and attending rituals in its Hindu temple that daily began its services before sunrise at 5 am. Following the morning rites I walked around the temple compound while trying to engage the

127

Adam's Peak

Kataragama

The Six-Headed Karttikeya, "Son of the Pleiades."

The three forms of Karttikeya: boy, peacock, and snake

129

Brahman priests, the Buddhist priests and the Islamic attendants of the mosque in dialogue about Sanat Kumara. I duly learned that Sanat Kumara had many names because he could manifest in a variety of forms, including a boy, a snake, and a peacock, which by no small coincidence are three principal manifestations of the Peacock Angel. The Muslims refer to Sanat Kumara as al-Khadir and they also refer to Kataragama as Khadirgama, the "Place of Khadir." As an old man with a long beard who wields the power to make everything green and full of life, al-Khadir has been occasionally spotted in his Green Man form by his Muslim devotees in and around Kataragama, especially at the crossing point of the two sacred rivers that run through the compound, the Menik Ganga, the "River of Gems," and the underground "Current of Grace." It is at the confluence of these rivers that many ages ago al-Khadir discovered the *Abu-Hayat,* the "Water of Life" or elixir of immortality. The Green Man drank the Water of Life and instantly achieved immortal life. Legend has it that afterwards he tested the magical water by placing a dead fish in it and then watched with wonder as it immediately returned to life. Today, many Muslim Sufis make regular pilgrimages to Kataragama in order to catch a glimpse of al-Khadir. His prophecies predict that he will soon make a physical appearance in the area and be seen by many fortunate devotees.

The Sufis also regard al-Khadir as the "Initiator" who arrives in their presence when they are ready for Baraka, the "Blessing," that will activate their inner evolutionary force and catapult them into spiritual life. Al-Khadir is the embodiment of Baraka, life force, which in its highest frequency is pure Kundalini power. Similarly, Sanat Kumara is identified by his Hindu devotees at Kataragama as Seyon, the Red One, as well as Agni, the Lord of Fire and the embodiment of the fiery Kundalini. Sanat Kumara's yantra or geometrical form body reveals his essential nature as the alchemical Kundalini force. The yantra of the Divine Son is the hexagram or six-pointed star, representing the alchemical union of the universal male-female polarity, Shiva and Shakti, that come together to produce the Serpent Power. Sanat Kumara's sacred yantra is engraved upon a precious stone (shown on opposite page) and kept in the holy of holies of Kataragama's Hindu Temple. It is only brought out for public display once a year during an annual celebration in July.

When I inquired specifically about the six-headed form of Karttikeya that was venerated at the Hindu temple at Kataragama the Brahman priests recounted a couple different legends regarding the Divine Son and his multiple heads. Some claimed that he had been born with seven heads but soon one of them was severed from his body. Others claimed that one of his seven heads has always been invisible. As the Son of Krittika (the Pleiades), he had inherited the seven heads from his "seven-headed" mother who shines in the heavens as the Seven Sisters. And like his mother, whose seventh head or star is invisible to the naked eye, the seventh head of Karttikeya is also invisible. Another priest informed me that Karttikeya's six heads denote the six corners of his yantra (geometrical form body), as well as the six-pointed star and the six directions of the unvierse he constantly dwells within. His seventh head is the seventh and invisible direction, i.e., the Spirit beyond the manifest universe. The six heads of Sanat Kumara also correspond to his six sacred temples in South India.

While the priests of Sanat Kumara inducted me into the mysteries of their deity I was overcome by an eerie feeling that the Divine Son was listening to every word that came out of their mouths. When I commented on the tangible, overriding presence that surrounded us as they spoke, the priests were quick to point out that the guiding presence of the Savior Son was everywhere at every moment at

Kataragama. If necessary, he might even assume an etheric and/or physical form. They told me about a tree near Kataragama where he manifested physically almost daily in order to take offerings left upon an altar for him. Sanat Kumara would arrive in the form of a snake, a dog or even a human to collect the offerings. Sanat Kumara has also been known to appear as a live snake or peacock in order to send a warning of impending danger to a devotee, or he often suddenly appears as a dog in order to accompany a devotee through a particularly dangerous part of the jungle. But his most significant manifestation is that of an eternally young and beautiful boy who wears a crown and carries a golden spear or "Vel." This is the form he has appeared in to such spiritual stalwarts as the Lemurian Sage Agastyar, the Alchemist Bogarnath, Swami Kalyanagiri, and the two-thousand year old Himalayan yogi known as Babaji, founder of the Kriya Yoga Path. In commemoration of Babaji's ensuing enlightenment through the guidance of Sanat Kumara, a small shrine currently sits within the precincts of the Kataragama temple compound.

When I inquired regarding the character of Sanat Kumara I discovered that there are two diametrically opposing sides to the Savior Son; he can be both an angelic saint as well as a devilish trickster. He thus reflects the androgyny of his counterpart Tawsi Melek, whose peacock form has been described as possessing the beauty of an angel and the cry of a devil. Sanat Kumara also mirrors "androgynous" Masau'u, who is both a creator and destroyer of the Hopis.

I was surprised to find that Sanat Kumara's legends are full of annoying pranks he has pulled on his angelic peers as well as his unsuspecting devotees. He has a reputation for confusing a devotee, making them completely lost, and even hiding their clothing and valuables from them. Some Hindu scriptures have explicitly denounced his unconscionable actions, referring to him by such derogatory terms as dhurta, meaning "rogue," as well as "...a philanderer, a thief, a scoundrel and a friend of criminals and politicians..."[9]

Sanat can also manifest as an eccentric madman, and there are many stories of outrageous sadhus suddenly appearing at Kataragama in order to communicate a lesson or message to one of the Divine Son's unsuspecting devotees. During one of the long July festivals at Kataragama, for example, a retired court justice with a lingering ailment was approached by a madman who gazed wildly at him while shouting "Well off to the north! Off to the north and you will be alright!" The wildman then disappered into thin air. The justice knew in an instant it was the Savior Son and followed his directions by immediately traveling to the northern part of Sri Lanka where he was duly healed by a famous Ayurvedic physician.

Like Masau'u, Karttikeya's androgyny extends into his lordship of the underworld, which yogis claim can be entered through an etheric portal situated along the Menik Ganga.[10] And there is even a myth that Sanat Kumara underwent a Luciferian fall similar to both Masau'u and Tawsi Melek. This event occurred when the Savior Son was living with his family on the summit of Mount Kailash and lost a bet to his brother, the elephant- headed Ganesh. Ganesh wagered that he could encircle the world faster than Karttikeya, but his brother was determined to prove him wrong. When the race began Sanat Kumara shot off like a bullet and sped rapidly around the globe while Ganesh slowly walked in a circle around his parents, Shiva and Parvati. Upon his return an exhausted Sanat Kumara noticed that Ganesh had barely moved from his original position and declared himself the winner. But then Ganesh pointed out that while Sanat had encircled the world, Ganesh had encircled *his* world, which was comprised solely of his beloved parents. By doing so he had completed his journey long before Sanat had. With his pride deflated, Sanat Kumara had to admit defeat and soon left Kailash in disgrace. He then descended, or "fell," from his exalted position on the holy mountain and eventually settled first in South India and then Sri Lanka. Interestingly, this legend of Sanat's "Fall" exactly parallels a description of Lucifer's "Fall" in the *Holy Bible,* wherein he is referred to as "the annointed cherub" who was cast down from the "Holy Mountain of God" (Ezekial 28:14-16). Sanat Kumara's link to Lucifer, the "annointed cherub," is also confirmed through his name of Skanda, which is a title once used in Greece for Lucifer.

Before completing my wave of research involving Sanat Kumara I discovered one more important link that unites him with Tawsi Melek, Masau'u and Lucifer. All four deities are related to the planet Venus and the asterism of the Pleiades. As Karttikeya, Sanat Kumara is the "Son of the Pleiades," but he is also the "Lord of Venus," a title accorded him by the Ascended Masters. Similarly,

Sanat Kumara with Peacock Crown

Sri Krishna with Peacock Crown

Lucifer is Latin for "Light bringer," which is a name for Venus in its appearance on the horizon as the Morning Star. And Lucifer's connection to the Pleiades is revealed by his Pleiadian name of Samjassa, the leader of the Fallen Angels in the *Book of Enoch*. Tawsi Melek's link to the Pleiades is ostensibly revealed during the Autumn Festival of the Yezidis, which they celebrate when the celestial Court of the Peacock Angel is directly overhead in the night time sky. At that time of the year the principal asterism that occupies the zenith position in the heavens is the Pleiades. As for Masau'u and his link to the Seven Sisters, it is ostensibly revealed in Navajo mythology by their Black God, the Navajos' counterpart of Masau'u. The Black God is a Fire God who like Masau'u wears disheveled clothing while walking upon the Earth during the dead of night with only a torch to light his path. According to one Navajo legend, the Black God is intimately associated with the Pleiades. He created the asterism and wears its seven stars tattooed to his head.

The People of the Peacock Angel

After returning from the East I made plans to visit America's largest colony of Yezidis in Lincoln, Nebraska. My goal in visiting the more than 500 Yezidis living in Lincoln, most of whom had fled Iraq during the savage regime of Saddam Hussein, was to learn more about the Peacock Angel. My hosts were to be Kawwal Hasan and his daughter, Laila, whom I had previously contacted after my eventful meeting with the Peacock Angel in the Andes. Kawwal was a Faqir, a Yezidi teacher and record keeper, and Laila served as his English translator.

I brought along my friend Larry, as well as the gift of peacock feathers and a Hindu aarti lamp. One of the significant links between the Yezidis and the Hindus are their ceremonial oil lamps known as aarti lamps (Hindu) and Sanjaks (Yezidi), both of which are typically surmounted with small images of peacocks. In lieu of not having a resource for buying a Sanjak replica, I arrived with a Hindu aarti lamp as a gift for Kawwal's family.

Larry and I were met at the door by Kawwal, a short, friendly man with a thick salt and pepper beard and a great love of tobacco. Kawwal and his family had been living in Lincoln since 1998, when Lutherans helped them move from the refugee tent camp in Syria they had lived in for nine years after fleeing Iraq. Most of the other residents in Lincoln's Yezidi community also arrived about this time.

Larry and I were led into a small living room that was sparsely decorated with pictures and photos displaying images of the Peacock Angel and the Yezidis' most sacred temple city of Lalish in northern Iraq. One outstanding photo that drew my attention was that of Kawwal's uncle, another Faqir, who looked mystical and dignified in his multi-colored ceremonial robes. There are three principal castes in Yezidi culture, the Sheikhs, Pirs and Murids, or "Commoners." A Faqir can be of any of the three principal castes, but they typically stand alone as their own sub-caste.

I presented the Hindu aarti lamp to my host and instantly a huge smile flashed across his face. Anything "peacock" is greatly prized by the Yezidis, but this was even more treasured because of its resemblance to the sacred Sanjaks. As I was to learn, the Peacock Angel had anciently given the Yezidis seven Sanjaks, most of which had, over many millennia, been either lost or stolen. The remaining two are only released for public viewing once a year, when singers and dancers known as Qewels escort them to the Yezidis' towns and villages in Kurdistan.

After we had all been seated in the living room and served Middle Eastern tea, I brought out the photos I had taken at Kataragama for Kawwal and Laila to look over. I watched with excitement as they poured over each photo while issuing joyous squeals of recognition. They felt such a kinship to every scene and image at Kataragama that you would have thought they were looking at photos of their beloved Lalish. And their enthusiasm continued to grow when I explained the symbology and legends associated with Sanat Kumara, including his status as Creator and King of the World, which were also epithets of their beloved Peacock Angel. To my surprise Kawwal had already felt a special affinity and kinship to the Hindus. In fact, his Yezidi ancestors had come from India!

Kawwal then shared with Larry and I a detailed history of the Yezidis. He told us that following the Garden of Eden scenario, which was in an area that includes Kurdistan and southern Turkey, the Yezidis participated in the founding of the Sumerian civilization. When a cataclysmic flood covered the Fertile Crescent around 4000 BCE and destroyed their native land, most of the Yezidis migrated to safer regions in North Africa, Afghanistan and India. Then, around 2000 BCE, many of the Yezidis returned to their ancestral territories in the Middle East where they participated in the creation of the Assyrian and Babylonian civilizations. Kawwal's family returned to Kurdistan during a later migration from India, leaving behind a community of Yezidis in the sub-continent that would eventually number hundreds of thousands. I was told that the remaining Yezidis in India are "Adawis" and recognize the Peacock Angel and Sanat Kumara as the same entity.

Larry and I sat in rapt attention as Kawwal spoke about the greatness of Tawsi Melek and how his sovereignty extends throughout the cosmos. The Peacock Angel first became Emperor of the Universe and then King of the World. He specially chose our planet as his galactic home base, but he also holds court on many other planets and stars throughout the cosmos. After arriving on Earth and playing an important role in the Garden of Eden with the other six Great Angels by producing Adam and Eve, Tawsi Melek resolved to create a tribe of people that would be exclusively his. To do so he isolated some of Adam's sperm in a jar and magically grew it without the help of Eve. The sperm grew into a male child known as Shehid bin Jar, "Son of the Jar," who later chose as his wife an houri, a spirit from Paradise. Together they begat the race of Yezidis.

When we reached a lull in the conversation I took it as an opportunity to recount my experiences with the Peacock Angel. With great anticipation I asked Kawwal if other Yezidis typically had similar experiences of Tawsi Melek. I had previously read that, like Sanat Kumara, the Peacock Angel takes the form of one or more peacocks, a snake, or as a boy with peacock plumes growing out of his hind end. It can, however, assume any form it desires.

Kawwal was suddenly reticent. The experience of the Peacock Angel is personal and varies from person to person. When he was ready he to speak again he shared his own special visitation from Tawsi Melek when he was just seven years old. At that time the young Kawwal was in the throes of a severe illness. The Peacock Angel manifested at his bedside in the form of a Yezidi Faqir who took him by the hand and led him to a small spacecraft in his back yard that was invisible to everyone except them. He then transported the young boy to another world. Upon arriving at their destination they were met by ten other Qewels (singers) who were sitting in a circle. A Faqir, whose seat was raised above the Qewels, pointed to Kawwal and asked why his people (the Yezidis) were being killed and forced to convert to Islam. He inquired if this persecution was continuing on Earth and Kawwal sadly answered "yes." Tawsi Melek then cured Kawwal by inserting a vacuum-like tube down his throat and sucking all the dark toxins out of him. Afterwards, the renewed boy was taken home.

As soon as their ship landed back on Earth, Kawwal immediately ran to his mother, imploring her to explain what had happened to him. With an urgency that betrayed her profoundly caring nature, she quickly left the house and then returned with a local wise man who examined the young boy, both physically and mentally. Realizing that Kawwal's story must be true since the boy was fully healed from his malady, the wise villager inquired whether Tawsi Melek had also given Kawwal any other gifts, such as prayers to repeat. Kawwal responded affirmatively and then proceeded to sing the prayers he had received long into the night. This shocked and amazed the village wise man. He informed Kawwal's mother that her son had been greatly blessed by Tawsi Melek and she should immediately sacrifice a lamb to the Peacock Angel. From that time onwards Kawwal fully developed the ability known in Kurdish as *eb daftare kat,* during which he would become unconscious for an hour or more while praying and chanting the entire time. He had become a mystical Faqir.

When it became time for lunch Kawwal's wife entered the room and spread a large plastic sheet in the center of the carpeted floor. She then covered it with all kinds of Middle Eastern delicacies typically eaten by the Yezidis, including boiled goat. This was the finest delicacy of the meal and considered a real treat among the Yezidis, so I pretended to munch on it rather than impolitely informing my host of my predominantly vegetarian diet. After all the dishes had been brought and laid out, Larry and I were told to sit in the center of them while Kawwal watched us eat. I could not remember seeing so much food served for just two people. I hated not being able to eat everything in front of me, but there was so much oil in the dishes I was quickly stuffed. Fortunately, the left over food did not go to waste but was later consumed by the other family members.

At one point while eating both Larry and I suddenly felt the floor underneath us shake with the intensity of an earthquake tremor. We looked at each other in startled disbelief, but then noticed that Kawwal was not the slightest bit disturbed by the rumble. A few moments later we both had the same epiphany: we had experienced the thunderous presence of Tawsi Melek in his form of the explosive Kundalini power. For sometime I had desired an experience of the prodigious power I knew he wielded, and now I had been blessed with it. And there would be more to come. The power of the Peacock Angel and its accompanying tremors became a staple of our experience over the next few days, even during our long drive home.

After lunch Kawwal began calling many of the other Yezidi men in his community and inviting them over to his home. One half hour later I watched through the window as at least twenty men wearing red and white turbans and sporting huge mustaches parked their cars and quickly headed for the house.

Kawwal's living room was filled to capacity. As we slowly went around the room and introduced ourselves, nearly every Yezidi man in attendance reported how his family back in Iraq had been persecuted by the Moslem Kurds. Most of their relatives had either been physcially tortured and/or denied the relief food and water sent them from countries around the globe. Kawwal had already debriefed me regarding the attacks the Yezidis had been subject to since the dawn of Islam. Over the course of 72 genocidal attacks directed against them nearly 20 million Yezidis have been murdered for refusing to convert to the religion of Mohammed. Helping to promote this carnage has been the biased education of the Moslems, who are taught from a very young age that the Peacock Angel is Satan and the Yezidis are his worshippers. So throughout life each Moslem man feels perfectly justified in persecuting and killing Yezidis anytime they want. In fact, a great reward of 72 virgins is said to await each of them in Paradise if they distinguish themselves as Yezidi murderers. Such deadly propaganda has spoiled the minds of the Moslem faithful and produced suicide bombers ready to blow up entire Yezidi villages. Their most recent massacre was in 2007 when four trucks laden with bombs drove into the Yezidi town of Sinjar. The bombs were detonated and at least 500 Yezidis were killed and countless others wounded.

I offered to help my new Yezidi friends anyway I could, but I knew that any assistance would provide no more than a band-aid to their current persecution. It seemed clear to me that only after fanatical Moslems (as well as the rest of humanity) had opened their collective minds to the truth about who and what the Peacock Angel truly is would the Yezidis finally find both peace and protection. So, as a first step to educating the world I came up with the idea of creating a website called Yezidi Truth; so instead of there only being only websites featuring the Yezidis as "Devil Worshippers," there would also be one that would give accurate information regarding both the Yezidis and Tawsi Melek. Everyone in the room agreed this was the best solution for the time being. The website was posted soon after I returned home with the internet address of www.YezidiTruth.org. Since then it has been visited many times by the inquiring public, politicians, and humanitary organizations seeking to help the Yezidis. So it has served a valuable purpose. But it has also been visited innumerable times by inimical hackers who have tried to disrupt and destroy it. At one point my webmaster threw up his arms in frustration and threatened to abandon the website, but I was able to convince him that this kind of assault is nothing new to the Yezidis and that the best option is to stay the course, however possible.

Faqir Kawwal Hasan and his daughter, Laila

Kawwal Hasan's late uncle, also a Faqir

The Royal Road of the King

During my visit to Lincoln Kawwal and I had also discussed at length the importance of the Yezidis' sacred city of Lalish. For the People of the Peacock Angel it is the Center of the Earth where Tawsi Melek had initially landed on our planet before spreading his feathers around the globe. It was also the site of the Garden of Eden and the location where Tawsi Melek's court convenes during the seven day Autumn Festival. As we spoke I recalled other places on the globe with similar pedigrees, i.e., locales that had at some time in history been venerated as Centers of the Earth, Gardens of Eden, and Courts of the King of the World. I made a mental note to plot these holy places on a global map when I returned home to see if they have any noticeable pattern. And indeed they do.

After purchasing a large map of the world I inserted colored pins in the regions corresponding to the Hopi Mesas, Giza in Egypt, Mount Kailash, Jerusalem, Eridu, Kauai, and the Yezidis sacred city of Lalish - all of which have been denominated by their respective inhabitants as the "Center of the Earth," as well as a "Garden of Eden," and a "Court of the King of the World." Some of these places are associated with the ancient swastika symbol which signifies, among other things, the Center of the World. Many are famous for their tridents - symbols associated with the power and authority of the King of the World - which manifest as trinitized mountains, hills and/or pyramids. They also mirror the three stars of Orion's Belt, thus designating them terrestrial homes of the Celestial King.

As I had predicted a very noticeable pattern emerged. All these places exist within a 20 degree band that encircles the globe and has 30 degrees north latitude as its midpoint. This band is not, technically, at the geographical center of the Earth, which is marked by the equator. But when the land masses south of 30 degrees north latitude are joined together as one continent (not including the Arctic or Antarctica), and the land masses north of 30 degrees north latitude are similarly joined together, both synthesized continents are approximately 26 million square miles in size. So the band and its midpoint represents the center of the landmasses that exist between the poles. It is this region that has been denominated by many past civilizations as the Center of the Earth.

I theorized that the central 20 degree band might be the legenday Royal Road of the King where the Earth's monarch had anciently encircled the globe while amalgamating new territories into his global kingdom and teaching the mysteries to his subjects. The monarchs Osiris, Dionysus, Sanat Kumara, and the Peacock Angel are all averred to have traveled around the globe while blessing our planet and spreading the sacred rites designed to uplift humanity.

Here are the co-ordinates of those places within the 20 degree band that have been Gardens of Eden, Centers of the Earth and Courts of the King of the World:

Sedona, Arizona 34.8600 N, 111.7892 W

Four Corners 36.9990 N, 109.0452 W

Hopi Second Mesa 35.82 N, 110.50 W

Mt. Kailash 31 N Lat 81 E Long

Varanasi 25.2820 N, 82.9563 E

Ahaggar Mountains 23.10 N 5. 50 E

Giza 30 N Lat, 31 E Long

Lalish 36 N Lat, 43 E Long

Eridu 30.8158 N, 45.9961 E

Jerusalem 32 N Lat, 34 E Long

Kauai 22.0833 N, 159.5000 W

Mount Kurama 35.1239 N, 135.7714 E

Leading my list are Sedona, the Four Corners and the Hopi Mesas, all of which were originally part of Tuwanasavi, the Hopis' Center of the Earth," which is the region that Masau'u, the King of the World, gave his favored tribe to settle. As the premier territory inhabited by the Hopis after their emergence onto the Fourth World, Tuwanasavi also merits the title "Garden of Eden in North America." Sedona receives this status twice. When the Yavapai settled there after a huge flood forced them from their underworld home, Sedona became their Center of the World and Garden of Eden.

Mount Kailash, which is on the opposite side of the globe from Tawanasavi, has been accorded similar epithets. Kailash is the physical counterpart of legendary Mount Meru, the premier mountain at the Center of the Earth from which all other peaks around the globe were seeded. The Hindu *Puranas* maintain that Meru-Kailash once marked the middle of Jambu Dvipa, which in the historical texts is a name for both a legendary continent at the Center of the World as well as the Earth in its entirety. Similarly, the Persian history contained within the *Aveinidad* refer to Meru-Kailash as Hara Benzati, (shortened as Albourz or Elbourz), the Emerald Mountain at the Center of the Earth that once united Heaven and Earth and served as home to Mithras, the ancient King of the World. Tibetan Buddhists similarly regard Meru-Kailash as being in the Center of the World, as do the practitioners of the Tibetan Bon religion, who refer to it as the "Swastika Mountain." Kailash, the "Crystal Mountain," is considered so sacred that no human other than the famous Tibetan recluse Milarepa has ever been allowed to climb it.

Many of the Asian peoples first appeared in the Garden of Eden that surrounds and includes Mount Kailash, including the Persians, Scythians, and the earliest Tibetans. The neighboring Bon Shamans claim that the region was the site

143

of their ancient Garden of Eden known as Olmolungring, while some Tibetan Buddhists identify the area as Shambhala, the location of the throne of the King of the World that is occupied by physical incarnations of the Dhyani Buddha Amitibha, Sanat Kumara's counterpart in Tibetan Buddhism. The incidence of so many Persian-speaking tribes in the same region once occupied by Olmolungring has prompted some ethnologists to speculate that the Bon were once part of a huge Persian Empire and even had Persian kings!

As one of the premier Courts of the King of the World Mount Kailash is both the home of Sanat Kumara before his "fall" and descent into the lowlands of India, as well as his permanent abode. Even though Shiva, the father of Sanat Kumara, is normally acknowledged to be the eternal figure seated upon the summit of Kailash, Shiva's true nature is that of the transcendent, infinite Spirit that is beyond any form or limitation. Shiva with a limited, tangible form is his Son, Sanat Kumara (aka Rudra).

Mount Kailash's status as the Center of the World, as well as the giver of life to its surrounding Garden of Eden and home to the Son of Shiva, is corroborated by its shape: a gigantic Shiva Lingam. A Shiva Lingam, which represents the union of the male and female sexual organs, is a symbol of both the primal Son and the source of life.

South of Mount Kailash is another throne of the King of the World. It resides in Varanasi, India, the most sacred city of the Hindus and their Center of the World. Here three sacred hills come together to form a trident, the symbol of Shiva and his Son, Sanat Kumara. At Varanasi or Kashi, the "City of Light," is the principal entrance to the King of the World's underworld or afterlife kingdom. As Lord of Death and Destruction, Shiva as Rudra accompanies the newly released soul into the next world while blessing it with a mantra that will grant instant spiritual liberation. It is for this reason that the greatest desire of a Hindu is to die and be cremated in Varanasi.

Another throne of the King of the World comprised of three hills or mountains resides in Algeria. Here, the Ahaggar Mountains form a perfect trident at the Center of the World of the desert-dwelling Taureg people, knicknamed the "Blue Vengeance." In ancient times these three mountains existed upon a sacred island in

The Hopis used the symbol of the Swastika to delineate thair migrations. The center of their Swastika is Four Corners, the Center of the Earth.

A Maze or Labyrinth is related to a Swastika. Each represents the middle and/or Center of the Earth from which all things emerge and return.

the center of the Triton Sea that covered much of North Africa. As merchant mariners the Tauregs regularly sailed between this island and their Atlantean homeland. After discovering the sacred island and the throne of their trident-wielding King Neptune, the Atlantean version of the King of the World, the Tauregs proceeded to hollow out the three united mountains and then construct a subterranean temple with adjoining library inside. The texts and scrolls they brought from Atlantis and then stocked within their library both described their homeland of Atlantis and recorded its sacred history. When the Triton Sea was subsequently drained to become the Algerian desert, the trident mountains became part of the Ahaggar Mountain Range. Legend has it that the library and temple of Tauregs still reside within the three mountains, and it is there that the Blue Vengeance often perform a special Atlantean Crown Dance that is also observed by their cousins on the other side of the globe, the Mescalero Apaches, who similarly claim to have originated on Atlantis.

Giza, Egypt is another Center of the World. Over many years of meticulous research "archaeocryptologist" Carl Munck proved that Giza was designated by the ancients as the Center of the World and made it the crossing point of the earliest Prime Meridian of longitude. All ancient temples and pyramids around the globe were once measured from it. Today, Giza remains the site of a trinity of sacred mountains in the form of three towering pyramids. These are the home of the terrestrial Green Man and King of the World, Ptah-Osiris, and according to Egyptologist Robert Bauvall, they reflect the belt of his celestial counterpart, Orion. Legend has it that Neptune-Poseidon was brought to Egypt by the Atlanteans where he became Ptah-Sokar-Osiris, the deity whose three names and three powers of the fiery life force - creation, preservation and destruction - were once symbolized by the three prongs of Neptune's royal trident. On Atlantis, one of King Neptune's forms was a great fire dragon that lived under the ground and within volcanoes. In Africa and Europe, the Atlantean fire dragon evolved into the Egyptian fire god Ptah and his counterparts, the Greek Hephaestus and the Roman Vulcan.

At Memphis, the capital city of dynastic Egypt, the ruling pharaohs incarnated the spirit of Ptah-Osiris and were, therefore, monarchs of not just Egypt but

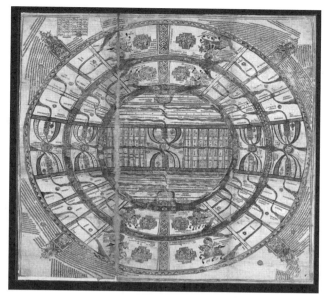

Ancient Jain depiction of Jambu Dvipa with Mt. Meru-Kailas at the center. Jambu Dvipa is a name for both a continent as well as Earth itself.

Mount Kailash: A gigantic Shiva Lingam

the entire world. Memphis had been built upon a sacred mound in the Center of the World that contained the soul of Ptah-Osiris, the Green Man. According to legend, the Memphite primal mound was the first plot of solid land to emerge out of the cosmic sea at the beginning of time and must, therefore, be considered an African counterpart of the Hopi city of Sip-Oraibi.

Northeast of Giza is Lalish, another Center of the World, where the Peacock King first landed before spreading his plumes and completely covering the Earth with flora and fauna. Some Yezidi Faqirs contend that Lalish was the first solid land to emerge from the water that initially encircled our planet, so it is the Asian counterpart of both Memphis and Hopis' Sip-Oriabi. Lalish later became the center of a Garden of Eden that encompassed the regions of modern Kurdistan and southern Turkey. It is said that the King of the World, Tawsi Melek, returns to Lalish each October during the annual Autumn Festival. At that time Tawsi Melek and the members of his celestial court hover over the sacred city and all the Yezidis gather below to directly commune with their beloved deity.

Recently, the discovery of Gobekli Tepe in southern Turkey has contributed solid evidence in support of the Yezidis' Garden of Eden. Gobekli Tepe is an archeological excavation of megalithic carved blocks placed in ceremonial circles that date back to at least 10,000 BCE. Under these blocks are believed to be more blocks, and under them are even older blocks. Thus, when the excavations are completed Gobekli Tepe could eventually reveal a Garden of Eden in northern Iraq and southern Turkey that existed hundreds of thousands of years ago. Researchers who have visited Gobekli Tepe, such as Andrew Collins, author of *Gobekli Tepe: Genesis of the Gods*, believe that its location is described in the *Holy Bible* and some earlier Sumerian tablets that refer to a primal Garden of Eden in the Middle East.

Previous to the discovery of Gobekli Tepe, Eridu, the home of their King of the World Enki, was recognized by western researchers as the original Garden of Eden. It was, and still is, considered by many to be the site of a Garden of Eden where Enki appeared to Adam and Eve in his form of the Serpent on the Tree. Afterwards, Eridu became the Court of the King of the World and the headquarters of the world's government. A passage in the Sumerian King-List plainly states:

Ahilya Ghat in Varanasi. Photo by Ken Wieland

The Ancient Triton Sea

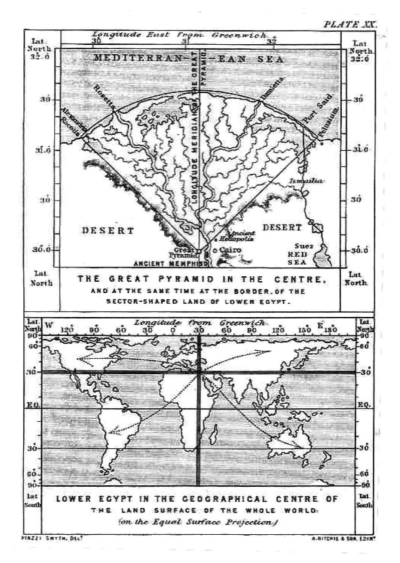

Maps made by early Egyptologist Piazzi Smyth

In the upper map Giza and Memphis unite Upper and Lower Egypt, thus placing them at the center of the Egyptian world.

In the lower map Giza and Memphis are shown to be in the Center of the World

"When kingship from heaven was lowered, the kingship was in Eridu." The translation of the name "Enki" is "Lord of the Earth."

Jerusalem is included in this list of the Courts of the King of the World because it was the ancient city of King Melchizedek, the Middle Eastern monarch who has been touted as our planetary ruler. He appears to have been a reflection or incarnation of Sanat Kumara by virtue of his being "without [physical] father or mother or genealogy, and has neither beginning of days nor end of life..." (Heb 7:1-3) Melchizedek was the King of Salem, which is an ancient name for both Jerusalem as well as the Earth in its entirety. Literally translated Salem simply means "Peace."

All the world maps created In Europe during the Middle Ages placed Jerusalem in the Center of the World. In the center of Jerusalem is the primal mound at the very center of the Earth known as the Eben Shetiya, the Stone of Foundation, that unites Heaven and Earth and from which the Prophet Mohammed was able to physically or metaphorically soar into Heaven. Today the Dome of the Rock encloses the Eben Shetiya, but in very ancient times the rock was surmounted by the Holy of Holies of Solomon's Templar and its indwelling Ark of the Covenant.

Kauai is the oldest of the Hawaiian Islands and said to be approximately six million years old. When Sanat Kumara arrived on Earth he made Kauai one of his palatial courts. He also projected his spirit into the island of Kauai (Sanat's spirit filled the Earth, although in certain parts of it, such as his Courts and the sacred mountain that became the Island of Kauai, his spirit is exceptionally strong). Today, Sanat dwells in the volcanic mountain in the center of Kauai known as Wai ale ale. The seven chakras of Sanat Kumara are marked by seven sequential temples that rise up the side of the volacano. Sanat Kumara's sacred animal, the cock or rooster, runs freely throughout Kauai, and Sanat Kumara's six-headed form as Karttikeya sits within a large banyon grove at the island's Hindu Monastery. Natives call Kauai both the Center of the Earth and the Garden of Eden.

Mount Kurama is located just outside the city of Kyoto in Japan. Legend has it that at approximately the same time Sanat Kumara transmitted his spirit into Kauai, he also merged with Mount Kurama. The Buddhists contend that as

Lalish, the Yezidis' Center of the World

Mideaval map of Jersusalem at the Center of the World

"Sonten," Sanat Kumara arrived from Venus six milliion years ago and then merged his spirit into the mountain. Known as both the Creator of the Universe and Spirit of the Earth, Sonten currently blesses all those who ascend Mount Kurama with both worldly and spiritual gifts. After Dr. Usui ascended the mountain in the 1920s and performed a 21 day fast, Sonten blessed him with the laying-on-of-hands healing system known as Reiki. Reiki, meaning "Universal Life Force Energy," is a name for Sanat Kumara who arrived on Earth as pure energy. So it can thus be said that the spirit of the life force taught Dr. Usui the system of life force healing. Part of Reiki training is to learn a set of symbols that look like bolts of lightening and serpents. These are symbolic representations of Sanat Kumara in his form of pure energy.

Shrine of Sonten on Mt. Kurama

The six-headed form of Sanat Kumara-Karttikeya on Kauai

The Great Flood

It is estimated that there are at least 170 flood legends scattered around the globe that recount gargantuam deluges that have decimated our planet. When I first began coming to Sedona I was told one of these flood legends. The prevailing legend stated that the red rocks had been shaped by a great sea or a massive flood that completely covered Sedona. As the flood waters lowered, the red rocks acquired their characteristic rings as they were smoothed and contoured into their current forms. I have since discovered that throughout its very long history Sedona has been underwater just as often as it has been above water. So the next time you are out hiking a trail in Sedona imagine yourself 200 feet below the surface of a huge ocean. It's a mind-numbing thought!

In this chapter:
  * Sedona's Flood History
  * Worlds, Deluges and Temples
  * Native American Legends of the Underworld

In 2001 Arizona beckoned again, so Andrea and I packed a U-Haul truck and moved from Washington State down to Flagstaff, Arizona. Andrea did not feel ready for either the brutal summer heat or the stimulating vortexes of Sedona, so I agreed to live in nearby Flagstaff until she was. After three frigid Flagstaff winters and inummerable commutes to Sedona, we were both more than ready to re-locate to my heart's home in the spring of 2004.

By this time I had completed my apprenticeship in Wachuma shamanism with A.C.. In the midst of a recent journey to Peru he had surprised me by an-nouncing that the Wachuma "Masters" dwelling in other dimensions had informed him that I was ready to lead my own ceremonies. A.C. gave me his blessings to begin my vocation as a Wachuma shaman in Sedona with one condition: he would be the Wachuma shaman in Peru while I would serve that function in the US.

So when we moved to Sedona in 2004 the stage was set for me to help people achieve a higher level of consciousness through the aid of a shamanic entheogen. For many years I had debated on whether the sacred Peruvians cactus could significantly and consistently enhance my inter-dimensional vision of the red rock temples, and whether it could assist others in seeing them as well. I first began to seriously contemplate using an entheogen when I visited Sedona with sound healer Tom Kenyon, who at the time worked as a psychotherapist at the healing center that Andrea and I owned and operated in Washington. Being natu-rally more psychic than myself it was not long after we arrived in Sedona before Tom began seeing interdimensional temples that I had only been able to perceive on very rare occasions. As we hiked Boynton Canyon his psychic senses allowed him to not only view many of the red rock temples that are hidden to most people, he even detected (and I believe later recorded) a complete melody issuing from one of them. He seemed to possess the enviable ability to switch on his interdimensional senses at will. Our hike took a comical turn when we found our-selves high upon the red rock shelf with the huge red monolith and dripping with sweat. After peeling down to our underwear and setting our clothing out to dry in the Arizona sun, Tom and I found two large red rocks to serve as rustic chaise loungers and then sprawled over them. Little did I know that we were next to an Anasazi cliff dwelling that is one of the stopover points of every helicopter tour through the canyon. So, within five minutes we heard a familiar whirling sound followed seconds later by a helicopter full of tourists that hovered directly over our fully exposed bodies. Tom and I decided that we were too tired to move and, laughing, decided to cater to the tourists by giving them a much more risque photograph of Boynton Canyon than they had bargained for.

My experience with Tom revealed to me that I could increase my research work in Boynton Canyon exponentially if I had the ability to elicit my second sight on command. Now, with Wachuma, I could potentially live out that dream. Moreover, there was no question in my mind that Wachuma was going to be the perfect entheogen to use on other people in Boynton Canyon. Both the plant and the vortex provide a very heart-centered experience and can thus enhance and synergize each other. The loving energy of the sacred cactus comes from the Universal Goddess, its indwelling spirit, and the loving ambiance of Boynton Canyon is derived from its female dweller, the Yavapai matriarch Kamalapukwia, the Goddess of Sedona. Boynton also generates a balanced heart energy by virtue of being the only vortex with the perfect electric and magnetic, or male and female, balance. By sympathetically uniting the male-female polarity within a person the canyon can assist in opening the heart chakra, which is one of the principal subtle energy centers in the body where the polarity unites.

My logic proved correct. From the start my Wachuma experiment bore very positive results. While guiding a series of ceremonies in Boynton Canyon it became easier for both myself and others to see interdimensionally, and many of the participants of my cereremonies reported intense feelings of love towards themselves, each other and all life. They also felt supremely safe and nurtured, which I attributed to the spirit of the Universal Goddess in the cactus that moved through them and surrounded them. Some even felt transported back "home" to the Garden of Eden. This made perfect sense since some Peruvian shamans claim that the cactus originated on the continent of Mu, the Pacific Garden of Eden, and carries the frequency of that fabled land.

Many of my new Wachuma initiates were eventually blessed with visions of some of the red rock temples of Boynton Canyon, and others could perceive the images of peacocks or peacock eyes that stared intently at them from the surrounding trees and bushes. Since I was also under the influence of the Wachuma during these ceremonies I was often able to confirm their visions.

When not leading others in ceremony I occasionally imbibed Wachuma to further my research. Sometimes I would blessed with a visitation from Tawsi Melek who would arrive to give me a lesson. On one special day the Peacock Angel taught me the intimate connection between the peacock and dragon. After appearing in his radiant peacock image, I closely watched as Tawsi Melek transformed himself into a dragon. What amazed me about this transformation is that the peacock form needed to be tweaked only slightly to become a dragon. Amazingly, in many ways the peacock and dragon were twins of each other. At last I understood why different cultures worldwide have referred to the King and Creator of the Universe as a dragon *or* as a peacock; it is because they are so closely connected. They are truly one. I also understood why the Chinese Taoists have traditionally conceived of Earth as the body of a great dragon while the Yezidis see it as covered with the peacock plumes of Tawsi Melek.

It was during this stage of my research that my relationship with Boynton Canyon and its temples moved to a new level. The catalyst of this evolution was a pivotal revelation I received in relation to the red rock temples. During one crystal clear morning the spirit of the cactus activated my Third Eye and I was guided to climb to a high vantage point overlooking much of the canyon. There, in front of me, were many of the temples I had not seen since February, 1987. Wachuma had fully activated my Ajna Chakra in the same way prayer had awakened it back in 1987. I reveled in the striking panorama of trees and temples for a few hours; and then, right on cue, the temples began to slowly disappear as the effects of the cactus wore off. But this time the end result was much different; the temples did not completely disappear from my view as they had in the past. Instead, they remained as very damaged or "ruined" red rock-shaped temples.

In order to confirm my new revelation I climbed down from my high perch for a closer inspection. The results were the same. Everywhere I looked I saw the ruined foundations of red rock temples, and they did not dissapear even when I was standing right in front of them. In fact, I realized that this is how everyone normally sees the red rocks; they do not recognize them as temples and continue walking right by them. Unless one has second sight and has seen the temples in their original perfection, it is nearly impossible to identify them in normal waking consciousness. But I had seen them in their interdimensional perfection, and now I could identify them in their normal 3-D shapes. So without hesitation, I decided I could both confirm and add to what Sakina Blue-Star had told me years before: "The Red Rocks of Sedona were [and are!] the sacred Temples of the Ancients."

Soon after this pivotal experience I began researching Sedona's cataclysmic records in order to determine how Boynton's red rock temples could have aquired their worn down, "ruined" appearance. Since their condition appeared to be the result of water wear I decided it expediant to focus primarily on Sedona's flood history. I knew I was on the right track when I subsequently discovered that not only had Sedona been completely covered by flood waters in the past, it had been submerged many times.

Sedona's Flood History

Much of Sedona's flood history can be discerned through its geological strata. According to the tale it tells the red sand that comprises Sedona red rock formations first arrived in the area about 280 million years ago. This was during the time when North America was part of the universal continent known as Pangea. The windblown sand arrived in Sedona from the region of what is now the Grand Canyon and then formed as great dunes over the Land of OZ, which was then the shoreline of an inland sea. This was the Pedregosa Sea, which covered most of what is now southern Arizona. Then, over millions of years of periodic flooding from the sea waves along with alternating ages of extreme heat and cold, the sand hardened into Sedona's famous red rocks. Their final shaping and polishing occurred over the last 3 million years, when they were either surrounded or completely covered over by the deluge-like flooding that was precipitated by the glacial melting that followed the last Ice Age.

Another excellent record of Sedona's flood history can be found in the local legends of many tribes living in the American Southwest. Almost every southwest tribe - including the Hopis, Yavapai, Navajo, Zuni and Apache - has at least one legend featuring a massive flood that once covered the southwest and/or much of the planet. Obviously some of these deluges would have severely damaged Sedona's red rock temples, while others would have been much gentler on the red rock. Of these deluges, the natives contend that the most cataclysmic floods occur at the end or beginning of very long cycles of time, which the Hopis, Zunis and Yavapai refer to as "worlds." At the conclusion of a world most or all civilization on Earth is said to be completely destroyed, and then at the beginning of the next world a new civilization rises up from its ashes. According to the Hopis, the worst flood occurred at the end of the Third World, thus making it a good candidate for much or most of the destruction that occurred to the Boynton Canyon temples.

Worlds, Deluges and Temples

In order to get a better grasp of the Native American "worlds," I referred to *The Book of the Hopis* wherein author Frank Waters fully delineates all Four Worlds known to the southwest natives. Waters' information reveals both how and when the temples of Sedona might have been destroyed by flood waters, as well as how and when they could have been built.

According to the wisdom he gathered from Hopi Elders, especially the late White Bear Fredericks of Sedona, Waters asserts that the First and Second Worlds were a highly spiritual epochs of Earth history. Humans sought to live righteously during these eras by keeping their "Kopavi" or Crown Chakra open, thereby maintaining a continual contact with the Great Spirit. The **First World** is known in Hopi history as Tokpela, "Empty Space," and corresponds both with the era of the Biblical Garden of Eden and the "Dreamtime" of the Australian Aborigines. During this First World all people and animals lived peacefully together and any significant differences between life forms went unnoticed. But their unity consciousness began to degenerate near the conclusion of the First World, thereby precipitating a planetary cleansing by fire which was most likely orchastrated by the active, spewing volcanoes that covered much of the Earth at that time. The **Second World**, known as Tokpa, "Dark Midnight," saw the development of even more separateness within the human race and the gradual shutting down of the Crown Chakra. This world came to an end via a polar shift. The **Third World**,

160

known as Kuskurza, "Underworld," is esoterically associated with the rise and fall of Atlantis, when ego and intellect became fully developed and the greatest degeneration of the human race resulted. On the positive side, this led to great technological achievements, including the construction of pátuwvota, "shields made of hide," which is the Hopi term for the ancient saucer-shaped crafts that could levitate and fly to any part of the globe. But it also led to the development of advanced weaponry that was used by the Atlanteans to conquer and subjugate other civilizations. As Plato tells us, this is what ultimately led to the downfall of the Atlantic Motherland, which was subsequently broken up by earthquakes and volcanoes and then sent to the bottom of the ocean by massive tidal waves.

The rock temples of Sedona were most likely constructed sometime during the first three worlds, which collectively constitute the era of the Dreamtime "Gods" of the Aborigines. The ancient builders could have been extraterrestrials from other realms, which the Hopis refer to as Kachinas, and/or they could have been primeval colonizers from Lemuria or Atlantis who psychically "received" the design and functions of the temples and then constructed them. At some point, perhaps in the **Fourth World,** the ancient Hopis also contributed to the construction or rebuilding of the temples because they *were* the Lemurians. This was the result of spending many years immersed in the civilization of the Lemurians while "island hopping" across the islands of Mu. It is said that when the Hopis finally reached the west coast of the Americas they looked back from whence they had come and watched as the planetary deluge ending the Third World engulfed many of their island stepping stones and sent them to the bottom of the Pacific Ocean.

One Hopi clan that continues to retain legends regarding the tribe's "island hopping" migration is the Water Clan, whose name in Hopi is Patki or Patinyamu, meaning "Dwelling-on-Water Clan." The history of the Water Clan states that its members reached the Fourth World after "a very long water crossing"[1] and that they have been administering all the Hopi water rites ever since. The syllable "Pa" links this clan with Palatkwapi, which is the name of a fabled temple city in Hopi legend that many believe Sedona now sits upon. The syllable "Pa" also links the Water Clan with other people around the globe who similarly migrated from Mu and continue to associate it with water. It links them with the people of India, for example, whose term for water is "pani."

Through references to Palatkwapi, the Water Clan may possess the ancient secret regarding when the red rock temples of Sedona were destroyed. An important rite currently observed by the clan commemorates the existence of Palatkwapi, while also revealing that it was destroyed at the end of the Third World. During the rite the name Palatkwapi is used both as a name for an ancient sacred city, as well as the "World before the Emergence," i.e., the Third World. Thus, if Palatkwapi was indeed Sedona, then its temples were destroyed before the beginning of the Fourth World.[2]

The neighboring Yavapai of Arizona echo the Hopis and their legend of a huge flood. The Yavapai claim that they once existed inside the Earth but a deluge that occurred both inside and upon the surface of the planet forced them out of their subterranean motherland. Presented in its entirety below, the Yavapai flood legend became part of Sedona history in 1904, two years after the city's incorporation in 1902. The excerpt that follows is the accepted version of the legend as told by Mike Harrison and John Williams:

"We [the Yavapai] came out at Sedona, *the middle of the world* [italics mine]. This is our home. We call Sedona Wipuk. We call it after the rocks and the mountains there. All Yavapai come from Sedona. But in time they spread out.

"North of Camp Verde there is Montezuma Well. This lake has no bottom and underneath the water spreads out wide. That's where the people come out first. Long time ago there was no water in that lake. And people were living down there... And there is one man, a little hummingbird, we call it "minamina" and it goes up...and it sees there is a good world up there.

"So all the people they go up on a corn. They go around, go around, and where the ears of corn come out between there, they sleep. The turtle, he almost got caught up in there. He can't go fast. But he made it up. Lots of people come up from there, deer, quail, rabbits, jackrabbits...and when they look back the water is coming. The flood is in the well. But the water doesn't come out. He just stays level in there.

"The corn that came out from Montezuma Well, we get the seeds from there first. Blue and white and red and black. After some time there comes another flood. The people put a girl in a hollow log. Put food in that log for her. Then they tell her, "The flood will raise you. You will hit the sky. But you just stay still. If you lay still you will get out in a the end" Then the people glued the log together with pitch.

"The girl lay still in there all the time. After some time the water went down. The girl had a dove with her and she sent that dove out. The dove came back with a little weed. So the water has gone. There at Sedona is a high place. It is the highest place all around. And when the water went down, the girl hit that high place. It stopped right there. And the girl came out from the log. That girl called Kamalapukwia. Means "Old Lady White Stone." She is the first woman and we come from her. She came to Sedona and that's where all the Indians come from."

Kamalapukwia landed in Boynton Canyon. In time she would raise a daughter and then a grandson in a large cave in in the canyon. She and her descendents eventually multiplied until they had settled much of Sedona and the Verde Valley. To commemorate their red rock beginnings, the Yavapai currently hold a special ceremony and celebration in Boynton Canyon, which they identify as their official birthplace upon the surface of Earth.

Could the Yavapai flood be synonymous with the Hopis' deluge? According to Chris Coder, an archaeologist of the Yavapai Cultural Center in Arizona, they are one and the same. As to when the massive flood occurred, Coder associates it with the melting of the glaciers that occurred at the conclusion of the last Ice Age. He maintains that the deluge recorded by the Hopis and Yavapai, as well as a massive flood remembered by the nieghboring Apaches, was either the result of glacial flooding that occurred 9,500 years ago, or by the more massive deluge of 12,800 years ago. This later date is interesting since it corresponds to the destruction of legendary Atlantis, the civilization that is said to have met its demise at the end of the Hopis' Third World. Could the Hopis' Third World have come to a cataclysmic end just 13,000 years ago?

Native American Legends of the Underworld

The Yavapai and Hopi flood legends noticably dovetail. Even if the Hopi "island hopping" legend is not in complete agreement with some of the details of

163

the Yavapai myth, there is an alternate Hopi flood legend that is. This alternate legend maintains that many of the Hopi ancestors retreated and then re-emerged from a subterranean underworld during the great flood. They traveled to the kingdom of the Ant People through a hole in the bottom of Grand Canyon, a Sipapu, that is now marked by a commemorative plaque. And then they returned to the surface through this same hole at the end of the deluge.

When I first read about the underworld of the Yavapai and Hopi I didn't know whether to take the legends literally or metaphorically. The Hopis themselves interpret their legends literally and an underworld theme runs prominently through much of their rites and beliefs. This includes their ceremonial kivas which simulate the underworld they once inhabited. I eventually found confirmation for the Hopi and Yavapai underworld civilization from other Native American tribes, such as the Navajo, who like the Hopi retreated to an underworld sanctuary when the world was covered with water. They state:

"...at one time all the nations, Navajos, Pueblos, Coyoteros, and white people, lived together underground, in the heart of a mountain, near the river San Juan. *Their food was meat, which they had in abundance, for all kinds of game were closed up with them in their cave;* but their light was dim, and only endured for a few hours each day. There were, happily, two dumb men among the Navajos, flute-players, who enlivened the darkness with music. One of these, striking by chance on the roof of the limbo with his flute, brought out a hollow sound, upon which the elders of the tribe determined to bore in the direction whence the sound came. The flute was then set up against the roof, and the Raccoon sent up the tube *to dig a way out,* but he could not. Then the Moth-worm mounted into the breach, and bored and bored till he found himself suddenly on the outside of the mountain, and *surrounded by water.*"[3]

I also discovered that there are tribes thousands of miles away to the east and south of the Navajos and Hopis that also speak of their emergence from the underworld. These include the Mandans, Creeks, Seminoles, Choctaw, Chickasaw, the Natchez Tribes, and some of the southern indigenous tribes of Mexico. Their legends consistently mention a subterranean world full of caverns, tunnels and even entire underground cities that their ancestors once inhabited. The Mandans claim to have lived in subterranean cities before eventually being led by the "tattooed ones" to the surface of the Earth through tunnels. The Choctaw and Creek Tribes claim that their people orignally emerged on to the surface through a big hole in the ground. They arrived on the surface very pale from having lived in the darkness of the underworld for so long and had to "bask in the Sun until their skin darkened."[4] In Mexico, the native Zapotecs assert: "We lived in cave-cities. Our forefathers came out of the caves of the underworld where it was crowded. They came out by tribes, each led by the spirit of its own animal totem."[5]

The Mescalero Apaches of Arizona maintain that they traveled to their current location in southern Arizona through an ancient tunnel system that unites all the Americas. Their history states that after fleeing the Old Red Land (Atlantis), their ancestors resided in the Peruvian Andes while helping to build the megalithic temples that still dot the South American mountains. Then they traveled north in an underground tunnel system all the way from Peru to Arizona. The Apache Chief Geronimo is believed to have had knowledge of this tunnel system and often hid in with it when pursued by the US Calvary. It is said that when the Calvary chased Geronimo into a box canyon they would suddenly loose him. A day or two later he would appear in a location 50 miles away that he had traveled to via the tunnels.

Today, we can find contemporary "urban legends" regarding underground cities in many parts of the American Southwest. Alien researchers claim, for example, that there is enough evidence to positively locate a subterranean base under Area 51 in Nevada, and another under Dulce, New Mexico. Furthermore, there are at least twenty other locations throughout the southwest that are allegedly colonies of ETs. Although some of these underworld cities are said to have been built in recent times, many are believed to be extremely ancient. Could the Star People have made these underground cities in an ancient age and then invited the southwestern tribes to live within them during times of planetary cataclysm? It is interesting to note that the Hopis' "Ant People" could refer to the race of ETs known as the Greys that allegedly now occupy the underground cities of the American Southwest and have been ascribed the physical features of ants. The Yavapai, who refer to the ancient Star People as the Kakaka, represent them in their sacred dances as possessing the features of Greys.

A Hopi descending into the "underworld" Kiva

Hopis observing ceremony in their "underworld" Kiva

After completing my research into the flood history of Sedona I returned to Boynton Canyon with a fresh perspective. I decided to try imagining the bottom of the canyon covered with water, which to my surprise is completely consistent with the placement of its red rock temples. They all sit about the same level, which would be just above the height of the water level if the canyon floor was fully submerged. It is not hard to imagine a water craft easily maneuvering between the temples, gradually going from one to the other. When I later shared this notion to a visionary hiker in Sedona he informed me of similar "water visions" he had had in other canyons and vortexes during his travels. Then he told me he found his visions accurately portrayed by Roger Dean, the visionary artist who designed the album covers for the progressive rock group *Yes*. For the cover of one of the group's albums Dean painted a scene that perfectly reflects what my friend claimed Sedona looked like in very ancient times. Every feature is there, including interdimensional temples, the spiralling red rocks of Sedona and even an American bald eagle. This was amazing to me since Dean is a Brit who has spent little time in the American Southwest. Perhaps I should not have been surprised; visionary artists are known to be natural channels for interdimensional scenes of the past they can summon through their clairvoyant vision. Below, and as a color plate in the center of the book, is what I now call "Ancient Sedona: Land of Blue Water & Red Rocks." It is Roger Dean's visionary painting entitled *Blue Desert*.

Courtesy of Roger Dean   www.RogerDean.com

Palatkwapi: City of the Star People

A legend among the Hopis states that there was once a great temple city of wisdom built by the Star People, the Kachinas. Many of the Hopi clans visited this city during their respective migrations throughout the Americas and later shared stories of it when all the clans reunited at their final destination on the Hopi Mesas. This mysterious city, known as Palatkwapi, the "Red House," was where the Star People taught important rituals and secrets of the universe that are still enacted and honored by the clans. Eventually destroyed by a flood, some believe that Palatkwapi is an ancient name for Sedona, and that its temples still exist in a "ruined" condition as the ponderous and magnificent red rock formations in the Land of OZ.

In this chapter:
* Who were the Star People?
* The Star Nations & Their Missionaries
* The Location of Palatkwapi
* Building Palatkwapi
* The Destruction of Palatkwapi

The legend of Palatkwapi begins with the arrival of the Hopis in North America. Soon after their arrival on the continent the Hopis were instructed by the Ruler of the Fourth World, Masau'u, to separate into clans and then embark on migrations to the extremities of the Western Hemisphere. Each clan was to travel as far north as possible, as far south as possible, and to the shores of the Atlantic and Pacific Oceans. Only after they had completed their migrations could all the clans reunite and live together in Tuwanasavi, the special home Earth's monarch had prepared for them.

The Blue Flute, Fire, Spider, and Snake Clans first headed north to the Arctic Circle while the Bear, Condor, Eagle, Grey Eagle, Sun, Kachina, Parrot, Flute and Coyote Clans began their migrations by heading south. Once they reached South America some of these clans participated in the construction of the lofty megalithic temples that punctuate the Andes today, just as the Apaches are reputed to have. Later, when they returned north, they brought with them the Cross-Stair Step symbol, the Andean "Chacana," that is today prolific throughout both the Andes and the Hopi Mesas. Joining each clan to mentor, protect and guide its members were the Star People, the Kachinas. They assisted the migrating Hopis in reaching their destinations, and they also helped them construct cities of spiritual light. The most sacred city visited by the clans during their migrations was Palatkwapi, a city built solely by the Star People many thousands of years earlier.

Who were the Star People?

The Star People, or Kachinas, of Hopi legend were missionaries and culture bearers who came to Earth in very remote times to teach fledgling humanity the sacred and mundane arts. In *Genesis* they are referred to as the "Sons of God" who married the "Daughters of Men." In many other Creation Myths around the world they are referred to as the early "Gods" or "Angels" who either mysteriously walked onto our world through interdimensional doorways or arrived here from other planets and stars in pátuwvota, flying saucers. Author Frank Waters asserts in *The Book of the Hopi* that the Kachinas came from "neighboring stars, constellations too distant to be visible, from mysterious spirit worlds."[1] Clifford Mahooty of the Kachina Clan of the Zunis adds that these ETs would suddenly

169

appear from other dimensions in the same way Captain Kirk and his Star Trek crew would spontaneously appear after being beamed down onto a planet. Once on Earth the Star People would share their knowledge with worthy humans, but they also selected certain persons to take back with them to their native planets. Their "kidnapping" continued until a treaty was made between the early tribes and the Kachinas that prohibited such abductions (see interview Chapter 11).

The Hopis locate the celestial homes of the Star People in the seven lower universes (there are nine universes in total) that were created by the Creator Sótunknang at the beginning of time. Sótunknang was himself an ET who traveled around the cosmos in a pátuwvota. His seamless, silver tunic is consistent with the uniforms reportedly worn by modern alien visitors. In one Hopi legend of Palatkwapi Sótunknang landed his flying shield on Earth in order to assist two lost children. As his pátuwvota arrived the children heard "a loud roaring noise over-head." Disembarking from his craft, Sótunknang appeared "clothed in a glittering costume of ice that sparkled like silver, and his head and face shone like a star." Sensing the overt fear of the children who were hugging each other for safety, Sótunknang calmly announced "Do not fear, I am Sótunknang, the heavenly God and because of the sympathy I have for you I have come to help you, so come and get on this pátuwvota of mine and let us be on the way." They then rose up to-gether "into the heavens" and sped away.

Like Sótunknang, many ancient Star People traveled to Earth as ETs in pátuwvota and some of their bodies as depicted by modern Kachina artists are also recognizeable by UFO researchers. The three solitary orifices in the head of many Kachinas, including Masau'u, are strikingly similar in appearance to many modern extraterrestrials, such as the Greys and Zetas. Similar iconic images can also be found among the Yavapai, who also interacted with the with the Star People. The Yavapai know the Star People as the Kakaka and currently honor them in ceremonial dances just as the Hopis do the Kachinas. During their cer-emonial Mountain Spirit Dance, Yavapai dancers cover their heads in buckskin to create the bulb-like appearance of their ancient ET mentors. If asked for a de-scription of the Star People the Yavapai describe them as very close to an average Grey or Zeta. They are 2-3 feet in height and have nondescript bulb-like heads.

Yavapai Mountain Spirit Dance

Kachina pátuwvota etched into stone on the Hopi Mesas

The Star Nations & Their Missionaries

Just as each Native American tribe refers to itself as a "nation," the cosmic homes of the Star People are similarly referred to by the Hopis and other native tribes as "Star Nations." Many tribes believe that they were directly descended from the ancient Star People and they can point directly to those Star Nations they came from in the evening sky. They claim ancestry from missionaries from the Star Nations of the Pleiades, Sirius, Orion, Andromeda, Arcturus, and Alpha Centauri.

Some Native American tribes claim descent from a specific ET ancestor. The Iroquois, for example, trace their beginnings back to "Woman-who-fell-from-the-Sky," and the East Coast Anishinabe claim descent from "Man let down from the Sky."[3] Many Native America tribes claim descent from Star People they refer to as the "Twins." The Twins are typically portrayed as young, pre-pubescent and androgynous boys. They are represented as two boys, a "brotherhood" of 4 to 7 boys, or they might be part of vast fleets of 144 or more Star People. They can often be found referred to in Creation Myths as the Twin Sons of the Goddess who were "created" and arrived on Earth during the creation of our planet. Once here, they assisted their mother in fabricating our planet's flora and fauna - *as well as many of its rock formations, such as those in Sedona.* Later, they taught fledgling humankind the martial arts, natural healing, divination, and alchemy.

The bi-sexual portrayal of the Twins as pre-pubescent boys found in Native American mythology may have started as a way of emphasizing the androgynous nature of the Star People. According to author Alan MacGillvray in *Sipapuni*, because of their bi-sexual nature many natives commonly refer to the ETs of the past as the "Blue Stone He/She People" who arrived from "outer space" and "seeded mankind."[4] The Twins may have also been represented as pre-pubescent and androgynous boys in order to emphasize the immortal nature of the Star People. In some cases it is said that these extraterrestrial visitors never aged and taught humankind the priceless secrets of both physical and spiritual immortality.

Most Native American Creation Myths make at least a perfunctory reference to the Twins. The legends of the Hopi remember the Twin Boys as Palöngawhoya and Pöqánghoya, great warriors and Sons of Goddess Spider Woman. They assisted the Hopis - whose service to humanity was to stabilize the

Earth's electro-magnetic field and keep our planet from toppling over and remaining in a steady orbit around the Sun - by stationing themselves at the North and South Poles. In their Creation Myth the Dene or Navajo remember the Twins as Monster Slayer and Child of the Waters, and the third prominent pueblo nation, the Zuni, continue to venerate the Twins as the fearless Ahayutas, patrons of the Warrior Clan. Among the central and eastern dwelling Iroquois and Winnebago the Twins are today spoken of as Taweskare and Tsentsa, and Flesh and Stump, and in Mexico they are forever remembered by the Maya and Toltecs as Hunapu and Xbalanque and Quetzlcoatl and Tezcatiliopoca respectively. On the other side of the Earth they have been called the Kaberoi, the Kumaras, the Dioscouri, the Ashwins, as well as Seth and Horus, Enlil and Enki, etc. Some of the creation myths that feature them also maintain that in time the Twins became the rulers of humankind, with one of them typically ascending the throne of our planet as its soverign monarch. King Masau'u had a Twin brother, as did his counterpart King Sanat Kumara, who was half of a Twin pair with Sananda Kumara.

The Twin Boys of the Hopis and Zunis are featured in Native American history as great warriors who fought side by side with their adopted Earth people. They and the other Star People or Kachinas had physical bodies and lived regular lives among the Hopis; many even aged and died like normal humans. The Hopi legends portray the Kachinas as teachers and magical deities who could change the weather and manifest either drought or abundant rain, but other Kachinas lived less distinguished lives as simple farmers, herders and craftsmen. Those that became husbands, wives and parents exhibited normal human emotions like jealousy and anger. They were mortals who could be slain by humans, and many were. Legend has it that during one skirmish some Hopis pursued a band of Kachinas into the mountains and then savagedly murdered them all. In order to gain a measure of revenge some other Kachinas then manifested a horrific hail storm that destroyed the annual crops and killed many Hopis.[5]

The Star People remained among the Hopis for many hundreds and thousands of years; in fact, it is claimed that they did not become invisible until after the advent of the European invasion on the North American continent. Their transition from physical to invisible entities was concurrent with the final destruction of their sacred city of Palatkwapi, which means that they could have once populated ancient Sedona in their physical forms. The Kachinas, meaning "Respected Spirits," (ka-"respect," chinas-"spirits"), could have left Earth permanently if they had wanted to, but out of compassion for the Hopis they committed to living half the year, between February and July, on the Hopi Mesas and the other half on the summit of the San Francisco Peaks in Flagstaff. They can still return to their Star Nations through interdimensional portals in both Hopiland and upon the San Francisco Peaks at any time they desire. Any Kachinas still remaining in Palatkwapi-Sedona would, of course, have no trouble traveling home through the abundant interdimensional portals dotting the landscape.

During the months that the Kachinas reside in the Hopi Mesas their invisible spirits enter the bodies of ceremonial Hopi dancers. These sacred dances, which were anciently taught by the Kachinas when the Hopis dwelled at Palatkwapi, require the dancers wear masks with the features of the Kachinas they embody.

When the Kachinas return to the San Francisco Peaks from July to February they use the mountains as antennae to transmit and receive messages to and from the Hopis and their celestial Star Nations. States Frank Waters in *The Book of the Hopi*: "The real Kachinas, as we know, are spirits from other planets and stars, but the high mountain to which messages are directed to them is San Francisco Mountain, southwest of Oraibi, near Flagstaff."

Today, more than 400 different Kachinas are known, each of which represents a force of nature, an ancestor, or a place or thing that directly influences the lives of the Hopi. They can personify a planet, a star or a constellation, as well as the Sun, an animal, a plant, one of the four elements, fertility, and even an idea. They supply both protection and wisdom when invoked with prayers and offerings. Typically, most Kachinas are summoned because of their influence over rain and the fertility of the Earth.

A worthy Hopi can become a Kachina at death. States Waters: "An individual who obeys the law of laws and conforms to the pure and perfect pattern laid down by the Creator becomes a Kachina when he dies and goes immediately to the next universe without having to plod through all the intermediate worlds or stages of existence…He then comes back with other Kachinas to help mankind."[6]

The Location of Palatkwapi

Over the last one hundred years there has been much speculation regarding the location of Palatkwapi. An abundance of ethnographers have located Palatkwapi in the Sedona-Verde Valley region, but there have also been other academics who have placed it much further south. Most everyone agrees, however, that the City of the Star People was someplace south of the Hopi Mesas. One Hopi legend of the Patki or Water Clan recounted by ethnographer Alexander M. Stephen in *Hopi Journey* states: "...no one knows just where the Red Land is, but it is someplace in the far southwest [of Hopiland]." Distance is, of course, relative, especially when you are traveling by foot.

Some researchers claim that Palatkwapi was Palenque in the Yucatan Peninsula of Mexico, which is *not* to the southwest of Hopiland. Outside of having once possessed buildings painted red, this jungle city seems to contradict many of the known facts regarding the "Red House." For example, one of the definitive Hopi legends regarding Palatkwapi maintains that the city was surrounded by "high walls," and that the city's name "seems to be derived from a high bluff of red stone."[7] There are no high bluffs of red stone in Palenque, nor was its temple compound completely destroyed by an ancient deluge. If there was a major deluge in the city's past it is recorded in the "Maya Flood Myth," which is, however, an astronomical event depicted on its temple walls. Moreover, Palatkwapi's destruction began with the burning of the pine forest surrounding it and Palenque is in the middle of a sweltering tropical jungle consisting of cedar, mahogany, and sapodilla trees. And if Palatkwapi is linked to the Mayan city of Paleneque simply because of the similarity between their names, let it be known that Palenque is not the city's original name. Its orignal Mayan name was Lakamha, meaning "Big Water." Palenque is a Spanish name given it by the Conquistadors meaning "Fortified Place." By contrast, Sedona and the Verde Valley possesss almost all the characteristics that are ascribed to Palatkwapi, and this is why the most renowned Hopi historian and ethnographer, Jesse Walter Fewkes, conclusively identified it as the location of the ancient holy city. Fewkes was so convinced of his identification that he was prompted to name one of the most heavily petroglyph-adorned Hopi ruins in the Sedona area Palatki, which is a shortened version of Palatkwapi.

Palatkwapi-Sedona "surrounded by a high wall" below Lizard Rock.

The "high walls" and "high bluffs of red stone" in Palatkwapi-Sedona

One difficulty in assigning a definite location for Palatkwapi are the many recorded land routes to it. This is the result of the various Hopi clans having arrived at the Red House via divergent pathways during their migrations. However, the routes taken by most of the clans when they left Palatkwapi and traveled north to the Hopi Mesas are very consistent and in many cases identical. It is this common route that has allowed ethnographers to definitively locate ancient Palatkwapi as the Sedona-Verde Valley area. In fact, this route still exists today and is known as the Palatkwapi Trail.

After closely studying the routes taken by 30 different clans after leaving Palatkwapi and traveling to the Hopi Mesas, Jesse Fewkes and other ethnographers synthesized a "universal route." This universal route is fully delineated in *The Fourth World of the Hopis* by Harold Courlander. An abridged version of it, complete with northern Arizona place names, is presented below:

"The clans that went north from Palatkwapi [Sedona-Verde Valley] stopped at one place and another, building winter villages, and then moving on. It is said that they settled at a place called Kunchalpi for some years. There they rested and grew their blue corn. Old people died and children were born, and thus in time there were many for whom Palatkwapi was only a word in the mouths of the grandfathers. But one night there was a bright shooting star in the northeastern sky, and it was taken as a sign that the migration should be resumed. So the people abandoned Kunchalpi and travelled again, drifting a little to the east, until they came to a site they named Hohokyam. There they settled again, planting their fields and resting from the journey. After many years they departed from Hohokyam and moved to another place, Neuvakwiotaka, which is now known as Chavez Pass, and there they remained for a long time. And later on, after many harvests at Neuvakwiotaka, they went on until they came to the little Colorado River near where the present town of Winslow stands. There they made a settlement that they called Homolovi, Small Mound, consisting of two villages, a larger one and a smaller one. The people of the Water and Sand Clans occupied the smaller village. Sharing the larger village were the Tobacco and Rabbit clans, the Sun Clan, and various others, including the Eagle, Hawk, Turkey, and Moon clans. After a time they were joined by the Badger Clan and a group called the Reed Clan...."

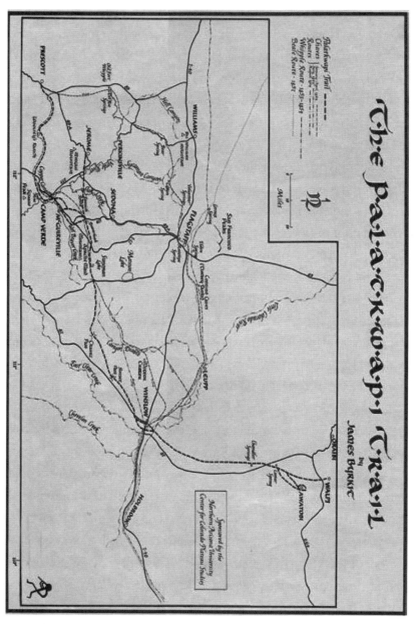

Map of the Palatkwapi Trail by James W. Byrkit

"After many moons the various clans at Homolovi were attacked by the Apaches, who also decided to move into the area and attacked the people in their fields and took away their crops. In order to protect themselves the clans then invoked the Twin Sons, Palöngawhoya and Pöqánghoya, who then met the Apaches on the battlefield. At first the Apaches laughed at the sight of the two boys, saying "Are there no men left in Homolovi?" Then the warrior brothers slung their heavy stones and killed some of the enemy, whereupon the laughing stopped. The Apaches shot some arrows, but Palöngawhoya and Pöqánghoya moved quickly this way and that and escaped the arrows. After that the Apaches rushed forward, and now each of the brothers took out a lightning arrow and shot it. The Arrows struck with a great flash and a thunderous noise. Many of the enemy lay dead or dying on the ground. Again the Apaches attacked, and again the warrior gods loosed their lightning arrows, and the ground was now covered with corpses. Those Apaches who were still alive fled from the field...."[8]

When it became time to resume their migration from Homolovi to the promised land, some of the clans decided to split off and travel north to the San Francisco Peaks and then to Wupatki, finally completing their journey at Oraibi in the Hopi Mesas. Meanwhile, the majority of the clans remained together, journeying first to Little Ruin Mound near Walpi, then to Awatovi, and finally to Oraibi.

Building Palatkwapi

"....it was the Kachinas that built Palatkwapi."[9]

As previously mentioned, although the destruction of Palatkwapi appears to coincide with the end of the Third World the period of its initial construction is nearly impossible to pin down. If, for example, one subscribes to the time periods known as the Hopi Worlds or the Dream Time of the Australian Aborigines, then Palatkwapi could have been constructed as recently as 10,000 years ago or as anciently as a million or more years ago. This is because the "Worlds" and "Dream Time" are very inexact time periods. And then there is the question of how the city could have been constructed in the distant past. If the building of the ancient megalithic circles and temples occurred during the time the Hopis refer to as the First or Second Worlds - when humans had their crown chakra wide open and remained

179

in continual communication with the Creator - their designs could have been spontaneously implanted by the Creator into the minds of their builders. The creative "Gods" could have also received some supernatural abilities to build the temples from the same source. While constructing the temples in Sedona these "Gods" would have also been assisted by the natural earth energies of the area. The amplifying vortexual power combined with the iron and crystal-infused particles would have first magnified the thought forms of the "Gods" and then magnetically united the Sedona sand into the solid formations delineated by the builders' mental blueprints.

The extent records of Palatkwapi imply that its original builders were the Kachinas. They also reveal that the city's initial construction preceded the Fourth World. Some Fourth World construction (or reconstruction) is, however, said to have been overseen by the Kachinas and carried out by the Hopis and/or the members of other tribes residing at Palatkwapi. States Waters:

"Under the supervision of the Kachinas, Palatkwapi was built in three sections. Completely surrounded by a high wall, the first section was reserved for ceremonial purposes; the second section, adjoining it, contained storage rooms for food; and the third section comprised the living quarters for the people of all clans. Underneath all three sections ran a river.

"The ceremonial section was the most important. There were no kivas then, as there are today, divided to accommodate initiates and ceremonial participants. Instead, there were two buildings, one for the initiates and one for ceremonial purposes. The ceremonial building was four stories high, terraced like the pueblos we see today. The main door opened to the east, and there were two smaller doors facing north and south.

"On the first or ground floor the Kachina people taught the initiates the history and meaning of the three previous worlds and the purpose of the Fourth World to which man had emerged. On the second floor they taught the structure and functions of the human body and that the highest function of the mind was to understand how the great spirit worked within man. The spirits or Kachina people taught this so that the people would not become evil again and this Fourth World be destroyed like the first three.

"In the third story initiates were taught the workings of nature and the uses of all kinds of plant life. Although the people were still relatively pure and there was little sickness, some evils would come, bringing resultant illnesses; and for each on there was a plant remedy for the people to remember.

"The fourth story was smaller that the three below, making the ceremonial building resemble a pyramid. To this top level were admitted initiates of great conscience who had acquired a deep knowledge of the laws of nature. Here they were taught the workings of the planetary system, how the stars affected the climate, the crops, and man himself. Here too they learned about the "open door" on the top of their heads, how to keep it open, and so converse with their Creator."

(Note: The "open door" or Kopavi, that the Kachinas taught the Hopis about is known in the Hindu occult system as the Sahasrara or Crown Chakra that is situated at the top of the head.)

"Just below (kopavi) lay the second centre, the organ that man learned to think with by himself, the thinking organ called the brain. Its earthly functions enabled man to think about his actions and work in this life. But the more he understood that his actions and work should conform to the plan of the creator, the more clearly he understood that the real function of the thinking organ called the brain was to carry out the plan of the creator.

"The third centre lay in the throat. It tied together those openings in his nose and mouth through which he received his breath of life, and the vibratory organs that enabled him to give back his breath in sound. This primordial sound, as that coming from the vibratory centres of the body of earth, was attuned to the universal vibration of all creation. New diverse sounds were given forth by these vocal organs in the form of speech and song, their secondary function for man on this earth. But as he came to understand its primary function, he used this centre to speak and sing the praises of the creator.

"The fourth center was the heart. It too was a vibrating organ pulsating with the vibration of life itself. In his heart man felt the good of life, its sincere purpose. He was of one heart. But there were those who permitted evil feelings to enter. They were said to be of two hearts.

"The last of man's important centres lay under his navel, the organ some people call the solar plexus. As this name signifies, it was the throne in man of the creator himself. From it he directed all the functions in man."[10]

The alchemical activation of all the human chakras at Palatkwapi were part of the universal Mysteries of the Feathered Serpent, which were known by initiates worldwide and transmitted to the Hopis by the Kachinas. Through these mysteries a man or woman learns to "fly" by ascending his or her consciousness. The Mysteries begin with the activation of the inner Fire Serpent or Kundalini, which is sympathetically facilitated by the dynamic, serpentine energy flow that spirals up and down within the vortexes of Palatkwapi-Sedona, as well as by the deep red color of its rocks that naturally vibrates within the human Muladhara Chakra (in some Tantric systems Kundalini is said to exist in the area of the solar plexus). Once awakened, the inner serpent rises up the spine while clearing out and fully activating the chakra centers that lie along it. When the serpent fire reaches the head and activates both Kopavi and the Second Center (the Hindus' Ajna Chakra) below it, the unused nine-tenths of the brain become fully enlivened. Then, the person intuitively knows the secrets of human existence and all the mysteries of the universe. He or she has become an immortal Plumed Serpent. The Serpent (i.e., the material matrix of the physical body) has sprouted wings and become the Plumed Serpent (pure energy). Such an evolved human resides principally in the etheric body comprised of the seven chakras. He or she has overcome death and become equal to the Kachinas in both wisdom and power.

Additional rites taught by the Kachinas in Palatkwapi would have included the ceremonial dances that the Hopis later observed on the Hopi Mesas. Such dances have since provided a way for the Star People to enter the Hopi rites by incarnating their spirits into the ceremonial dancers. Many other tribes that sojourned along with the Hopis at Palatkwapi also learned dances from the Kachinas, including the Yavapai, who remember the Star People as the diminutive Kakaka. The Mountain Spirit Dance taught by the Kakaka gave the Yavapai a vehicle through which they could request assistance from their patronizing Star People, while fully embodying their invisible mentors.

The most exalted teachers at Palatkwapi were the Star People known as Eototo, the chief and "father" of all the Kachinas, and his "lieutenant," Aholi. Chief

182

Eototo was the principal teacher of the Bear Clan, which during the Fourth World was chosen to lead all the other clans. Besides being the fountainhead of all the Hopis' important ceremonies, Eototo also possessed the supernatural power to control the rain and all the seasons. Aholi's role at Palatkwapi was comparably important. He taught the mysteries to the Corn Clan, which was destined to bring together all the clans and races during the Fourth World. Aholi taught the Mysteries of the Plumed Serpent at Palatkwapi, and he is said to have later established the regular observance of these rites on the Hopi Mesas.

Eototo's presence in Palatkwapi as the Chief of the Kachina Star People is extremely significant since it reveals that King of the World Masau'u was also a resident of the Red House. According to the field research of Dr. Jesse Fewkes, Eototo is another name for Masau'u, thus making Palatkwapi one of his royal courts. In a book authored by Fewkes about prehistoric pottery that includes research associated with Sikyatki, a Hopi village that existed north of Walpi but was abandoned around the year 1540, the archaeologist writes:

"Eototo, **also called Masau'u** (italics mine), was the tutelary deity of Sikyatki, as Alosaka or Muinwu was of Awatobi."[11]

Fewkes had stumbled upon some important and very pertinent knowledge about Masau'u. There is no question that Masau'u and Eototo do indeed resemble each other in both appearance and function, and that they could be synonymous. Like Masau'u, Eototo is similarly recognized as the personification of nature, i.e., the Green Man, and his white, Kachina image closely resembles what the Lord of Fire most likely looked like before falling into the fiery pit of the underworld and acquiring a red, scarred and bloody body.

The Destruction of Palatkwapi

There are two principal legends regarding the eventual destruction of Palatkwapi. One maintains that the destruction of the City of the Star People was the consequence of a raid by the Spider Clan, which had been prevented from settling in the sacred city because of its past indulgence in black magic. The resident Hopis put up firm resistance, but after many days they were finally defeated by the Spider Clan and driven from Palatkwapi. The second legend reveals that

Eototo Kachina

the destruction of Palatkwapi was caused by a massive flood orchestrated by the two principal Kachina teachers of the Red City, Eototo (Masau'u) and Aholi, who decided that the Hopi residents of Palatkwapi were becoming both complacent and degenerate and needed to complete their migrations as instructed by Masau'u. When the two elder Kachinas determined that the time had arrived for the Hopis to evacuate Palatkwapi they approached the leaders of the Water Clan to hatch a plan for the destruction of the sacred city. The Water Clan elders were consulted because, next to the Kachinas, the Patki or Water Clan had been the most influential in the construction and maintenance of the Red House throughout its history. In fact, some historians believe that much or most of the building of Palakwapi during the Fourth World was done by the Water Clan. As previously mentioned, Palatkwapi and Patki are closely related, and both names derive from the same root, "Pa," denoting "water."

The plan eventually devised by the Water Clan was launched when an old man living in Palatkwapi suffered some intentional abuse from a young miscreant. The abuse was reported to both the village chief and the warrior chief, who then met at the old man's house to discuss what to do about the degeneration of morals that had, sadly, befallen the young people of the Red City. The final resolution of their deliberations set in motion a chain reaction of events that culminated in the destruction and abandonment of Palatkwapi. The beginning of the end began with a stern command from the village chief to his son:

"Run to Pine Ridge (Löqö'nmuru)," he instructed.

The chief's son ran hard to the ridge and when he returned his father inquired:

"How are you feeling now, are you strong?"

"Yes," the son replied, "my legs are strong."

The chief then gave his son four Kachina masks. The first mask resembled that of Masau'u except that it had small clumps of hair on each side and in front. The son placed all the masks on his head together, beginning with the mask of Mána Kachina and followed by the masks of Lâ'nang Kachina, Áha Kachina and Yáhponcha Kachina. The chief then attached to his son's wrist some fingers that he had severed from old, dry corpses. They would serve as rattles.

The chief also created a long cedar-bark fuse that he handed to his son.

Then he said: "Now you run back to Pine Ridge and set the pine trees there on fire; come back here afterwards." The son did as instructed, and the destruction of Palatkwapi offically began. Returning like a phantom to his father's house, the son ground corn on his sister's small milling stone while singing: "Tû'tawunaha! tû'tawunaha!" He then left the house again to set other trees on fire.

The following night the son returned to his father's home to grind corn before replacing his masks over his face and departing to burn more trees. This time the village people became suspicious, and when they assembled in their kivas the next morning they inquired who had been moving about the night before. "Some one went into the house of the chief and then ran away again," they protested. It was subsequently decided that some young men would hide the following night to catch a glimpse of the intruder. By this time the chief's son had ignited several fires that could be seen in the distant forests.

The young men hid at different places in the village that night. Again the son of the chief lit several tree fires while scurrying back and forth to the village. The boys saw him enter the village and climb to the house of the village chief, where they then heard him grinding corn and singing. Because of his Kachina masks they decided he must be a ghost or spirit. When the son eventually left the house he passed by one of the boys who jumped up. But the ghostly figure of the son ran by him at full speed across the plaza. Another boy was waiting for him at the other end of the plaza, but the son's ghost-like image was so scary he feared to move. So the son dashed away again and lit more fires.

The villagers discussed the problem again the next morning and decided to post watchers all over Palatkwapi to catch the ghost. Each would be stationed at a different location, with one positioning himself on the path that led down from the village and through a creek.

Again the fires blazed that night, but this time the young men saw the ghost when he returned to the village and jumped him. The chief's son was so quick and powerful that he easily broke free from their grasp.

The masked boy continued ahead and ran straight across the plaza, which was surrounded by people waiting for him. He eluded them all and then descended the trail to the river where the other boy was waiting. The boy jumped up and grabbed the chief's son, holding him with all his strength. He then cried out: "I have the duálangwu (ghost)!" Everyone rushed to the creek and saw that the young man had indeed caught the masked intruder. They then led the chief's son back to the village and down into a kiva for a special meeting.

All the villagers soon assembled in the kiva to confront the masked man. The old men of the town began the meeting by saying: "There is some reason for this, certainly it is not without some purpose that this man is acting the way he is. He certainly wants to do something bad." The village chief commanded that the man's mask be removed. The mask was fastened securely with strings around the man's neck, so a knife was used to cut the strings. As the first mask was removed a wave of surprise shot through the kiva when it became evident that was another mask underneath.

The second mask was removed, and then the third. When the fourth mask that resembled Masau'u was removed all the people looked dumbfounded at the person in front of them. It was the chief's son!

He was a clean, handsome youth who wore turquoise ear pendants and many nice beads. On his face were two black lines that ran from the upper part of his nose to his cheeks. Having had his identity laid bare for all to see, the chief's son looked soberly at the villagers and then began to instruct them. "Take báhos (prayer sticks) and thrust them into the ground, one at the plaza, and the others in the different corners of the village," he ordered. The chief's son told them that for four days they should have a feast, and he then left the kiva.

The villagers did not know what to think of the boy's instructions but decided to comply just in case they were designed to help them ward off some black magic directed against them. They killed their sheep and feasted for four days as instructed. On the fourth day they watched with trepidation as the sun rose and set, but still nothing happened to them. Thinking that the evil had passed they returned to their homes.

Three years passed without any untoward events occurring in Palatkwapi, but the fourth year brought destruction to the Red House. It turned out that the chief's son had not prepared the people with the right instructions. The "evil" was destined to befall the village in four years, not four days.

So in the fourth year the evil came as expected. The old man, who four years before had complained to the village chief of the bad conduct of the young men of the village, was still alive and angry. In this fourth year he plotted to get his revenge. He began by fashioning some báhos out of hard wood that had very sharp points.

During the fall of the fourth year, after the people of Palatkwapi had gathered in their crop, the village chief told the people they had been lied to four years previously and now was the true time they needed to feast for four days. But the people were full of fear and mistrust now. They were afraid that at the expiration of the four days some evil would befall them no matter what they did, so they did not prepare a feast as requested.

The village chiefs met with the old man again. The man told them to dress him up and put him into the tiwónyapavi. This was a shrine to the Kachinas that held an image that once belonged to the Kachinas. So they dressed him up and painted his back black, his chest and abdomen red, and both sides of the front of his body green.

On the old man's arms, chest, and legs they made the typical marks of Pö'okong (two short lines). On the back of his head they fastened a póhtakni, the tail feathers of a sparrow-hawk, and on the top of his head they attached a horn. They also painted his face black. In his new costume the old man had become the Bálölöokong, the great water serpent.

That night they went to the plaza and dug a hole for the old man to completely immerse himself in. They gave him all the báhos that he had made, along with a Bálölöokong whistle. They also gave him a little bowl with some water to blow the whistle in, just as it is still done in some ceremonies.

Finally, they covered over the hole with a rock and dirt so there were no traces of it. Placing a piece of native cloth upon the dirt they began to sing some sorcerer's chants. When they got to the third song they heard the old man in the ground saying "I have been successful, I have reached my objective." "All right," they said in response, and left the plaza.

The next day the villagers noticed something emerging from the hole. The old man had thrust four fingers out of the hole and was singing:

"Ala kwikwi, ala kwikwi, Ala kwikwi, ala kwikwi"

When he completed his song the old man lowered his little finger. The next morning he sang the same songs and finished by lowering another finger. And at sunrise on the third morning he again sang the songs and lowered his third finger. The villagers were now very scared that some evil was about to befall them. And their fear was well founded. Soon, those places where the báhos had been placed four years previously by the chief's son began to emit water. These báhos had really been disguised Bálölöokongs, and the water serpents were now bringing the water out of the ground.

As the waters increased the villagers began to fear that they were witnessing a huge flood that would soon destroy Palatkwapi. Believing that they would all die, they killed their sheep and had one final feast. On the fateful fourth day just before sunrise the old man sang the same words from within his hole while lowering his final, fourth finger. He then completely emerged from his hole in the form of a huge Bálölöokong. Simultaneously, other Bálölöokongs shot forth from the ground in all parts of the village. They came forth from the fireplaces in the kivas, and even from the water vessels within the houses. The water that came with them now completely covered Palatkwapi.

Soon the houses began to collapse, one by one, burying the inhabitants inside. A number of villagers fled to a house on the east side of the village that was on higher ground. Since the water did not reach the house many of the people were saved, including the chiefs, who then called a council meeting in order to decide a course of action. They began by making many báhos. They took beads and turquoise, first crushing them and then grounding them into powder.

From the bead powder they made two balls, which they placed onto a tray that also had báhos on it. Calling to them the Village Chief's son, whom they believed was responsible for the destruction of Palatkwapi, they dressed both him and his sister in special costumes. The young girl was given the costume of the Flute-manas to wear. They placed a white robe over her, fastened an eagle-breath feather in her hair above her forehead, placed beads around her neck, etc. Her chin was painted black, white lines running from ear to ear over her upper lip.

The chief's son was clothed in a plain white kilt and his legs, arms, and the back and front part of his body were painted with black zigzag lines. The villagers hoped the two costumed siblings would be able to drive back the Bálölöokongs. The water was still coming rapidly out of the ground and the Bálölöokongs were still moving swiftly through the water. The old man was the largest and most powerful of the Bálölöokongs.

The rumbling of falling houses could still be heard throughout Palatkwapi. The two siblings waded into the waters; the young man carrying some of the báhos and his sister holding the tray containing the two balls and the rest of the báhos. They went straight at the largest Bálölöokong, the chief of all the water serpents. The young man grasped the serpent with both arms and held him down under the water, whereupon all the serpents, as well as the young man and his sister, disappeared under the water and never returned. They had been sacrificed.

Immediately the water began to recede and disappeared in a comparatively short time. The bead powder made of turquoise caused the ground to dry and become hard quickly. The water-serpents had all disappeared, but so had the young man and his sister. Where the village had once stood all that remained was mud. Everything was destroyed.

The survivors in the eastern part of the village prepared to abandon Palatkwapi. They baked píki and made other food for provisions. Early the next morning they took some of the food which they had prepared and made a food altar (tonö'sh-pongya), a little ways east of the village. Packing up the things, and especially the food which they had prepared, they all passed by this food altar, with the village chief at the head of the line. Each one took a little quantity of each kind of food and ate it. They then left Palatkwapi.[12]

The serpent Bálölöokong remained in the Red City even after all the residents had departed because it was his home. He was the snake Guardian of the South. He still resides in Palatkwapi today as the tortuous serpent that twists and turns along the high ridge of red rocks in the center of Sedona that includes Capitol Peak (Thunder Mountain). Bálölöokong was discovered by Nicholas Mann when he identified the shapes in the terrestrial landscape of Sedona.

Thus ended the life cycle of the City of the Star People. A final flood completed the destruction of red rock temples that began thousands of years earlier.

190

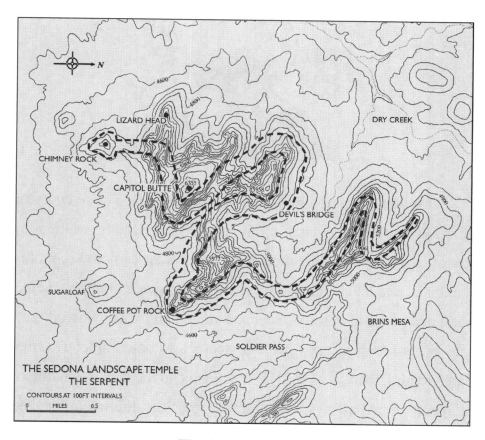

The Sedona Serpent
From *SEDONA: SACRED EARTH* by Nicholas Mann

Sedona's Court of the King

When I began to fully embrace the existence of an entity or spirit known as the King of the World he seemed to be waiting for me at every turn. Earth's monarch knew I was ready to accept his guidance and teachings. If I took one step towards him, he would take one hundred in my direction. Even when I was involved with places, groups and activities that seemed to be completely unrelated to him, there he would be, staring me in the face. I eventually realized he had always been right by my side...lifetime after lifetime...

In this chapter:
* The Ancient Of Days
* The Knights Templar & The King of the World
* The Discovery of Boynton Canyon's Court of the King
* The Court of Masau'u, Sanat Kumara and the Peacock King

The Ancient of Days

After relocating to Sedona I continued to return to Boynton Canyon every few months for more interdimensional research and to conduct shamanic ceremonies. It was during this period I founded *The Kumara School of Wisdom* (KSW) that was dedicated to continuing the work of the late Sister Thedra and her *Association of Sananda and Sanat Kumara* (ASSK). My new school taught esoteric information regarding Mu, as well as the continent's link to Sedona. It also served as a vehicle for any new messages that might arrive for humanity from Sanat and/or Sananda Kumara.

Andrea's destiny as the principal channel for the KSW was revealed during a short pilgrimage we took to Mount Shasta soon after the new school was established. We arrived at the towering vortex in late spring when much of the winter's snow had melted, thereby enabling us to renew our spirits on the upper slopes of the ancient volcano.

After parking at the 7000 foot level we decided to let our intuition be our guide and set off along a snow-covered trail. After half an hour of crunching the grainy spring snow under our feet we noticed ahead of us an inviting patch of tall, grass with a dry log at its center to rest upon. Feeling a little beat from our hike, Andrea and I hastened to the large log and slumped down upon it. Our droopy eyes closed shut and we both drifted into a deep meditative state.

Some time passed when I was abruptly jostled back into my body by a new voice loudly issuing from Andrea's mouth. The voice was deep, powerful and commanded my attention. "I am the Kumara, the synthesis of all the Kumaras," it firmly announced. I sat bolt upright, and stared directly at Andrea. As the rays of the late afternoon Sun flickered upon Andrea's newly animated face, I watched as the robust spirit continued to speak forcefully through her. "Kumara is not a name but a vibration," it instructed, "it is the vibration of love...and all those who are called Kumara are the embodiments of love." There was a pause and I knew it was my turn to say something to keep the fledgling dialogue alive. So, with the excitement of a child entering a candy store the size of a Walmart superstore, I immediately reached for my "heady" Virgo mantle and prepared to embark on an assault of esoteric questions I keep in special reserve for otherworldly entities like

Mount Shasta: A special home of Sanat Kumara

The Ancient Of Days

this "Kumara." Sensing the gathering onslaught, the Kumara's indomitable energy suddenly turned soft as he moved my attention from my head to my heart. "Kumara is a mantra that will open the heart," it instructed, "if you continue to repeat Kumara, you will become Kumara." My new mentor proved to be as accurate as he was inspiring. Just a few repetitions of the Kumara name made my heart sing with joy. "Do you have any more questions, my dear boy?" inquired the Kumara as I reveled in my newfound inner bliss. Surprisingly, I didn't, which of course he knew. He had completely disarmed me. In my new state of love all questions seemed to suddenly evaporate.

A few minutes later I ended my conversation with the Kumara with his assurance that we would meet again in Sedona. By that time I had concluded that the Kumara was my mentor, Sanat Kumara, the King of the World and indwelling spirit of Mount Shasta, and so his presence would also be in Sedona. I was, however, still a little confused by his introduction. Is Sanat Kumara also the "synthesis of all the Kumaras?"

After returning home to Arizona I switched into research mode and discovered that Sanat Kumara is indeed often referred to in both the scriptures of the East and in the occult literature of the West as the first Kumara, as well as the synthesis of them all. According to most *Theosophical Society* and the Ascended Masters teachings, Sanat Kumara is synonymous with that entity much of the world currently addresses as the "Ancient of Days" or as simply "God." He is, therefore, the synthesis of everything; or at least everything with a form. Technically, he is not the transcendant, invisible and impersonal God that is pure, witness consciousness without qualities (Nirguna). Rather, Sanat Kumara is the Demiuge, the Creator God with qualities (Saguna). In India, where the Nirguna and Saguna manifestation of God is clearly delineated, the Supreme God without qualities is Brahman or Shiva, and the Creator God with qualities is his "Son," Sanat Kumara. Sanat emerges directly from his infinite Father, and it is through his Son that the Father is able to create the universe. Thus, the Father and Son are One. This timeless occult wisdom runs through many organizations patronized by Sanat Kumara in the past, including the *Theosophical Society, Summit Lighthouse,* the I AM Church and various other Ascended Masters groups around the globe.

195

Sanat Kumara is also the "synthesis of all the Kumaras" by virtue of being the Lord of the Seven Rays. Many esoteric and scriptural sources directly refer to Sanat Kumara as the synthesis of the Seven Kumaras that separate out of Sanat Kumara during the creation of the universe. The Seven Kumaras are the guiding consciousnesses of the Seven Rays that emerge within the primordial soup of energy that crystallizes to become the physical universe. Their influence is to determine the septenary characteristics that will distinguish all the forms of physical matter in the cosmos, i.e., their 7 colors, 7 tones and 7 crystaline matrixes.

The Knights Templar & The King of the World

I helmed the KSW for a few years and during that time my understanding of Sanat Kumara and his role on Earth and in the universe grew immensly. I also came to realize that this entity had always been with me, beginning with my lifetime on Mu. He had accompanied me throughout many past lifetimes, patiently waiting in the wings until I was ready to consciously accept him as a guide. At other times he had been an anonymous guide, such as when he led me from Shasta to Sedona in 1987.

The Kumara taught Andrea and I much about alchemy. He taught us that a Kumara adept was Ma (female) and Ra (male) united as Ku (the Son, pure energy). He also instructed us in ways we could assist in uniting our inner polarity, as well as the polarity of those in the KSW. We were guided to facilitate alchemy in others by many approaches, including conducting a retreat in Sedona followed months later with a second retreat in Mount Shasta. Since Sedona was predominantly a "male" vortex with a vibrant red color and dry, hot, desert climate, and Shasta was predominantly a "female" vortex with a soothing green color and a moist, cool mountain climate, this sequence of retreats proved profoundly balancing and alchemically transforming for all participants.

Then one day I knew it was time for a change. There were aspects of the KSW that had become very challenging for me and I needed a break. Besides having regularly attracted much of the New Age "granola" (its fruits, nuts, and flakes), the KSW also magnetized to itself certain individuals claiming to be physically incarnated Kumaras. One or two even claimed to be Sanat Kumara himself.

They would show up unannounced and not only expect me to recognize their spiritual status, but to also instantly jettison them to the highest ranks of the Order. Thankfully, just as I had reached my breaking point in dealing with their New Age egos, another more conservative and credible organization stepped in to take the place of the KSW. This was *The International Order of Gnostic Templars*, a branch of the ancient Order of the Knights Templar. Not surprisingly, I would soon discover that the Knights Templar were also an order patronized by Sanat Kumara!

My Knight Templar phase began with a message from the Goddess in Boynton Canyon. During one sunny afternoon as I was seeking guidance from my loving mentor, a familiar voice emerged from my heart. "It's time for another book," it firmly announced, "this one will be on the Holy Grail." I knew it was the Goddess because of the loving and nurturing energy that accompanied Her voice. And I also knew not to ignore Her instructions. Technically, they were coming from my own higher self and were, therefore, in my best and highest interest. Besides, my new "marching orders" would give me an opportunity to further study the Holy Grail lineage that I believed originated with Sanat Kumara, the primal Fisher King. So, with a batch of fresh anxiety beginning to brew in my gut, I hiked out of Boynton Canyon intent on embarking on a new adventure that would culminate in my fourth book: *Guardians of the Holy Grail: The Knights Templar, John the Baptist and the Water of Life.*

I proceeded with the research for my new book just as I had with the previous ones, by being as thorough as possible in collecting information. With the cavalier attitude that the Goddess "had my back" and I was fully protected, I decided to go right to the jugular of my new subject matter and interview a series of high profile members of certain "Secret Societies" that were linked to Grail lore. This included the Knights Templar, Freemasons and Rosicrucians. I even contacted members of the so-called "evil" Illuminati.

After finding contact information I shot an email to many chiefs and grandmasters of the various Secret Societies. Very few replied, but that was to be expected. After all, they were initiates of Secret Societies and needed to keep a low profile. Among those that did reply, however, was a robust man from Scot-

**IOGT ceremony at Noss Head, Scotland
with Sir Ian Sinclair (center) and Sir Andrew Sinclair (left, seated)**

Mary Magdalene, Johannite Grandmaster

land named Sir Ian Sinclair. Sir Ian was a Knight Templar and "laird," or land owner, living in a home that adjoined a lighthouse in northern Scotland overlooking the North Sea. Sir Ian was, at the time, a Preceptor of *Milti Templi Scotia* (MTS), which was the principal Knight Templar organization in Scotland. During our ensuing phone interview Sir Ian graciously gave me a plethora of information regarding himself, MTS and the Sinclair (French: St. Clair) Clan, which I came to learn had always nurtured a deep and abiding relationship with the Knights Templar, beginning with the marriage of Catherine de St. Clair to the first Knight Templar Grandmaster, Hughes de Payen. I was so taken by Sir Ian's forthright and commanding Templar spirit that at the end of the interview I inquired about my own chances of joining MTS. I was thrilled when Sir Ian responded matter-of-factly, assuring me that my admittance into his order would be "no problem" and require no more effort than submitting an application. He repeated his belief at the conclusion of our phone call while also adding that he would find out specifically what was involved at the next meeting of his Templar order.

My follow up phone call to Sir Ian two weeks later was not nearly as uplifting. Sir Ian had approached the leaders of MTS with my request and was not at all happy with the result. With a fiery edge to his already indomitable voice, he informed me that the big wigs of MTS - which he roundly referred to as "self-important pontificators" - had ruled that no person outside of Scotland could become a member of their order. While Sir Ian burned with fiery indignation at their verdict I slouched back in my chair, certain that my career as Knight Templar was over before it had begun.

I would soon learn that there was a long history behind Sir Ian's anger toward MTS. This was not the first time he had had problems with the governing body of MTS; nor was he the only disgruntled member of that Templar order. In fact, internal dissension within MTS would soon come to a boiling point after my interview with Sir Ian and the organization would be completely dissolved. Many of the disbanded members would then continue on in the reconstituted *Jacques de Molay 13*, while others, such as Sir Ian, would found their own Templar orders. Sir Ian's new order was duly named *The Scottish Knight Templars* and initially it was composed of two divisions. One was conservative and a clone of

MTS; the other, which I helped Sir Ian create, was esoteric and gnostic. It became known as the *The International Order of Gnostic Templars* (IOGT).

Over the next few years Andrea and I made a series of visits to Scotland so Sir Ian could indoctrinate us in traditional Scottish Templarism and initiate us through its ascending ranks. During these visits Sir Ian and I collaborated on the rites for the fledgling IOGT, which began as clones of the MTS rites until I added some gnostic ideology and symbology. I intentiionally gave the rites of the IOGT a "Johannite" veneer that the other modern Templar orders around the globe did not possess, and I did so in order to to align it with the ancient Johannite Templars. The Johannites were the inner core of early Knights Templar, who in 1118 CE inherited a gnostic tradition that stretched back to John the Apostle, Mary Magdalene, Jesus and John the Baptist. The name "Johannite" refers to the grandmasters of this tradition, all of whom assumed the titular name of "John," meaning "he of gnostic wisdom and power." It was the Johannite beliefs and practices of the inner circle that eventually got the entire Knights Templar Order in trouble with the Inquisition and culminated in its mass arrest for heresy in 1307. Many or most Templar Knights survived the ensuing attacks from both the Inquisition and the French monarch, King Philip IV, although they and the surviving Johannites were forced to exist clandestinely until the 19th century. At that time a new Templar Grandmaster, Bernard Fabre-Palaprat, rose into prominence and made Johannism the centerpiece of his new Templar Order, *The Johannite Church of Primitive Christians*. Unfortunately for Faber-Palaprat, the new grandmaster had many enemies who did not agree that the original Templars had been Johannite Gnostics. So, after his death they expunged any trace of gnosis from his revived Templar order. In the process they made the Knights Templar a predominantly military and charitable organization.

When I learned this Johannite Templar history I resolved to take it upon myself to revive the gnostic teachings and rites of the orignal Templars. But before I was ready to set the world afire again by introducing a reconstituted Johannite Templar sect, I decided it imperative that I first learn all I could about it.

Almost from the start I became aware that any available information about the Johannite Templars was spotty at best, no doubt the result of its many hundreds of years underground and its 19th century purge. Consequently, I felt like an explorer searching for a very obscure and little known island. I was sailing on choppy waters that few people had navigated, and many of those that had had suffered martyrdom. But I plowed forward anyway. I think something inside me knew that on the distant shore Sanat Kumara would be waiting for me...again.

I was able to trace the history of the Johannite Templars back to John the Baptist and then to the Mandaeans, an ancient sect of gnostic baptizers that currently reside in southern Iraq and refer to the Baptist as their last great prophet. Before coming west to the Middle East, the Mandaeans had arrived on the world stage thousands of years previously in their "Garden of Eden," Sri Lanka (or Serendib as it was known), when the island was part of the continent of Mu. After leaving their Lemurian homeland the Mandaeans successively became part of the Sumerian, Persian and Egyptian civilizations, finally merging with the Jewish Essenes to produce the gnostic sect of Nazarenes or Nasoreans.

I took pause when I learned that the Mandaeans' origin was on ancient Sri Lanka. The Garden of Eden on Sri Lanka is often identified with Kataragama, a world "throne" of Sanat Kumara. This was my first clue that I was about to meet the King of the World again.

Since the Mandaeans claimed to have been gnostics since the time of their Garden of Eden they were most probably students of Sanat Kumara, the Jnana Pandita or "Lord of Gnosis" whom Gnostics claim manifested as the Sri Lankan Serpent on the Tree. The Mandaean link to Sanat Kumara apparently continued when this gnostic tribe migrated to Sumeria, where they continued to venerate the Lord of Gnosis and Serpent on the Tree as Enki, a deity who shares innumerable characterisitics with Sanat Kumara. Today, the Mandaeans of southern Iraq venerate a deity known as Manda'd'Hiya, the "Embodiment of Gnosis," who is arguably an evolution of both Enki and Sanat Kumara. Like these two ancient Lords of Gnosis, Manda'd'Hiya bestows gnosis on those Mandaeans worthy enough and ready to receive it. And like his Hindu counterpart, Manda'd'Hiya typically manifests as a forever young boy. Therefore, over the course of hundreds and thousands of years, Sanat Kumara seems to have morphed into Manda'd'Hiya.

Another credible link that unites the Mandaeans with Sanat Kumara are

201

the gnostic sect's enlightened masters, the Nasurai, whose name begins with the prefix nas, meaning "serpent." Like other sects of "Serpents" worldwide, the supernaturally endowed Nasurai undoubtedly had their origin with a mythical serpent. Their legendary serpent was no doubt Sanat Kumara, the Sri Lankan Serpent on the Tree.

And then there is the Mandaean-Johannite link to Sanat Kumara through his name of John. The Sanscrit name of Sanat Kumara is Jnana, which in its Hebrew and English versions is Yohanan and John. The name Jnana or John probably passed to the Johannite grandmasters directly from Jnana of Sri Lanka.

Not surprisingly, John is also a name of Enki. Enki's Greek name of Oannes is nearly a facsimile of Ioannes, which is Greek for Jnana or John. Thus, through the Mandaeans the Johannite Knights Templar were connected to the King of the World in his "John" forms of both Sanat Kumara and Enki, the dragon goat-fish. One manifestation of dragon Enki in Egypt was the Goat of Mendes, who among the Knights Templar became venerated as the dark goat Baphomet. By another name Baphomet was Rex Mundi, the "King of the World."

When I decided I had sufficently rescued the esoteric history of the Johannite Templars from its musty cobwebs I could fully understand why the Goddess had led me to become a member of the Templars. It was another path that would reveal more secrets and lead me back to Her Son, Sanat Kumara. I also understood why it was necessary for me to contact a Sinclair. The Sinclair family mausoleum and church of Rosslyn Chapel near Edinburgh, Scotland is arguably the current world headquarters of the Johannite Templar Tradition. It is the final resting place of the Templars' Johannite documents that were brought from the Holy Land to Europe by the orignal Temnplars in 1129 and eventually stored in the chapel's crypt. The chapel is also covered inside and out with an abundance of breathtaking, sculptured images related to the Johannite Templars, John the Baptist and the King of the World in his various forms of the Green Man, King Melchizedek and St. George. Both St. George and John the Baptist are authentic embodiments of the King of the World. Both St. George and the Prophet Elijah, John's incarnate spirit, are synonymous with the Sufis' al-Khadir, who on Sri Lanka is venerated as a form of King Sanat Kumara.

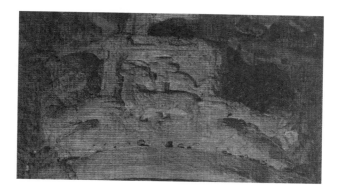

**Rosslyn's Images related to
John the Baptist & King of the World:
Agnus Dei (top)
St. George (middle left)
King Melchizedek (middle right)
Green Man Head (bottom)**

The Discovery of Boynton Canyon's Court of the King

After anointing Sanat Kumara and John the Baptist as the official patrons and etheric guides of the IOGT, I decided that Sedona was the best possible place for the Johannite revival. The red rock vortexes of Sedona alchemically activate the inner transformative Kundalini, which then fully awakens inner gnosis. Moreover, Sedona is truly the Land of the Holy Grail, which I now identify not as an object but as the alchemical power a Holy Grail object possesses. This power is ubiquitous in Sedona.

When I finally returned to Boynton Canyon after nearly a year away I found myself guided to a different part of the canyon than I had previously explored. New interdimensional temples subsequently appeared in this area, as well as what appeared to be enigmatic writing chiseled into the canyon wall. One line of the chiseled script looked remarkably similar to Chinese characters, so I asked a Chinese-American friend if she could interpret them for me. She immediately recognized three Chinese characters among them that she translated as "go up", "mountain," and "light." When taken together I decided that the characters were instructing me to "Go up to the Mountain of Light." Unfortunately, I did not know of any trails that ascended upwards in this new part of the canyon, so I decided to put the message on hold until one was revealed to me.

A week later I returned to Boynton Canyon to lead a ceremony with two friends from Kauai, M & V, who were closely aligned with Sanat Kumara. After imbibing the sacrament we all struck out independently in directions dictated by our intuition. For a couple of hours I wandered aimlessly, not feeling particularly inspired, and then slowly ambled back to camp. When I was within a couple hundred yards from our ceremonial area I noticed a little-used trail off to my right that led upwards along the canyon wall. Even though the trail was well camouflaged with leaves I was still amazed that I had never spotted it before. I must have passed it a hundred times. Now, my inner voice was urging me onwards. "Go up to the Mountain of Light," I heard it say.

After entering the trail head I found my new path to be very uneven and steep. On more than one occasion I lost my balance on its loose gravely earth and slid dangerously backward. But unused trails in Boynton Canyon had always been a source of excitement for me, and when I followed them I usually made some kind of unique discovery, Indiana Jones style.

Eventually the precipitous trail became horizontal and easier to negotiate. As I caught my breath I was slowly led along a ridge attached to the side of the canyon. As I continued forward I noticed to my left a magnificent panorama gradually opening up. "Just another fifty feet and I will be able to take it all in," I told myself.

When I finally stopped at an overview spot and gazed out onto my new discovery I could not believe what I saw. In front of me was a surreal panorama of red rock temples arranged in a horse shoe pattern around a central mound. My first impression was that I was surveying a grand court and the central mound was its throne. Could this wandering knight (me) have found a home?

Since I was still under the influence of my sacrament, a parade of colors, symbols and carvings moved over and around the temples, thereby making it very difficult to discern if what I was seeing were permanent features of the "court" or just part of a fleeting phantasmagoria. I decided to keep to my rule of thumb, which was to not accept any temple or temple feature as real unless I had consistently seen it at least five times, with the real litmus test being whether I could discern any traces of it when I was completely sober. In the past, only after revisiting temples numerous times had I felt confident to record their exact shapes and sizes, and, of course, this was my first experience at the "court."

As I gazed at the court its fluid features moved across across my field of vision. Human skulls intermittently manifested upon and around the temples, and at one point the ambiance of the entire court became decidedly cold, dark and eerie. As a dark shadow fell over the court I could feel the hairs on the back of my neck stand straight up. I was sure that I was about to be introduced to the diabolical owner of the court. But then the skulls disappeared as fast as they had arrived, and an aura of scintillating white light replaced the morbid darkness. If there was an owner of the court, I told myself, he must be a lord of both light *and* darkness.

After meditating on the unique features of the court for thirty minutes I decided to find my friends and escort them to my new lookout. After literally flying down the precipitous trail I re-entered our ceremonial area while loudly proclaiming: "I have made an amazing discovery!" My announcement was badly timed and fell on deaf ears. M and V were deeply engrossed in their own magical journeys and could not muster much of a reaction to my inspired news flash. So rather than giving a half-baked description of the court that would not have been well received, I decided it would be best if my friends could see it for themselves.

When we all finally arrived at the overlook I told my two friends to meditate for a few moments on the scene in front of them before I shared my own insights regarding it. Superlatives and one syllable vocables erupted in spurts followed by V's pronouncement of "Ahhhhhhhh, the Holy of Holies!" I then offered my revelation that the red rock temples formed a court of some kind and we all stood in stunned silence trying to visualize it. When M and I finally emerged from our reverie we looked at each other and laughed with giddy anticipation. We were two boys who had just been given the keys to a lost city and could not wait to explore it. Shaking hands, he and I resolved to spend the rest of our lives exploring and unraveling the secrets of the "court." I was thrilled to have found a buddy who could assist me in my ongoing research of Boynton Canyon. But, sadly, my excitement was pre-mature. When M later returned to Kauai he became violently ill and blamed his dangerous malady on the Sedona energy. So far he has yet to return to Boynton Canyon.

The Court of Masau'u, Sanat Kumara & the Peacock King

After my initial discovery of the "court" I returned to my new overlook in Boynton Canyon many times in the following days and weeks. Eventually I had accumulated a data base of interdimensional temple features I consistently recognized on and around the court. And, of course, I felt quite sure who the court belonged to. But definitive evidence of Sanat Kumara's "signature" still eluded me.

A significant breakthrough came during the fall of 2010 when I enrolled Larry, one of the knights of the IOGT, to accompany me on some sacramental research in Boynton. While hiking on the trail near the court we both received the same interdimensional vision of a red rock temple that had the shape of a knight's head. The helmeted head was straight out of the Middle Ages, and it could have passed as the bust of one of King Arthur's knights. Larry and I initially chuckled that our common discovery had resulted from the sacrament and was no doubt precipitated by our biased "knight vision," but later when we returned in a more sober state of mind the knight's head was still there. I was thrilled with this result, believing that the discovery of the helmeted head was a sure sign that the owner of the court was soon to be revealed. "This at least proves the owner of the court is a king," I told Larry, "and this is one of his knights."

My return to Boynton Canyon in the spring of 2011 finally and unequivocally revealed to me the owner of the court. A day that began as just another sacramental ritual ended being one of the most pivotal experiences of my life.

When I reached my perch on that fateful day I immediately noticed that something was amiss. Either the plant sacrament I had imbibed was extremely strong or an invisible power source was magnifying its effects. All the temples came into view as expected, but they were sharper and more ornate than ever before.

All the diverse features of the temples I had previously recorded were now on exhibit, as well as a host of new ones. I was seeing some detail that had previously been hidden from me because it vibrates on a very high dimension. But now every color, symbol, shape and minute carving was on full display, and they blended together perfectly as one magnificent, interdimensional tapestry.

Once the completed court was in perfect focus I saw my old friend, the Peacock Angel, there to greet me. As was his custom he manifested as the trees and bushes around the court that were now hundreds of peacocks. But he was also present in the court as peacock heads, feathers and complete bodies that were carved in and around the stone temples.

A silvery lightning-like flash from above suddenly drew my attention to a towering ridge of white sandstone that served as the backdrop to the court. The ridge seemed to be partitioned into long, crystal shaped columns that were both receiving and transmitting cosmic energy. I watched as the energy from the cosmos entered these huge crystals and then traveled down into the very center of the court. When it reached the area of the throne the silvery river of energy magically transformed into a cavalcade of radiant peacocks that descended directly into the middle of the throne/mound. I couldn't help noticing that as each new peacock entered the mound it increased the throne's interdimensional glow. There was no doubt that the throne-mound was the principal focus of the court and the gathering point for its power. It was indeed the throne of a king, whose power was nearly blinding in its intensity. It was assuredly the throne of Tawsi Melek, the Peacock King.

As I continued to scan the court temples I noticed that many of them displayed the features of numerous other animals besides peacocks. One of the temples located diagonally across from me possessed the features of an elephant, another adjacent to it had the appearance of a horse, and one next to it projected a distinct antlered deer motif. The central throne/mound was adorned with the body of a regal lion and the head of a mighty eagle, and nearby I could clearly perceive the head and body of an antelope or gazelle. Above them all was a huge snake. I had seen many of these animal shapes at different times, but now they were all appearing at once.

When I grouped together the animals on the right and left sides of the throne a distinct pattern emerged. If a monarch was seated on the throne the more yin or female-natured animals, such as the antelope, snake, and peacock, would be situated on his left, female side and the male-natured animals, such as the powerful lion, buck, and bustling elephant, would be located on his right, male side. This placement of yin/yang animals resulted in a perfect balance of energy in the center of the throne, and I knew that the king embodied and personified that perfect balance. He was the androgynous union of the universal male and female principles. He was pure energy itself.

My inner light bulb was now blazing, and with its luminosity came the final revelation. The court that I had been seeing for months was the Court of the King of the World; it was home to the monarch I had come to know over many years of research and direct experience as the Peacock Angel, Sanat Kumara, Masau'u and the Green Man. Now, all the contrasting imagery and symbols I beheld adorning the court were easy to identify. The peacocks, of course, represented Tawsi Melek, the Peacock King. The animals covering and surrounding the throne/mound represented the four legged subjects of the King of the World in his role of Green Man and the Lord of Nature. Even the Hindu temple design of some of the temples made perfect sense now; they were associated with the Lemurian-Hindu king, Sanat Kumara. And, finally, the skulls, skeletons and grotesque faces that often appeared among the temples, as well as the dark and forbidding feeling that accompanies them, were the calling card of Masau'u, the Lord of Death and King of the Fourth World who once reigned in Palatkwapi. I could now say with conviction that while most of the Kachinas may have left the Hopis' patron was still in the City of the Star People!

Having identified the central mound or "throne" as containing the power of the King of the World, my gaze locked on to it. There was no question that the king's dynamic energy was the seminal power of not just the court but the entire Boynton Canyon vortex. And, as if to say "You are right," the moment this realization occurred to me the rays of the Sun beemed directly onto the mound, fully illuminating it. "Yes," I repeated over and over while staring at the radiant throne-mound, "I am finally in the physical presence of the King of the World!"

I did not perceive an actual human-like figure seated on the throne or even the outline of one. I didn't need to. I knew that the power in the mound was the true essence of the king. I reflected on the many legends of the King of the World from various traditions that identify the King of the World with the dynamic energy of Kundalini or the "Serpent Power." "Yes," I murmured, "the legends are true."

I decided that of all the temples and rock formations I had ever seen or experienced in in Boynton Canyon or anyplace else in Sedona the court and its throne/mound was definitely the most powerful. And if Boynton Canyon is indeed the most powerful of the four principal vortexes as many people contend, then it must be the principal energy source of the entire Sedona vortex. An image appeared in my mind of one gigantic vortex covering Sedona that was sub-divided into many smaller vortexes and had the court and it throne/mound at its center.

As I prepared to leave the court I glanced to my right in the direction of the center of Sedona and noticed a direct line that connected the throne to the rock formation known as Bell Rock, one of the other four major vortexes. I then visualized energy emerging from the court and its throne/mound and then traveling down this line to the towering bell-like edifice at the opposite end of town. My first thought was that this corridor must be the "spine" of Sedona. If I was correct, then the throne in Boynton Canyon was Sedona's Root Chakra and Bell Rock its Crown Chakra. This would also reveal the directional flow of the energy moving along the Sedona spine. In any chakra system the Root Chakra is always the source of the power and the Crown Chakra its final destination. I made a mental note to explore the spine of Sedona during the next phase of my research, that of plotting the Sedona Grid. I then gathered up my belongings and began my trek home.

The Court of the King of the World

Left/ female side of the Court. A peacock peers around a corner.

Right /male side of the Court

The Elephant Temple with baby elephant in front

The "Temple of Masau'u"
A gruesome face is held by spindly fingers.

A Knight of the Court

The Throne/Mound of the King of the World

Temples leading to the Court of the King

The Court of the King

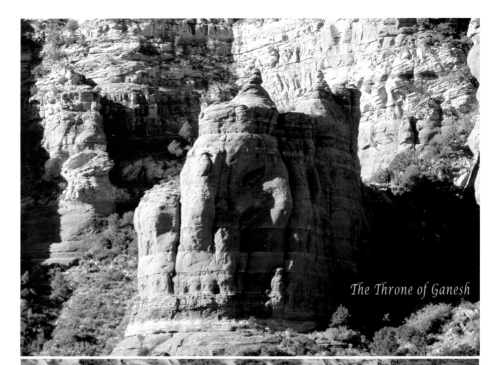

The Throne of Ganesh

The Elephant Temple

Mother and Baby Elephant

The Sedona Grid

Over the past fifty years many of us have come to identify Earth as a living organism. Like every human who walks upon it our world also possesses a Spirit, Soul and Body. And just as every human possesses an etheric sheath composed of meridians and vortices that chi or prana moves through to all parts of the physical body, the Earth has an intricate grid of energy lines and vortexes through which life force travels to all parts of the planet. In truth, all of Earth's continents, countries, towns and cities are living entities possessing their own grid systems of energy lines, vortexes and chakras. This includes the City of Sedona.

In this chapter:
   * The Spine, Chakras & Leylines of Sedona
   * The White House and The Court of the King
   * The Sedona Grid and The Tree of Life

The Spine, Chakras & Leylines of Sedona

When I was ready to delineate Sedona's spine and the grid of energy lines and chakras aligned with it I purchased a topographical map of the area that highlighted most of the principal red rock formations and vortexes. Then, guided by a rudimentary knowledge of geomancy and my trusted pendulum, I drew a line connecting Boynton Canyon to Bell Rock and then drew ley lines connecting this pathway to many of the other major vortexes and rock formations that were highlighted on the map. I also dowsed for additional vortexes that were not marked on the map and then traveled to them physically to measure their strength and integrity with L-Rods. As my grid gradually took shape it became evident to me that my schematic had been inspired. The corridor between Boynton Canyon and Bell Rock was indeed a central pathway that the other major ley lines in Sedona naturally fed into like major nerves feeding into the human spine.

I next plotted the chakras of the Sedona Grid. I began with Boynton Canyon and Bell Rock (which I now began to refer to as "Crown Rock") as the city's Root and Crown Chakras, and then I located Sedona's middle five chakras. I received a measure of confirmation when my chakra identifications proved consistent with Nicholas Mann's pentagram and hexagram landscape temples. My three "yang" or male chakras were all located in the region of Mann's "male" hexagram temple, and my upper three "yin" chakras were located in the region of his "female" pentagram temple.

I also received corroboration for the area I had assigned to be the city's **First or Root Chakra.** The ley line configurations that exist in that region ostensibly reveal that Sedona's Muladhara Chakra is indeed Boynton Canyon. As you will see in the the Sedona Grid maps on the following pages, one of the outstanding configurations of ley lines in the canyon is a square with the court right in the center. I interpreted this square grid of lines to be both instructive and symbolic. The square is the geometrical shape commonly associated with physical matter and the "earth" element of the Root Chakra. And, esoterically, the four sides of this square represent the four "petals" of a Root Chakra, inside of which is the Serpent Kundalini, which in the case of Sedona manifests within the throne/mound in the Court of the King.

216

The hexagram of ley lines that is tied to the throne-mound in the Sedona Grid is also instructive regarding the spirit and energy that resides there. As the symbol of the Son of God/Goddess, the hexagram identifies the throne-mound as the seat of the androgynous King of the World. In India, where the hexagram is the definitive yantra (geometrical form body) of the Divine Son, Sanat Kumara, it represents him as the androgynous union of his mother and father, God Shiva and Goddess Shakti. The six pointed star is also the premier symbol of alchemy, the science that unites the polarity and leads to the awakening of the androgynous Serpent Power. This fits perfectly with what is known about Boynton Canyon, which is the only electro-magnetic or "androgynous" vortex in the Sedona area. For those hiking, meditating or performing ritual, the canyon's dual nature makes it the ideal place for uniting the inner polarity and activating the serpentine force.

The Goddess's support for Her Son's reign is revealed by Isis Rock, a towering rock formation in Long Canyon that sits directly behind the king's throne/mound in Boynton Canyon. From Isis Rock, the Goddess, who throughout the ancient world was once kown as "the power behind the throne of the king," continually sends supportive energy to Her Son. Her supportive power was acknowledged in ancient Egypt, where Goddess Isis wore a throne upon her head to symbolize that she was indeed the power behind the throne occupied by Green Man and King of the World, Osiris.

Moving up the Sedona spine, we find that the **Second or "Water" Chakra** is marked physically by a small pond located just off the main road leading to Boynton Canyon. Circular ponds and lakes are natural vortexes that continually spiral energy in and out of the Earth. I discovered this pond after completing the Sedona Grid and was pleasantly surprised to find the city's water chakra was actually marked physically by a water source..

The **Third or Fire Chakra** of the Sedona grid manifests physically as the conjoined red rock formations of Chimney Rock and Little Sugarloaf, which are united by a raised land bridge. Chimney Rock, which gives the appearance of a massive oven surmounted by three united smoke stacks, is part of a fiery energy zone with Thunder Mountain at its center. Nicholas Mann asserts that Chimney Rock is the "Head of the Sedona Serpent" that slithers along Thunder Mountain

217

ridge. The Chinese recognize the high, jagged ridges like the one along the summit of Thunder Mountain to be natural pathways of the fiery, male dragon force. The Sedona Serpent's head and termination point, Chimney Rock, is thus a gathering place for this fiery force. Third Chakra activation can occur here.

The **Fourth or Heart Chakra** of the Sedona Grid is Airport Mesa, which serves as the point of union of Mann's pentagram and hexagram temples. Like the heart chakra of the physical body, Airport Mesa is both the dividing point between the male/female, upper and lower chakras, as well as a place where the polarity naturally unites. It is thus a place of alchemy where a hiker or meditator can awaken their own heart chakra, arouse the Fire Serpent, and undergo a powerful transformation.

The **Fifth or Throat Chakra** on the Sedona spine is marked physically by a high knoll that faces Cathedral Rock. A home with a complete 360 degree view of Sedona currently sits upon this knoll, thus making it a perfect place to communicate with all four directions. Communication is the specific activity associated with the Throat Chakra.

The **Sixth or Third Eye Chakra** is also a tall knoll aligned directly with Bell or Crown Rock. As the third of Sedona's chakras where the polarity naturally unites, the alchemical effect of this knoll is to unite the polar opposite hemispheres of the brain and awaken the Third Eye. Like the Ajna Chakra of the human body with its two petals (representing the two hemispheres), this power point on the Sedona grid sits between the "petals" of Twin Buttes and Cathedral Rock and unites the energies of these opposing landmarks. It is thus an excellent place for hemisphere synchonization and Third Eye activation.

Sedona's **Seventh or Crown Chakra** is Bell Rock (or Crown Rock), whose crown-like shape makes it the perfect Crown Chakra of Sedona. Bell Rock is considered an "up flow vortex," which means that spiraling energy continually moves up it. As it rises this energy gains both "velocity and frequency, forming an "energy beacon."[1] Bell Rock's power comes from the vortex or chakra it sits upon, as well as from the Kundalini force that travels up the Sedona spine from Boynton Canyon before shooting upwards and outwards at Bell Rock like an etheric geyser. This is an excellent place for Crown Chakra activation.

The Sedona Grid

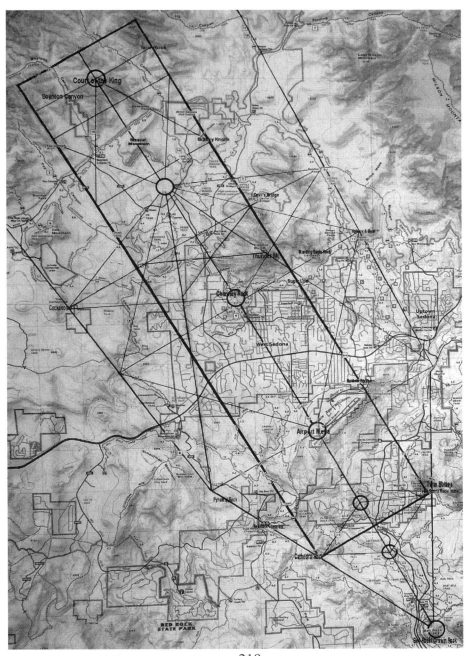

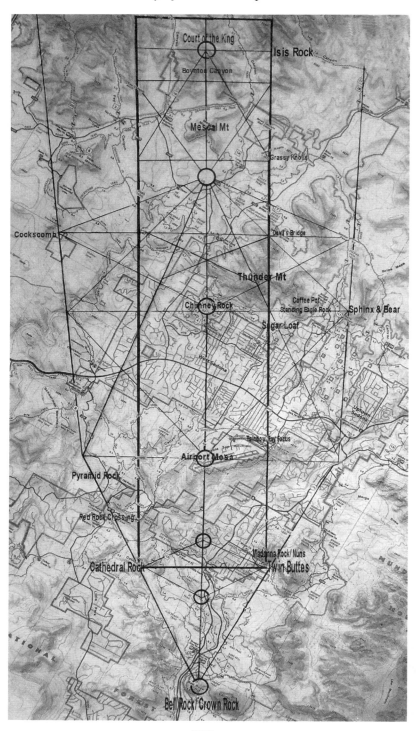

The Lower Chakras of the Sedona Grid

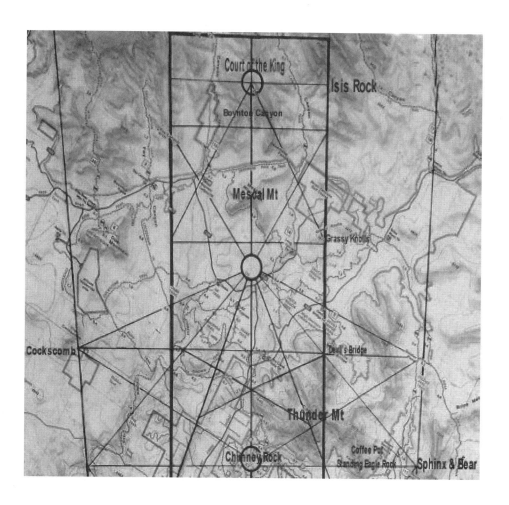

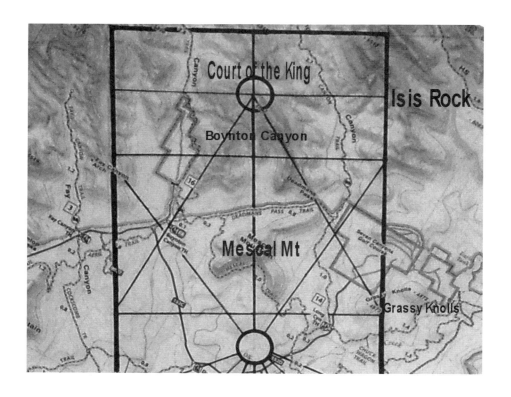

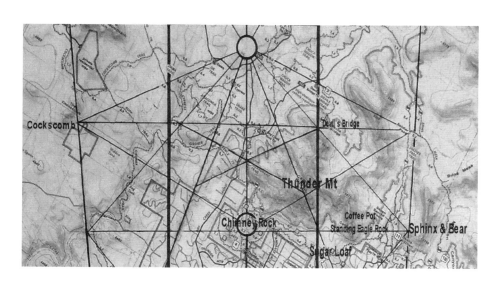

The Upper Chakras of the Sedona Grid

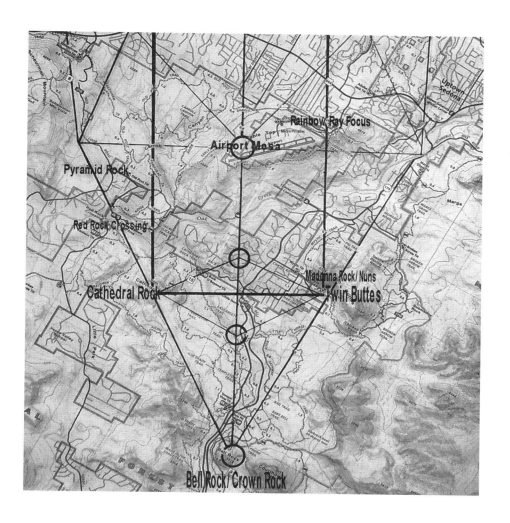

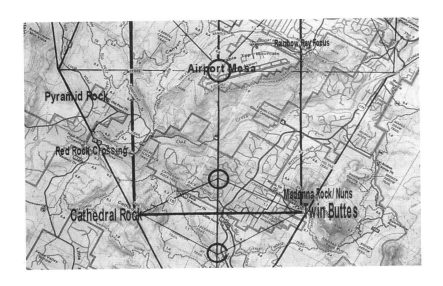

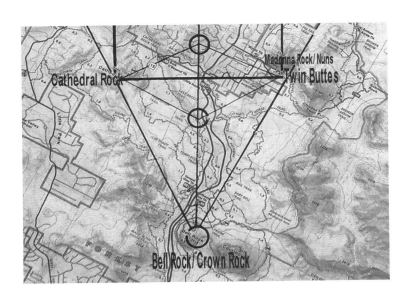

The White House and The Court of the King

The hexagram and pentagram of the Sedona grid reflect the ley line grid of Washington D.C., which is physically overlaid with streets and avenues. Just as they are in Sedona, the pentagram and hexagram can be seen to be united at a ruler's court, which in the US capitol is the White House. The most ancient and supportive relationship of the Goddess and Her governing Son was thus perpetuated by the Freemason designers of Washington D.C..

As seen below, while linking to and surrounding the White House the pentagram and hexagram can be found united in at least two different configurations.

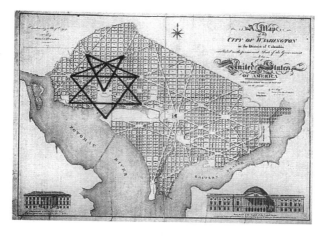

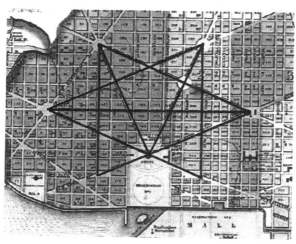

225

The Sedona Grid and the Tree of Life

The central corridor of the Sedona grid (the region between the two straight, thick lines) bares a striking resemblance to the Tree of Life of the Kabbala. This is instructive as it perfectly symbolizes Sedona's function. As an ancient Garden of Eden for both the Hopis and Yavapai, Sedona is a Tree of Life for the American Southwest.

When incorporating the Kabbala's Tree of Life into the Sedona Grid, Sedona's Root Chakra and Court of the King is found to correspond to the Sephera Malkuth. Malkuth denotes "Kingdom," and the Court in Boynton Canyon is indeed the court and "kingdom" of the King of the World..

Sedona's Second Chakra corresponds to the Sephera Yesod, the "Foundation." The Airport Mesa, sight of Sedona's Heart Chakra, is synonymous with the Sephira Tiferet, meaning "Beauty;" and the mound that functions as Sedona's Fifth Chakra corresponds to Da'at (Daath). Finally, Sedona's Crown Chakra, Bell or "Crown" Rock, corresponds to the Sephera Keter (Kether), meaning "Crown."

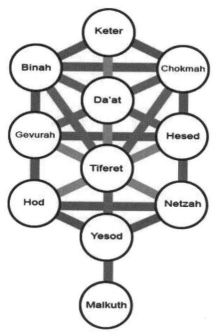

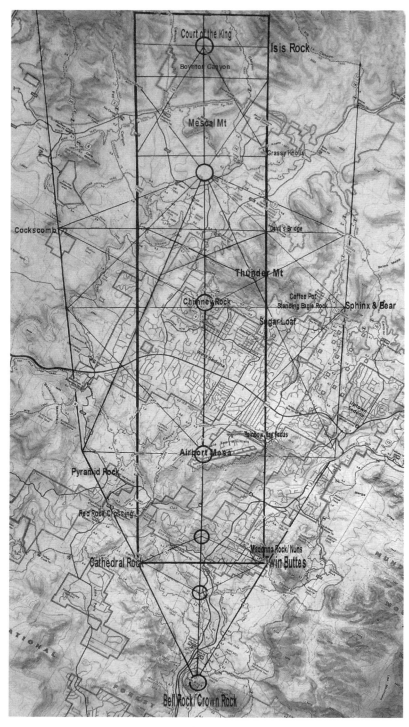

Sedona's Seven Chakras

Sedona's First Chakra: The Court of the King

Sedona's Second Chakra

Sedona's Third Chakra: Little Sugarloaf and Chimney Rock

Fourth Chakra: Airport Mesa

Sedona's Fifth Chakra

The Sphinx and the Honey Bear

The Faces
of Sedona

Venusian Pink Starship-Portal at
Cathedral Rock Vortex.
Photo by Shekina Rose

Moving into Pleiadian Light Portal.
Pleiadian Starship is in sky above.
Photo by Shekina Rose

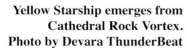

Yellow Starship emerges from
Cathedral Rock Vortex.
Photo by Devara ThunderBeat

Sedona's Sixth Chakra (mound in foreground)

Sedona's Seventh Chakra: Bell Rock or "Crown Rock"

231

Other Landmarks and Vortexes in the Sedona Grid

Cathedral Rock (Front)

Cathedral Rock (Back)

Courthouse Butte

"Pyramid Rock"

233

Isis Rock

Sphinx Rock

Ship Rock

Steamboat Rock or "Throne of Isis"

Sugarloaf Rock

Coffee Pot Rock
Native American Name: Standing Eagle Rock

Mescal Mountain

The Devil's Kitchen

The Devil's Bridge

The Two Nuns

The Twin Buttes

The Chapel of the Holy Cross

Elephant Rock

The Cockscomb
Native American Name: The Three Warriors

Grassy Knolls (next to golf course)

Red Rock Crossing

Lizard Rock
Native American Name: Nesting Eagle Rock

Condor Rock

Sedona and the World Grid

My perspective broadened dramatically the moment I began perceiving the Earth to be the physical body of the King of the World. I now identify our monarch's arteries and viens with Earth's rivers, his flesh with the solid ground, and his etheric body with the ley lines and vortexes of the World Grid. The Earth would be a much different place if we all subscribed to this perspective. We would then be much more careful about pouring noxious chemicals into the Earth's waterways, knowing that it is the king's blood stream. And when we strip-mined minerals or clear-cut acres of trees we might think twice about shearing away valuable portions of our ruler's flesh.

In this chapter:
* The Etheric Bodies of Earth
* Revival of the World Grid
* Sedona and the Arizona State Grid
* Sedona: Root Chakra of the Earth
* Masau'u and his "Twin," Pahana
* The Chakras of the Planetary Logos
*The Spine of the Sub-Continent of India

The Etheric Bodies of Earth

When I had completed the Sedona Grid I decided to continue my investigation to see how Sedona ties into the larger World Grid of ley lines and vortexes. I was anxious to see what special place Sedona might hold in the King of the World's body. But first I needed to review what I knew about the World Grid.

The World Grid has been known about for hundreds and thousands of years. No doubt its knowledge began when our more etheric and psychically attuned ancestors could both feel and see Earth's etheric lines and vortexes. According to the Australian Aborigines, during the Dream Time the Star People or "Gods" could not only see the energy lines and vortexes of Earth, they were also the creators of them. The World Grid they helped fabricate eventually became a massive grid composed of five interlocking grids, each of which was in the shape of one of the five Platonic Solids and served as the etheric body of one of the five elements that comprise the Earth: ether, air, fire, water and earth. The subtle body grid of the ether element is a dodecahedron; the etheric body grid of the air element takes the shape of an octahedron; the subtle body grid of the fire element is a tetrahedron; the subtle body grid of the water element has the form of an icosahedron; and the sheath grid of the earth element is a cube. When these five grid shapes are superimposed over the Earth and then interlocked at their nodal points, the World Grid is created.

The five sheath-grids of the Earth were apparently known of by the builders of Skara Brae, a settlement in the Orkneys of Scotland that has been dated to 3200 BCE. The five Platonic solids (below) were found at Skara Brae carved into the stone balls, suggesting that each one is superimposed over a sphere.

244

Revival of the World Grid

One of the first literary references to the World Grid that has survived over the centuries is found in the writings of Plato. According to the Greek philosopher when teaching his student Simmias, Socrates proclaimed: "My dear boy, the real earth viewed from above is supposed to look like one of those balls made out of twelve pieces of skin sewn together." Socrates was referring to that part of the World Grid that is the subtle body of ether and takes the shape of a massive dodecahedron, wherein twelve five-sided pentagrams are joined together and completely cover the planet.

In 1972 a revival of the World Grid began in earnest with biologist Ivan T. Sanderson, who published an article in *Saga Magazine* entitled *The Twelve Devil's Graveyards Around the World*. The article presents Sanderson's work of superimposing an icosohedron grid around the Earth and then discovering at the grid's nodes the location of twelve triangular vortexes that are notorious for the disappearance of ships, planes and other vehicles associated with them. Known as "Vile Vortices," the two most fatal of these vortexes are the Bermuda Triangle in the Atlantic Ocean and the Devil's Triangle off the coast of Japan.

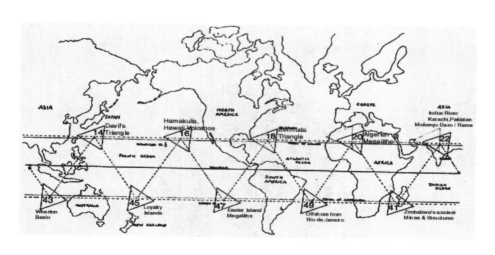

Earth's Ten Vile Vortices

Continuing Sanderson's work were three Russian scientists, Nikolai Goncharov, Vyacheslav Morochov, and Valery Makarov, who superimposed a dodecahedron grid over the Earth and then interlocked it with Sanderson's icosahedron grid. They anchored their new amalgamated World Grid at the poles and at Giza, which they chose as the Center of the Earth. Their new World Grid revealed twenty triangular vortices around the globe, ten of which are "Vile Vortices" and ten of which are "Healing Vortices." The ten Healing Vortices include Giza, Egypt, Machu Picchu, and Sedona. Sedona is part of a positive triangular vortex that begins at 31st N latitude in the Sonoma Desert of Mexico and then moves north to encompass much of Arizona, including Sedona and Hopiland.

The terms World Grid and Planetary Grid were officially inducted into western parlance in 1975, when geomancer Chris Bird published an article in *New Age Journal* that covered the work of both Sanderson and the three Russians. When geomancers Bill Becker and Bethe Hagens read the article they contacted Bird, and the three of them joined forces to complete the World Grid by incorporating into it the geometrical grids of the other three Platonic solids. In order to create their final Planetary Grid or "Earth Star," as they called it, they also added many smaller ley lines and vortexes to the grid by utilizing formulas that Buckminster Fuller had used in developing his geodesic domes. Becker and Hagens systematized Fuller's work and named it Unified Vector Geometry.

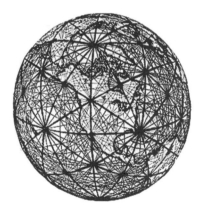

Becker-Hagens' Planetary Grid

246

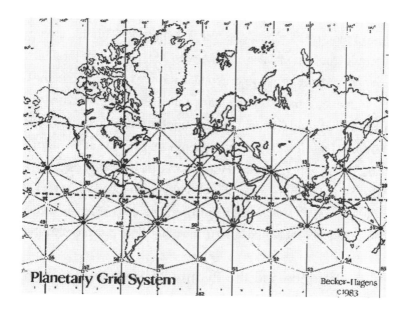

112 W Longitude runs straight through Arizona

Becker and Hagen's Earth Star and Planetary Earth Grid maps reveal both major and minor leylines and vortexes. One of the world's most important ley lines on their maps runs along 112 W longitude. This line emerges from the huge vortex in the Sonoma Desert in Mexico and then travels through the center of Arizona and such important energetic locations as Prescott and the Grand Canyon. Its influence can be felt for many miles on either side of it, including the regions in and around Sedona. Other important ley lines that radiate from the same Sonoma Desert vortex innervate both the eastern and western parts of Arizona. One of them traverses the Hopi Mesas, passing very close to Third Mesa, and it also moves within a few miles of Sedona. Sedona is thus very close to two major ley lines and receives energy from both. As their midpoint, Sedona acquires the same significance it would have if one of the lines ran directly through it.

Sedona and the Pyramidal State Grid of Arizona

In order to more fully plot out a grid of the State of Arizona I dowsed for additional ley lines and vortexes that were not on the Becker-Hagens' grid. When the lines and vortexes I discovered were united into a closed grid I found that the Arizona Grid takes the shape of a pyramid with Sedona at its apex.

To construct the Arizona State Grid I began by taking the Yavapai Sacred Triangle grid of Mingus Mountain, Montezuma Well and Sedona, and then extended the triangle's ley lines both north and south. These extended lines run across Arizona and naturally unite many of the state's recognized vortexes with the Sacred Triangle. One of these extended lines moves north to the big vortex of Canyon de Chelly, and south through the city of Prescott. From there it moves along the Harcuvar Mountains and then to the vortex of Quarzite. Another extended line from the Sacred Triangle runs north to the mammoth vortex of Grand Canyon and south to Tonto National Monument. It then runs along the Tortilla Mountains to the big vortex at Saguaro National Park. A third extended ley line runs north through the ancient Hopi settlement of Wupatiki and south until it reaches the vortex of Organ Pipe Cactus National Monument. The vortexes of Quarzite and Organ Pipe are also joined together by a large ley line that runs along the Palomas and Growler Mountains in the southwest.

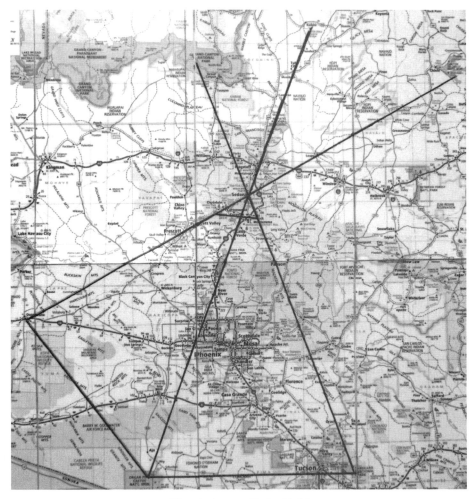

The Arizona State Grid

The spiral, symbol of a vortex, inscribed by ancient natives at Saguaro National Park.

249

My finished Arizona Grid takes the shape of a pyramid with the Sacred Triangle as its capstone and the city of Phoenix in its center. A pyramid is a structure with "fire in the middle," which in this case is Phoenix, the land of the fire bird.

Sedona: Root Chakra of the Earth

As part of the World Grid there have been numerous planetary chakra charts drawn up, each listing different vortexes around the Earth as its chakras. Most chakra systems name Mount Kailash as the Earth's crown chakra, although the identification of the other chakras varies considerably. Having already determined that the true Center of the Earth is the 20 degree band that surrounds our planet and has 30 N latitude as its midpoint (see Chapter 4), it is logical to look for Earth's chakras along that central band. If Mount Kailash, which is on the band, is designated the Crown Chakra, then logically an opposing point (another "Court of the King") on the other side of the planet should be the planetary Root Chakra. That turns out to be Sedona and the Hopi Mesas, two salient points also on the central band. When I joined Sedona and Hopiland to Mount Kailash by a rod inserted through the Earth, representing the planetary spine, I found that they are nearly exactly opposite each other with a differential of ten degrees of longitude. Certainly, with its bright red rock and Kundalini-like energy, Sedona fits all the criteria required to qaulify as Earth's Root Chakra, just as Mount Kailash perfectly fits the description of Earth's Crown Chakra. Sacred Mount Kailash is the physical manifestation of invisible Mount Meru, the mythical mountain that is the first, the tallest and the crowning peak of Earth.

As mentioned earlier, both Sedona and the Hopi Mesas are united by being part of a grid in the American Southwest that reflects the stars in the constellation of Orion. Since Orion's counterpart on Earth is the Hopis' King of the World, Masau'u, it can be said that Earth's Root Chakra is the terrestrial body of Masau'u. This makes sense considering that one of Masau'u's titles is "Lord of the Underworld," and Earth's "underworld" *is* its Root Chakra.

This designation of the American Southwest as Earth's "underworld" and Root Chakra is not new. In fact, thousands of years ago the area was mentioned as part of Earth's geography in the ancient Hindu legends, the Puranas. The authors of both the *Vishnu Purana* and *Shrimad Bhagavatam* referred to the American Southwest as Patala, the "underworld," that they knew existed on the opposite side of the world from Jambu Dwipa, a continent in the "upper world." Jambu Dwipa, an ancient name for Asia, was said by these early geographers to contain Mount Meru and its physical counterpart, Mount Kailash, at its center. Meru-Kailash was thus designated the Center of the World in the "upper world" and the American Southwest became known as the Center of the World in the "lower world" of Patala.

Masau'u and his "Twin," Pahana

But, as mentioneed numerous times in this book, Masau'u is King of the (entire) World, so his kingdom encompasses more than just the Earth's under-belly. He is lord of BOTH Jambu Dwipa and Patala. Thus, there should be mani-festations of him on both sides of the planet. And there is. Masau'u governs the "lower world" of the American Southwest as himself, and his "Twin", Pahana, governs the "upper world" of Mount Meru-Kailash of the Tibetan Himalayas, the "Roof of the World."

Masau'u and his "Twin" Pahana, the "White Brother," are a version of the ubiquitous Twins mentioned in Chapter 6. Their sibling relationship is reflected by these twin pairs, and especially by their counterparts of the Cheyenne Tribe known as Mausuam (a version of the name Masau'u) and Sweet Medicine Root. The Cheyennes' version of Pahana, Sweet Medicine Root, was a great culture bearer who taught his people the chunoupa rite (pipe ceremony), as well as many other rites that became the bedrock of their religious life. He also established a lineage of Peace Chiefs that continues to govern the tribe today. By contrast, the Chey-enne Masau'u was the founder of the Rites of Mausuam, wherein the observances taught by Sweet Medicine were performed backwards. These enigmatic rites are today observed by the tribe's sect of Contraries .

Like their Cheyenne counterparts the Hopis' Pahana and Masau'u are also polar opposites of each other. Like his counterpart Mausuam, Masau'u pa-tronizes the Hopis' sect of contraries, the Kwan or One-Horned Society, which observes its rites backward during those months when the traditional Kachina dances are forbidden. The actor who is chosen to impersonate Masau'u during these rites prepares for his role by spending many days fully emulating his character and performing all his daily activities backwards. He sleeps throughout the day and is active all night. He puts his moccasins on the wrong feet and runs around the reservation in a counter-clockwise circuit (traditional Hopis move in a clockwise direction). When he finally enters a ceremonial arena the Masau'u impersonator has become one with the Lord of the World. According to one observer, the masked Masau'u dancer then "chases down (each) dancer with clownish antics and hits him with his cylindrical sack. The man falls down as if dead and Masau'u strips him of his clothes, putting them on himself. But in the wrong manner."[1]

Hopi legend maintains that Pahana was separated from his "twin" and sent to the opposite side of the planet during the period leading up to the long migrations of the Hopi Clans. Pahana's mission in traveling to the other side of the world was to help give our planet balance, which is in keeping with the seminal duty of the Hopi Tribe given it by Masau'u. Once in the East Pahana's duty was to balance his "Twin," Masau'u. His long term instructions were, however, to eventually return to the West and help the Hopis usher in a new era or golden age on Earth.

In recent years Pahana has been identified by many Hopis as the Tibetans, the people living in the country surrounding Mount Kailash. Thus, it is now acknowledged by many that the Tibetans and their country are Pahana and the Crown Chakra of Earth, and that the Hopis and their territories are Masau'u and the Root Chakra of our planet.

The opposing natures of Pahana and Masau'u are reflected by the people they represent. In the Hopi language, for example, the word Nyima means "Moon" while in Tibetan it means "Sun;" and the word Dawa in Tibetan means Moon while in Hopi it denotes Sun. Moreover, the Hopi word for love is the Tibetan word for hate, and the Hopi word for hate is the word for love in the Tibetan language.

But since Pahana and Masau'u are also "Twins," there are also many similarities between the people they represent. Both the Hopis and Tibetans possess a similar rugged, dark-skinned Mongolian appearance, and they share some of the same DNA genetic markers, such as the D1 Haplogroup marker. The

The Tibetan and Arizona Flags

Mount Kailash and Thunder Mountain

View of Mt. Kailash and Thunder Mountain as Shiva Lingams

Hopis and Tibetans are both famous for their sand paintings and their fondness for silver, gold, coral and and tourquoise, which they use to ward off evil spirits. The swastika is a common symbol among both people, and since the founding of the State of Arizona the flag of the Hopis' current home state has been very similar to the Tibetan flag. And, perhaps most surprising, when Sedona's highest peak, Capitol Peak or Thunder Mountain, is seen from certain angles it is nearly identical to Tibet's Mount Kailash!

In order to remain in contact with Pahana and the Tibetans, as well as to evolve and harmonize the Earth, members of the Hopi Snake Clan annually perform a ceremony that sends waves of Kundalini power up the spine of our planet from its Root Chakra in the American Southwest to its Crown Chakra of Mount Kailash in the Himalayas. The Serpent Power alerts Pahana that "he is not forgotten and that he must come [back]." [2]

During their ceremony of activating the Planetary Kundalini the members of the Hopi Snake Clan take turns stomping a "sounding board" over a special hole in the ground, or "sipapuni," that leads to the underworld home of the Kundalini snake. As the Serpent Power awakens....

"...a faint rumble (comes) from underground...Never elsewhere does one hear such a sound, so deep and powerful it is. It assures those below that those above are dutifully carrying on the ceremony. It awakens the vibratory centers deep within the earth to resound along the world axis the same vibration....For this is the mandatory call to the creative life force known elsewhere as Kundalini, latently coiled like a serpent in the lowest centers of Earth and man, to awaken and ascend to the throne of her Lord (the Crown Chakra) for the final consummation of their mystic marriage."[3]

According to an ancient Hopi prophecy regarding Pahana, the White Brother was destined to eventually turn dark in color and clothe himself in a red robe before returning home. Thus, when the red-robed and dark skinned Dalai Lama of the Tibetans met with the Hopis in 1979, a hue and cry went out that Pahana had indeed returned and the new era had arrived. A meeting of the representatives of Pahana and Masau'u occurred in the Wilshire Hotel in Los Angeles, where the Dalai Lama met with three Hopi elders. Grandfather David Monongye's first Hopi words to the Dalai Lama were: "Welcome home."

Pundits have since claimed that this great event was prophesied by Padmashabhava, founder of Tibetan Buddhism, when he anciently decreed: *"When the iron bird flies, the red-robed people of the east who have lost their land will appear, and the two brothers from across the great ocean will be reunited."*

The Dalai Lama meets with Hopi leaders in 1979

The Chakras of the Planetary Logos

Once I had designated Sedona as the Earth's Root Chakra and Mount Kailash as its Crown Chakra I then identified some of the chakras on the spine connecting these opposing nodal points. The Planetary Heart Chakra was easy to identify; it is Shambhala, the land of immortals at the Center of the Earth which Tibetan legends locate as either being at the base of Meru-Kailash or close by it. Shambhala certainly meets all the criteria of a planetary heart chakra. Like the human heart chakra which is the seat of joy and an etheric "lotus" of eight petals (there are two Heart Chakras: the Anahata of 12 petals and the Hrdaya of 8 petals to the left of it), Shambhala is the "Place of Joy" and similarly divided into eight portions or territories like a huge eight petal lotus. Moreover, like the human heart chakra that is the dwelling place of the inner Spirit, the center of Shambhala's eight territories is the residence of the monarch of Shambhala, who is the embodiment of the Spirit and King of the World, Sanat Kumara.

Shambhala: Heart Chakra of Earth

Below Shambhala and functioning as the Third or Solar Plexus Chakra of Earth is the central mountain of Aghartha, the cavernous kingdom located inside our world. States Ferdinand Ossendowski, the throne of the King of Aghartha is surrounded by millions of incarnated Gods" and located in a palace at "the top of [the] mountain covered with monasteries and temples."⁴

It should be noted that each of the Earth's chakras is a throne of the King of the World. But although these are his principal thrones it must be remembered that all vortexes around the globe are the seats and dwelling places of the Planetary Logos and Green Man. The notion that the entire Earth is the physical body of the King of the World has been embraced for thousands of years by the Chinese philosophers who recognize the Earth to be the body of a great Dragon King, and the planet's vortexes to be his dragon "lairs." It is because there are hundreds of huge vortexes or Dragon's Lairs around the Earth that there are so many planetary chakra systems.

The Spine of the Sub-Continent of India

The Earth's spine that connects Mt. Kailash to Sedona and the American Southwest is closely mirrored by the spine of the sub-continent of India, which unites Mt. Kailash with Kataragama on Sri Lanka. Sri Lanka is united to South India by an underwater bridge that was anciently raised above the water, so it is naturally part of the sub-continent.

In the model on the next page the spine of the Indian sub-continent corresponds with 81° E longitude, which has both Mount Kailash and Kataragama situated along its length. At the top of this spine is Mt. Kailash as the Crown Chakra, and at its bottom is Kataragama, another Court of Sanat Kumara, as its Root Chakra. One of the predominate venerated forms of Sanat Kumara at Kataragama is that of the Serpent Kundalini, the dynamic power that dwells in the Root Chakra of the Indian sub-continent.

The Great Dragon protects his lair of Sedona

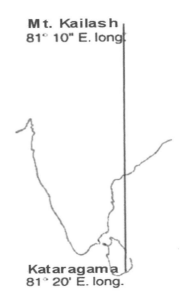

Mt. Kailash
81° 10" E. long.

Kataragama
81° 20' E. long.

The Redemption of the King and his People

My discovery of the Court of the King in Boynton Canyon was timely. A few years later the Yezidis would be savagely massacred by ISIS - Islamic State of Iraq and Syria - and the surviving refugees would need new homes in countries far away from Iraq. A home in the United States, in the same city as the Court of their beloved Tawsi Melek, would, of course, be perfect. A member of the Yezidi royal family appeared in Sedona and declared its potential of becoming the "Lalish of the West." His son came soon afterwards with 50 Yezidis to see the Court of the King. It is just a matter of time and money before a mass exodus of Yezidis come to Sedona to live there permanently.

In this chapter:
* Sanat Kumara also reigns in Sedona as Amitabha
* 12-21-2012: Beginning the Fifth World in Sedona
* The Hindus identify the Peacock Angel as their Sanat Kumara
* When the Hindus and Yezidis were ONE PEOPLE
* The Yezidis Come Home to Sedona

Sanat Kumara also reigns in Sedona as Amitabha

Once I was sure that an important planetary court of the King of the World existed in Boynton Canyon I discovered that his presence in Sedona had previously been acknowledged and he was already well known by the residents. He had arrived a few years earlier in the Land of OZ, albeit by the name of Amitabha, the Dhyani Buddha of Limitless Light, who is the Tibetan Buddhist manifestation of Sanat Kumara. His arrival in 2004 corresponded to the completion a 36 foot tall Buddhist stupa built by an organization headed by an American born woman who had been recently identified by high ranking Tibetan lamas as a tulku, a reincarnation of a Tibetan deity or saint. She was informed by the Tibetan adepts that in her last life she had been the Indian consort of Padmashabhava, the great Indian missionary who brought Buddhism to Tibet in the 8th century. In her current incarnation she had been born and raised in Brooklyn, New York, and since her endorsement as a tulku she had been living with a group of her followers in the Washington D.C. area. This was the second stupa she had overseen the construction of. So why chose Sedona for her second stupa, especially when it was so far from her home? When I contacted some of her local followers with this question the only answer I could get was that their teacher, who is now known as Jetsunma Ahkon Lhamo, chose Sedona because it is a high energy vortex area. That's it. Perhaps, like myself, Jetsunma had been directed to Sedona to alert the world of the return of the King of the World. Or perhaps she had been inspired by celestial forces to contribute to the wave of Tibetan culture now arriving in Tuwanasavi that signaled the official return of Pahana.

The stages of erection that went in to building the Amitabha stupa were followed according to traditonal Buddhist protocols and required literally hundreds of ceremonies to consecrate the edifice and the millions of prayers stored within it. When Amitabha was finally installed in the stupa his new home was a micro manifestation of his old one in Tibet. The King of the World took residence in the Sedona Peace Park that stretches across 14 acres of red rock just below Thunder Mountain, the American Southwest's version of Mt. Kailash.

I was overjoyed to learn of Amitabha's stupa. To some extent it meant that the "cat was out of the bag" and the world had already been notified that

Amitabha's Stupa in Sedona's Peace Park

261

Sedona was a home of the King of the World. I decided this would definitely make it easier for me to disclose my own discovery to the public. Of course, accepting a statue of Amitabha was not the same as acknowledging the existence of an etheric monarch who had been on Earth for millions of years and retained a court in Boynton Canyon for much of that time. So I decided not to push the issue and wait for the time of the court's unveiling to come to me from on high.

12-21-2012: Beginning the Fifth World in Sedona

The "command" came much sooner than I expected. During one spring day in Boynton Canyon I was studying the King's Court when I suddenly felt overcome with the sensation of energy entering and expanding my crown chakra. My eyes detected rays of vibrant white light descending from above that completely engulfed me and covered my canyon overlook with a glowing interdimensional fog. As the light flowed through my sahasrara and filled my head, my psychic vision became as clear as it was the day I first beheld the entire Court of the King of the World. From within came the knowledge that the white light I was experiencing would begin arriving on Earth December 21, 2012 and it would eventually transform millions of people on the planet. It would raise their consciousness and allow many to see the interdimensional structures of Boynton Canyon I had beheld for years. Humanity was about to move into the Fifth World, and what had been hidden from it during the entire Fourth World would now be unveiled. Collectively, we were returning to the Garden of Eden, the Fifth Dimensional realm we had left millions of years ago by becoming intellectual and ego-centered. Along with humanity's new shift Palatkwapi would arise from its ashes, and eventually Sedona would become recognized as one of the greatest centers of spiritual light that ever existed on Earth. My instructions from on high were explicit: organize a seminar in Sedona on December 21, 2012 and invite people from around the globe to attend. This would assist the descent of the new light and serve as the first step in precipiting the new era.

After returning home I began to jot down on paper the details for a Winter Solstice conference that would take place over a three day period and culminate on 12-21-2012. Both lectures and purification rituals would be offered to assist the attendees in preparing for that fateful day. I placed myself on my list of speakers for the event along with some cutting-edge lecturers who were known for their prophetic insights regarding what was ahead for Earth in the coming Fifth World. I made sure to add Hopi and Yezidi speakers since the revival of Palatkwapi and its Court of the King was especially relevant to them. My list of purification rites included Kundalini Meditation, a Native American Sweat Lodge, Sacred Dance, a Hopi ceremony, and a Vedic Yagya or Fire Ceremony. Vedic Fire Ceremonies have been recognized for thousands of years in India for their ability to not only purify people in a local area or country, but people all around the world.

With great expectations, the conference finally arrived. The Winter Solstice of 2012 had been touted around the world as one of the most important days in the history of humankind. As the Solar System aligned with the exact center of the Milky Way Galaxy on December 21st it was believed that our planet would become the recipient of a tremendous influx of spiritual light that would rapidly evolve both the Earth and all those that lived upon it. Anticipation was clearly evident on the faces of the participants as they arrived to the conference from five different continents.

The ensuing lectures and purification rites were well attended, and most of us could feel a perceptible energy gathering in and around us as we moved closer to December 21st. The Vedic Fire Ceremony cranked up the energy considerably, especially when offerings were made into the fire in honor of Shiva and his son Ganesh, the elephant-headed deity and brother of Sanat Kumara who would remove all our obstacles to entering the Fifth World. For me, the high point of the conference was the ceremony and presentation made by Hopis from the Hopi Mesas. As two members of the Water Clan spoke about Palatkwapi and their patron, Masau'u, I joyously watched as inviting glances and nods of recognition from the Yezidis seated in the front row punctuated their lecture. Afterwards, some of my Yezidi friends from Lincoln, Nebraska, informed me that the Hopis could just as easily have been speaking about their own tradition. There were so many similarities, including the similarity between Tawsi Melek and Masau'u.

The much awaited day of December 21st began briskly under a panoply of twinkling stars. In preparation for the sunrise that would begin the new era I

263

Hopis Rueben Saufkie and AllenTalayumtewa

Yezidis at the Fifth World Conference
Standing L to R Kawwal Hasan, MAP, Mirza Ismail,
Basim Bebany, Salem Daoud

accompanied some of the younger and more robust participants of the conference through the early morning darkness and deep into the bowels of Boynton Canyon. Meanwhile, in another part of Sedona Andrea conducted a second group along a much shorter and easier trail that winds around Bell Rock. And a third group was led to a medicine wheel on Cathedral Rock. As the first rays of the morning Sun illumined the Earth, all three groups united their energies through the observance of a ceremony specially crafted by me for the reception of the new spiritual light from the center of the Milky Way. In order to assist the reception of the new energies onto Earth, we all spun around both clockwise and counterclockwise, thus making ourselves human conduits for the incoming light.

After completing the rite in Boynton Canyon I hiked over to check on my vantage point that overlooks the Court of the King. My intention was to lead the the members of my group up to it, one by one. But to my dismay I discovered that some recently fallen snow had melted the day before, and over the long frigid nightit it had become a blanket of sheer ice that completely covered the precipitous trail. Only those in our group with large treads on their hiking boots had any chance of scaling it. So, as fate would have it, just a few people chosen by destiny got to view the great unveiling of the Court that morning. And even though many of the inter-dimensional features of the Court remained hidden to them, there seemed to be more details of the temples available for observation in the Third Dimension then I had previously remembered.

One of the principal events of the conference occurred at the end of the day at sunset. To mark humanity's entrance into the Fifth World we launched *The Most Ancient Order of the Peacock Angel.* Through this vehicle the Mysteries of the Peacock Angel would now be freely promulgated to all those who sought the highest and most ancient truths brought to our planet by the entity that became its king. This new order also set the stage for the prophesied return of Tawsi Melek, the great savior who has been guiding and ruling our planet from an unseen dimension since the time of the Garden of Eden.

For the premier initiation into *The Most Ancient Order of the Peacock Angel* the candidates for membership formed a long line behind Faqir Kawwal Hasan, who then led them in an ancient Yezidi dance designed to release old thoughts and emotions while being reborn into a new life. Together, we moved in choreographed syncopation around a large circle that recalled a graceful Sufi dance. Those Yezidis in attendance for this first-ever Peacock Angel initiation in the US included Sheikh Faqir Mirza Ismail and Sheikh Salem Douad, a member of the Yezidi royal family.

At the conclusion of the initiation rite the new members of The Most Ancient Order of the Peacock Angel received a rainbow belt to wear at future gatherings and meetings of the order. The rainbow is one form that the Peacock Angel, the Lord of the Seven Rays, assumes for his devotees. As I handed out the belts I truly felt the presence of Tawsi Melek enwrap itself around each new member, and I knew beyond a shadow of a doubt that a new era had officially arrived.

The Hindus Identify the Peacock Angel as their Sanat Kumara

As amazing as it was to see the Yezidis and Hopis come together an even bigger surprise awaited me. Beginning in the summer of 2014 thousands of Hindus living in India and the US offically acknowledged Tawsi Melek to be their beloved savior Sanat Kumara. Many went so far as to maintain that the Hindus and Yezidis had always been one people since the beginning of human civilization!

The catalyst for this unforeseen development was the invasion of the Yezidi homeland by Muslims of the terrorist group known as ISIS (Islamic State of Iraq and Syria). At the end of July all Yezidis living in Kurdistan were given an ultimatum to either convert to Islam or die. Then, on August 3rd, ISIS began its rampage. During the first five days of their attack they killed over 3000 Yezidis, including men, women, children, the elderly and the disabled. They also kidnapped at least 5000 Yezidis, mostly women and girls, whom they then tortured, raped and sexually enslaved.

When word of the invasion reached the US I began fielding phone calls from concerned Yezidis in Lincoln, Nebraska, and Ontario, Canada. Yezidis everywhere were in a quandary as to how to help their relatives in Iraq. It was finally decided that a Yezidi demonstration outside the White House gates in Washington D.C. would be the best option to pressure President Obama into calling for airstrikes against ISIS. I was prepared to travel to the capital myself and assist the demonstration, but at the last minute I decided I could better serve the movement by staying at home. That decision proved correct.

When the demonstration occurred on August 7th I was flooded with phone calls from media outlets who wanted to know more about these strange people called Yezidis. The big guns of media, including CBS, FOX and Time Warner, contacted me after finding the website I had set up for the Yezidis on the internet (www.YezidiTruth.org). Functioning as a go-between, I was able to help set up phone interviews between the Yezidis and reporters as well as help organize important meetings between lawmakers and the Yezidis in Washington D.C. The demonstration proved successful and Obama ordered the first airstrikes a couple of days later.

Following the demonstration I received a series of e-mails from a group of Hindu activists in the US and India who felt a strong calling to help the Yezidis. They had found my website and its identification of Tawsi Melek as the Hindus' Sanat Kumara, as well as a history of the Yezidis I had cobbled together citing that they had once lived in India. The website also mentioned some obvious links between the two people, such as the Hindus' ceremonial aarti lamps and the Yezidis' Sanjaks, which are identical. The group latched on to the information I posted and they even added some of their own by listing additional correspondences they uncovered between the two cultures. They found that both the Hindus and Yezidis subscribe to a belief in reincarnation; that the holy men in both cultures anoint the blessed with a dot between the eyebrows; and that temples of the Hindus and Yezidis display marked similarities. But perhaps the most convincing of all their discoveries is a mural that covers a wall in the Yezidis' mecca of Lalish. This united Hindu-Yezidi themed painting portrays a woman wearing a Hindu sari and next to her is a ritual lamp that could be either a Yezidi Sanjak or a Hindu aarti lamp.

This group of Hindus subsequently formed the *Yezidi Sanatan Dharma Society* (YSDS), which served as a vehicle through which the Yezidis and Hindus could finally reunite after thousands of years apart. I saw this as a big breakthrough and a huge opportunity for the maligned Yezidis to receive international support. Finally, a people who truly understood the ubiquitous Tawsi Melek had come forward to help. I immediately pledged my full support to the new Hindu

A Yezidi man kisses a sacred Sanjak

A Hindu Aarti Lamp

A Yezidi girl stands next to a woman wearing a Hindu sari and holding a sacred lamp at Lalish

group and offered to assist them achieve their goals anyway I could.

When in late October it appeared that ISIS had released another ultimatum and was preparing for a final massacre of those Yezidis still residing on Sinjar Mountain, the members of YSDS, as well as myself and a group comprised of Yezidis and Hindus, met over a teleconference to deliberate on some quick strategy. The phone meeting was touted as both momentous and historical. It was the first time in thousands of years that the Yezidis and Hindus had come together with one heart and one voice. Then, during a follow up call one week later, I suggested that since the first demonstration was successful we should try another one. Unfortunately, this second demonstration did not prove nearly as effective as the first, but it helped the cause in other ways. It precipitated some events that were extremely pivotal in the evolving Yezidi-Hindu alliance.

As fate would have it, just as the second demonstration was to take place the Baba Sheikh, the highest religious official of the Yezidis, also arrived in Washington D.C. for talks with US government officials. Our group of Yezidis and Hindus capitalized on this fortuitous synchronicity and arranged for the Baba Sheikh to visit the Hindu Murugan Temple in the city. A special ritual was planned by the presiding Brahman Priests in the Baba Sheikh's honor.

I had been pushing for a special ritual that would officially unite the Yezidis and Hindus, but was not satisfied that the one in Washington D.C. was it. So I phoned up Abhaya Astama, head of the *Vishwa Hindu Parishad of America*, the largest Hindu organization in the US. In a previous conversation Abhaya had informed me that the national meeting of VHPA was going to occur in San Jose at the end of October and the organizers would welcome such a ceremony. I let Abhaya know I was determined to find a Yezidi to travel to the conference and represent the People of the Peacock Angel. After a short search I found Haji Hamika, a Yezidi man from Lincoln, Nebraska, who agreed to drive the distance to San Jose and represent the Yezidis.

Unfortunately, I had to hear second hand about Haji's short presentation and the ceremony that followed it in San Jose's Hindu temple. I would have loved to have been present for the event, but I had previously committed to leading a tour in Egypt at that time. When news of the successful event arrived via the

Yezidis demonstrating in front of the White House

The Baba Sheikh attends a ceremony at the Washington D.C. Murugan temple

The San Jose ceremony uniting the Hindus and Yezidis

internet to my cruise ship on the Nile River I could have walked on water!

Another event soon occurred in the US that served to fortify the fledgling Yezidi-Hindu alliance. This was a meeting between Yezidis and the Hindu holy man Sri Sri Ravi Shankar in Chicago. The meeting was arranged by members of YSDS, many of whom were devotees of the guru.

Sri Sri Shankar graciously received the group on October 25th and pledged his full support in their campaign to re-unite the Hindus and Yezidis. He also promised to rally political support for the Yezidis in their crisis with ISIS, as well as deliver aid packages of food, water, blankets, and tents to those Yezidis who had lost their homes and were now barely surviving in refugee camps.

Sri Sri backed up his promises with press releases, a donation drive, and meetings with important political advisors. Then, on November 21st, Sri Sri Ravi Shankar made a special visit to Iraq. While accompanied by Mirza Ismail, one of the founding members of *The Most Ancient Order of the Peacock Angel,* Sri Sri visited a large Yezidi refugee camp. This was followed by a visit to the sacred precincts of Lalish, thereby reciprocating Baba Sheikh's visit to Washington D.C.'s Murugan temple. Sri Sri was met at Lalish by the Baba Sheikh and other Yezidi leaders, and then given a full tour of the Yezidis' most holy shrine. This was acknowledged by myself and many others to be "icing on the cake" in the campaign to unite the Hindus and Yezidis.

The last, and perhaps crowning event of this sequence, occurred when delegations of the Yezidis traveled around India and were welcomed in many cities as part of the extended Hindu family. The first delegation arrived in November, 2014, while Sri Sri Ravi Shankar was visiting the Yezidis in Iraq. They came to India to speak on the Yezidi plight at the First World Hindu Congress in Delhi, India, that was attended by 1800 delegates from 50 countries. This special event was convened by the Dalai Lama himself and featured two minutes of silence to honor those Yezidis who had recently died at the hands of ISIS. The human rights violations against the Yezidis and their ongoing genocide were discussed at length numerous times during the Congress, and each time the Yezidis poured their hearts out to the the assembled dignitaries they received a huge outpouring of support. The second delegaton of Yezidis arrived in India in January of 2015, and then

Sri Sri Ravi Shankar touring a Yezidi refugee camp with Mirza Ismail

Sri Sri Ravi Shankar leaving the main temple at Lalish

The Baba Sheikh meets with Sri Sri Ravi Shankar at Lalish

spent three weeks traveling the length and breadth of India while connecting with their new Hindu brothers and sisters. Their campaign included stops in Mysore, Bangalore, New Delhi, Haridwar, Rishikesh and other important cities. Wherever the delegation traveled they were honored with prayer shawls, pujas (worship), and bandaras (feasts) during which they shared Yezidi history, culture and current affairs with Hindus of all social strata. They also attended many special meetings with important government officials, including Sushma Swaraj ji, Minister of Indian Foreign Affairs, and when they visited the ashrams of India's saints they were showereed with blessings from Sri Sri Ravi Shankar, Baba Ramdev, and H.H. Pujya Swami Chidanand Saraswamtiji. Throughout their journey the Yezidi delegation proudly displayed the flag of a future autonomous Yezidi Nation they hoped to create in Iraq with the help of the Hindus and other members of the international community.

Thus, in the end a very small movement to reunite the Hindus and Yezidis had snowballed beyond anyone's expectations and much of India now rallied solidly behind it. Finally, after nearly two thousand years of constant persecution and seventy-four genocides directed against them, the Yezidis had an important ally to call upon in their fight to retain their ancient religion and way of life. And this was not just any ally, but a country of more than a billion people.

The Yezidi Delegation in India with the flag of their future Yezidi Nation

During the the time the Yezidis were receiving special attention from the Hindus I spent many hours at the Court of the King praying to Tawsi Melek to help his people. On one occasion I visited the court with Sir Kurt Bagley, a knight in the IOGT, who snapped the above photo when the image of a pensive and sad face suddenly appeared above us in the clouds. Both of us knew instantly it was the face of Tawsi Melek, and that his distress reflected the deep grief he felt for his people and their tragic plight. Since it was a clear sign that the Peacock King was indeed watching over the Yezidis, we posted the photo soon afterwards on social media with the caption: "Courage Yezidis! The King of the World is always with you!" What is particularly fascinating about the image is that it resembles the face of one of the Peacock Angel's incarnations, Sri Krishna of India, who is nearly always depicted with one or more peacocks and wearing peacock feathers (one can be seen over his eye). Could this image reflect the newly created reunion of the Hindus and Yezidis?

When Yezidis and Hindus were ONE PEOPLE

In order to continue to facilitate a Yezidi-Hindu re-union I founded four Yezidi-Hindu groups on Facebook. The support for this union from the members of the groups was nearly overwhelming, but certainly not without its challenges. One challenge quickly emerged when many Hindus began claiming that the Yezidis had once been part of a huge Hindu or Vedic kingdom that stretched across Asia, thus making them a branch of Hinduism. This was offensive to many Yezidis who were proud of their own heritage as the First People that were created well before the dawn of Hinduism. On the other side of the fence were a group of Hindu scholars maintaining that there was not enough evidence to prove that the Yezidis and Hindus were anciently one people, nor can it be proven they are even culturally linked. Debates raged in my Facebook groups, with Hindus and Yezidis lining up on both sides of the argument.

Eventually, I resolved to let the historical records and legends speak for themselves. Their authority would decide the winner of the debate. I began by volunteering what I believed to be truth, that the connecting link between the Yezidis and Hindus was ancient Mu, the Pacific continent where Sanat Kumara-Tawsi Melek is reputed to have reigned as priest king. As previously mentioned this wisdom had been promulgated previously by a few antiquarian authors, including James Churchward, who claimed that the Nacaal or Naga Maya missionaries left Lemuria and colonized many countries west of the Pacific Motherland, including India, Burma, Babylonia, and even Egypt. It has also come from the research of Churchward's modern counterpart, Stephen Oppenheimer, who in *Eden of the East,* concluded that missionaries from "Sundaland," a part of Lemuria that was once connected to Southeast Asia, had "fertilized the Neolithic cultures of China, India, Mesopotamia, Egypt and Crete."[1]

Given the documentation supplied by Churchward and Oppenheimer there was no doubt in my mind that an east-west migration between Mu and Asia could have united the ancient world under a common ruler and culture. Now, if I could just identify a Garden of Eden that had given birth to both the Hindus and Yezidis I believed I could end (or nearly end) the Facebook argument. This turned out to be a very difficult task because many locations were recognized as *the* Garden of

Eden. They included the islands of Mu (Sri Lanka, Hawaii, etc.) as well as Middle Earth (the Himalayas, Mount Meru-Kailash) and the Yezidis' Lalish, an area that stretched across Kurdistan and much of southern Turkey, including the 11,000 year old settlement of Gobekli Tepe. Both Tamoanchan in Mexico and Tiahuanaco in Bolivia in the Western Hemisphere had also received the honorary epithet of "Garden of Eden."

After reviewing what I knew of humanity's beginnings I concluded that the entire Earth must have been the original Eden, and that all the early civilizations were part of it. This incipient planetary Eden would have manifested soon after Tawsi Melek landed on Earth and encircled the planet with his peacock plumes. Many of his peacock feathers would have then crystallized to create a paradise of flora and fauna on the third dimension, but other peacock plumes would have remained fifth dimensional and served as a subtle interdimensional backdrop to the emerging global paradise.

So it appeared to me that within this original global Eden many sub-Edens that are now calling themselves *the* Garden of Eden could have arisen. Wherever large groups of people manifested Tawsi Melek and his entourage of instructors from the Pleiades and other Star Nations would have soon appeared as culture bearers to teach them the sacred and mundane arts. These sub-Edens would then have eventually been united by missionaries traveling from a more advanced, regional Garden of Eden with the goal of establishing an homogenous worldwide culture. According to Churchward and Oppenheimer, the regional Eden that united the sub-Edens of Lalish, Mu, and Middle Earth was the flourishing Pacific Eden of Mu. Both these authors concluded that missionaries from Mu had traveled across Asia and left traces of their culture in their wake. One aspect of their teaching was related to the first primeval missionaries, the Twins, and another was related to the Divine Son and Savior who had been born from the union of the universal male and female principles. The Son was thenceforth called Sanat Kumara by the Hindus and Tawsi Melek by the Yezidis.

I rejoined my Facebook group with my new theory. I would not say I received an avalanche of accolades for my ensuing posts, but I was satisfied that the members of my groups gave the theory as much or more credence as any other. Anyway, in the end, we all had to agree that of those presented theories that had merit there really was not enough tangible evidence to positively and irrefutably prove any of them.

The Yezidis Come Home to Sedona

During the winter of 2014-15 thousands of Yezidis survived in refugee camps in northern Iraq. They suffered through continual floods, as well as bone-chilling cold weather. It is now the spring of 2015 and most are hoping to leave their unpleasant circumstances behind and relocate to other countries around the globe. Since the US has so far supplied most of the defense to combat ISIS and protect the Yezidis, it is in America that the majority of Yezidis feel drawn and seek sanctuary. A tremendous amount of funding is needed, however, if a significant Yezidi exodus to the west is to become a reality.

The two principal destinations of the displaced Yezidis in the US will likely be Lincoln, Nebraska and Arizona. In mid-2014 I was visited by Salem Daoud, a member of the Yezidi royal family and founding member of *The Most Ancient Order of the Peacock Angel,* who was scouting Sedona for land to accomodate a colony of immigrant Yezidis. I had told Salem about the Court of the King and fifteen acres of virgin land on Oak Creek I hoped to acquire and how this land would be perfect for some Yezidis to live on. After seeing the land Salem was hopeful, even declaring that because of its special relationship to Tawsi Melek Sedona could very well become the future "Lalish of the West." Then, on April 9, 2015, Salem's prophetic vision began to seemingly unfold when his son, Sam, led nearly fifty Yezidi men, women and children living in southern Arizona to the parking lot of Boynton Canyon. In a procession for the ages, we hiked together (I even carried Sam's three year old daughter half the way) into Boynton and then up the side of the canyon wall to see the Court of the King. It was exciting to be part of this extremely momentous event, which marked the first time in this cycle of time that Yezidis had visited the ancient western court of their king. Even though they could not see most of its interdimensional features, the Yezidis fully accepted the Court of the King as an earthly domicile of Tawsi Melek, and many pledged to make regular pilgrimages to it in the future.

Yezidis arrive at Boynton Canyon

Yezidis examine the Court of the King

Return of the Star People and King of the World

We stand on the cusp of the Fifth World and its plethora of new and ancient prophecies. One prophecy states that the Star People will soon return to those people on Earth that they once mated with and taught their mysteries to, such as the Hopis and Yezidis. Their return will coincide with the return of the King of the World, one of the leaders of the Star People, whose existence will again become known to the masses. And it will also mark humanity's return to the Garden of Eden, when many of us will re-enter the fifth dimension that has been occupied by both the Star People and Earth's ruler. It will then become evident that while humans might have left the realm of Eden when they shut down their psychic abilities and became egotistical and left brained, the Star People and King of the World have continued to exist there while overseeing the spiritual evolution of humanity.

In this chapter:
* Hopi, Yezidi, & Tibetan Prophecies of the Return
* The Second Coming of Christ?
* Interview with Zuni Elder Clifford Mahooty
* Interview with Yezidi Faqir Kamal Kaso
* The Current Return of the Peacock King

Hopi, Yezidi, & Tibetan Prophecies of the Return

According to Hopi prophecy, both the Fifth World and Return of the Star People will officially occur when the celestial Blue Star Kachina, the star Sirius, makes an unmistakable and dramatic appearance in the heavens. At that time a Hopi dancer portraying the Blue Star Kachina on Earth will remove his mask for the first time ever during a live ceremony.

In *Book Of The Hopi* Frank Waters maintains that Hopi prophecy foretelling the return of the Star People is symbolized by a "flying shield" or spacecraft engraved on a prophecy rock in the Hopi Mesas. He states:

"On Second Mesa near Mishongnovi an ancient petroglyph depicts a dome-shaped object resting on an arrow which represents travel through space and the head of a Hopi maiden, who represents pristine purity. As the Hopis believe that other planets are inhabited, this petroglyph represents a *paatuwvota* or a "flying shield" similar to a "flying saucer" that came here in the Beginning. So now at the End the sacred ones will arrive from another planet, said to be Venus, by flying saucers. Many Hopi traditionalists recently have reported seeing flying saucers, all piloted by beings they call Kachinas."[1]

The *paatuwvota* rock carving is reputed to have been inscribed by the ET Masau'u after the Lord of the Fourth World piloted his own *paatuwvota* to and from the North Pole while leading some of the Hopis on their migrations. Masau'u's *paatuwvota* inscription anticipates both a return of the Star People from Venus as well as his own return to prominence as King of the World. According to esoteric sources, Sanat Kumara-Masau'u is intimately related to both the Pleiades asterism and the planet Venus. His initial arrival on Earth from the Seven Sisters was by way of the Morning Star, where he acquired the title of Lord of Venus. Thus, Masau'u's *paatuwvota* symbol ostensibly represents the return of the Star People and himself from Venus and possibly the Pleiades. This makes sense in light of the fact that many Hopis believe that their ancestors came from both the Planet of Love and the Seven Sisters.

As Waters states, some Hopis believe that the Star People have already begun their return and have witnessed their flying saucers moving across the heavens as confirmation. Then there are others who contend that they never left. They simply became the invisible Kachinas of the Fifth Dimension. Many of those aligned with the first group maintain that the Return began as a massive UFO sighting that was witnessed above the Hopi Mesas on August 7, 1970 by dozens of onlookers and photographed by Chuck Roberts of the *Prescott Courier.* For many Hopis this sighting began the fulfillment of an ancient prophecy made by Masau'u regarding the Return of the Star People and the corresponding Purification Day, when worthy Hopis will be flown to other planets in "ships without wings." This was the opinion of the late Hopi Grandfather Martin Gashweseoma, the former keeper of a set of prophecy tablets anciently given to the Fire Clan by Masau'u. Grandfather Martin spent his life alerting the world of the Purification Day.

The Hopi prophesies also allude to the return of the Twin Sons, which as mentioned earlier is a name associated with both the King of the World and the leaders of the Star People. These Hopi prophecies assert that the return of the Twins will be seen in North Western skies. The Twins will come in their *paatuwvotas* to see who on Earth still remember the original teachings they gave to the Hopis. And they will bring many Star People with them.

Not surprisingly, there is a Yezidi prophecy of the future return of the Star People that is nearly identical to that of the Hopis. It states that after al-Qud, the "Blue Star," makes a special appearance in the heavens and ushers in the Fifth Age, Tawsi Melek will manifest as a rainbow around the Sun. At that time he will send two extraterrestrial messengers to Earth with 11,000 assistants. They will come "riding white horses with yellow streaks down their backs" - an apparent reference to their white space craft that will be spewing out yellow fire. According to the Yezidi Faqir Kamal Kaso (see interview), events that began in 2014 are destined to culminate in the arrival of these two messengers and their entourage of 11,000 Star People. Once they have arrived back on Earth they will return our planet to peace and prosperity. And at that time many people will again be able to see both the Star People and Tawsi Melek interdimensionally.

The Hopi and Yezidi prophecies are echoed by the prophecies of the Tibetans. One Tibetan prophecy states that the King of the World will leave his throne in Shambhala with an army of warriors riding white horses that will cleanse the Earth of evil. He will then reclaim his rightful place as King of the World. The

A "prophecy rock" on Hopiland inscribed with the image of a spaceship

Hopi Grandfather Martin Gashweseoma and MAP

most commonly accepted date for this event is 2327, but that date assumes that each Shambhala king has or will govern for 100 years. This has not been the case. Therefore, an updated schedule for the emergence of the King of Shambhala adhered to by many Buddhist Lamas has the event occuring any time now.

Like the prophecies of the Hopis and Yezidis, the Tibetan prophecy could also be referring to the arrival of an army of extraterrestrial warriors led to Earth by the King of the World. Nicholas Roerich, who studied the prophecy intimately while in Tibet, depicted the King of Shambhala riding his steed through the upper clouds in his paintings, thereby implying that his imminent arrival on Earth will be from above. His painting could also represent the King of Shambhala riding in a flying vehicle as he leads the "army" of Shambhala around the Earth to cleanse it. And it could also represent the monarch of Aghartha, the underworld kingdom intimately linked to Shambhala, as he leads the inner Earth People back to the surface of our planet. A prophecy made in 1890 by the King of Aghartha while visting a Tibetan Buddhist monastery in Mongolia predicted that in the year 2029 he and many of his people would collectively rejoin the terrestrial race of humans on the surface of Earth. Their emergence from Earth's tunnels and caves would precipitate a new planetary consciousness and a "Synarchy," a universal, synthetic culture. Humanity would finally unite as one people.

The prophecy of the return of the Aghartha monarch also anticipates the re-emergence of the Hopis' King of the World, Masau'u. This is because Masau'u's kingdom is part of Aghartha. This truth was disseminated by Mongolian Prince Chultun Beyli to Ferdinand Ossendowski when he stated to him that Aghartha "extends throughout all the subterranean passages of the whole world."[2] This notion was earlier alluded to by the 19th century visionary Marquis Alexandre Saint-Yves D'Alveydre, who wrote of it in *The Kingdom of Agarttha: A Journey into the Hollow Earth*. Saint-Yves D'Alveydre learned from Haji Sharif, an Afghan prince, that America's "subterranean regions belonged to Aghartha in very remote antiquity."[3] To reveal Aghartha's position under the American Southwest and other places worldwide, Saint-Yves D'Alveydre published a map that reveals the kingdom's mammoth size and tunnel openings.

The King of Shambhala by Nicholas Roerich

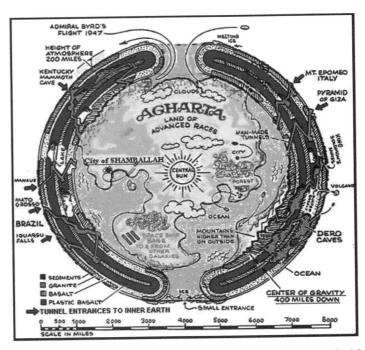

The Kingdom of Aghartha and its tunnel openings worldwide.

284

The Second Coming of Christ?

How will the Return of the King of the World be accepted by the masses? It is likely to be hailed by many as the Second Coming of Christ. This is because Earth's monarch was our planet's first Christ and Savior, and his return will mark the true Second Coming of Christ. We currently identify the Second Coming with Jesus Christ because the Christian Son of God co-opted the ancient legend of the King of the World. This also occurred among other Saviors, including Mithra and Dionysus, who made it their own and distorted it. (see my book: *The Truth Behind the Christ Myth: The Redemption of the Peacock Angel).* In its original form the original Christ Myth of Earth's monarch recounts the life cycle of the Divine Son (the Green Man and King of the World) whose spirit is born annually to the Virgin Earth Mother on December 25th when the Sun begins its return transit north. He then becomes all the forms of nature at the ensuing Vernal Equinox (aka his annual resurrection) and then dies with the falling leaves each autumn. One of the essential symbols of the King of the World that was co-opted along with his myth is the symbol of the Crucifix. The symbol orignally revealed that the King of the World was sacrificed on the Cross of Matter after transmitting his spirit into the material Earth and becoming the Planetary Logos. Through giving his (immortal) life as a sacrifice for the "sins" that would eventually be fostered by humanity, he helped lead us to our collective enlightenment.

Once the original Christ Myth and its true meaning are understood by the masses, the current notions regarding a Second Coming of Christ will be drastically revised for many. But this will only be true for those ready to "look outside the box" of limiting theological dogma. The legend of the Christed Divine Son will be acknowledged by them to be much more ancient than anyone ever imagined. He is an entity that the Gnostics assert arrived on Earth at least six million years ago from the stars (the Pleiades and Venus) to give birth to both the flora and fauna of our planet, while also endowing it with a mind and will. He functioned as a computer chip that entered the Earth and installed it with a program of evolutionary unfoldment for both our planet and humanity. This evolutionary program requires each soul to take a physical form, acquire an egoic sense of self and a discriminating intellect, and then go in search of true wisdom. Their search will inevitably lead them to the altar of Self-Knowledge and Christ Consciousness right inside themselves.

To be clear, the path of humanity to Christhood and the path of the Planetary Logos to Christhood are one and the same. We are in this together. The Planetary Logos is the Collective Consciousness of humanity. Only when the Planetary Logos is ready to achieve Christhood will the majority of humans also be ready to make the hallowed leap. At that time the Earth's Savior will literally take us upon his back (the Earth) and carry us to the goal.

The original Cross of the Christed Savior is part of the symbol of Earth. It represents the King of the World crucified on or within the planet.

An ancient Greek pre-Christian seal of Dionysus, King of the World, on a crucifix. Above him are his nursemaids, the seven stars of the Pleiades.

Prophecies of the Return of the Star People
Interviews with Indigenous Prophets

Interview with Zuni Elder Clifford Mahooty

MAP: What is your Tribal Clan?

CM: I am of the Sun Clan and a child of the Raven Clan.

MAP: I understand that you are also a member of the Kachina Society.

CM: Yes. The Kachina Society is a priesthood. The members are the representatives of the Star People. I am part of that priesthood. The Kachinas passed their Star Knowledge to this priesthood and we became their representatives. All male Native American children are born into this priesthood.

But it is not just the Kachina Society that has the knowledge. The Star People gave the spirituality to the indigenous people on all continents. They said: "This is your charge. We are passing this to you."

Unfortunately, the tribes are loosing the Kachina wisdom and ceremonies because they are not observing them they way they were taught. And of those that do the ceremonies, many do not understand them and perform them just for show, just for ego. Take the powwow circuit as an example. It is all commercial. All the dances are done for show. They have nothing to do with real spirituality.

MAP: So the Kachina wisdom once existed throughout the Americas?

CM: In the old days there was not the country of Mexico, not the United States…it was wide open. So the wisdom moved throughout the Americas. We know that the languages of the various tribes in different parts of the Americas is very similar. This proves that we were all interconnected in the past.

MAP: Where did the Kachinas come from?

CM: They came from many places, many star systems. We include their origins in our ceremonies when we include Orion, the Pleiades or Sirius. We have always referred to the Pleiades as "the Seven," way before the invention of the telescope, even though you can normally only see six of the stars. This was some of the wisdom the Star Brothers gave us.

I am part of the Milky Way Galaxy order that came from the center of the galaxy. This is an order that has members from all over the galaxy. This is an order of the Star Brothers.

The Star Brothers came to Earth to give knowledge of agriculture, building techniques, the arts and sciences, the healing techniques, how to live on this planet to take care of Mother Earth, to respect all the plants and animals, and all the relationships.

MAP: How did the Star People appear to the early Zunis?

CM: The Kachinas were the gods. They would suddenly appear from other dimensions like Captain Kirk and his Star Trek crew. They would spontaneously appear on a planet after being beamed down to it. Once in Earth's third dimension the Star People would share their knowledge. They had a great aura around them. We don't know exactly what they looked like, but people would fall in love with them because they were pure love. But there were the abductions. They would take humans back with them to their native planets. This continued until a treaty was made between the early tribes and the Kachinas that prohibited these abductions.

MAP: Have the Kachinas been here during the Fourth World?

CM: Yes, but they have had to make themselves invisible.

MAP: When were they visible? Hundreds or thousands of years ago?

CM: Nobody knows when.

MAP: How long is each cycle or "World" according to the Zunis?

CM: Nobody knows that either.

MAP: So a World could be thousands or even millions of years in length?

CM: Yes, it could be.

MAP: What do the Zunis say about Sedona?

CM: They came to Sedona when they emerged into the Fourth World in what is now Grand Canyon.

The Zunis were the first ones out of the lower world. They came out at Ribbon Falls or Rainbow Falls. Then the Hopis followed them and came out at their Sipapuni [in Grand Canyon]. After the Zuni came out they went on a migration route similar to Moses leading the Hebrews through the Sinai Desert. These people were not functional human beings when they first came out. The Warrior Gods [the Twins] acted as emissaries of the Creator to help the people become functional humans. There were very many of them. The people dispersed in different directions to many parts of the world. They traveled all over the Americas and settled in many different places. The Kachinas were with them at that time, guiding them.
As they were migrating all the plants and animals returned to the Earth with the help of the Star Brothers.

I have identified nineteen different places that the Zunis stopped on their migration route. The Star People guided them there. Sedona is one of them. They went to these places and made temples. These were vortex points. The people were guided there to receive downloads from the Creator. Ninety percent of these places are not on native lands anymore. They are stargates. We know where they are but we don't tell about them. People will go there and misuse the energy.

289

The nineteen are between Grand Canyon and Mexico City. Sedona was one of the first, so it was where the people became more humanoid.

There were plazas in Sedona. It was a ritual center.

At one of these places, about ten miles from the Arizona/ New Mexico border, the people received a download regarding the clan system.

MAP: How long ago was this?

CM: A long time ago. They say that Earth was still raw. When you walked your feet made an imprint. The Earth was not completely solid yet. Today we find imprints of dinosaurs next to human footprints. They were made at a time like the beginning of the Fourth World.

MAP: So at the beginning of each World we have to start over again?

CM: Yes. We have to start all over again.

MAP: Will we have to go through that now?

CM: It's possible. That is why we have to follow the ceremonies that the Star People gave us.

MAP: Is there a connection between the Zunis and the Lemurians?

CM: Yes and no. The Hopis are the Lemurian people. The people that became the Zunis came from all over the planet, not just one place. They came from the north, the south, the east. The Star People guided them to become part of the Zuni tribe.

MAP: How much of the Kachina wisdom is intact today?

CM: The ancient knowledge was so detailed, but we lost much of it.

Of course much of our spirituality has been taken from us. And now we are not allowed to perform many of our ceremonies any more. The medicine people use eagle feathers in their ceremonies, but if they are caught with an eagle feather they can go to prison. They can't go into nature to get feathers like they used to. There is only one place they can legally get them, it's a place in Oregon. But when that place has some feathers the true medicine men never get them. Those pow wow guys show up and get them all. Its all very political.

The tribes let the Catholics and their ideology into their spirituality. Now, many of the medicine people follow both the Catholic and the Indian way. This is not right. If you want to be a Catholic, be a Catholic. If you want to be an Indian Medicine Man, be a Medicine Man. Its like being a Jew and a Muslim at the same time.

So how can we do the rituals that the Kachinas gave us? They taught us to use the eagle feathers.

MAP: Will the Kachinas return?

CM: They are still here. They are just invisible. They have been making contact since the 1940s. Many come in flying ships. They are making contact now with many people to prepare humans for the Earth changes. Many people are drawn to the pyramids and the peaks of mountains, the natural pyramids, where contact is made.

We are now at the end of the Fourth World. The Star People told the Earth people that when the time comes to move into another world that you will survive by following our instructions about how to live, what ceremonies to perform, etc. They said it was important for all the people to join together at that time. The information has to come out now because we are on the verge of the next big change of the planet.

MAP: So you think it is coming soon?

CM: We are right in the middle of it now.

Interview with Yezidi Faqir Kamal Kaso

MAP: As a Faqir what special duties do you have among your people?

KK: A Faqir's duty is to teach the knowledge of Tawsi Melek, the Peacock Angel. They also act as mediators when there is conflict between the Yezidi people.

MAP: I have heard that many Faqirs are descended from Sheikh Adi and the six archangels. Is your birth family also descended from Sheikh Adi?

KK: We are not directly descended. But yes, you can say that all the Faqirs are like the "family" of Sheikh Adi. We represent Sheikh Adi.

MAP: What can you tell me about Tawsi Melek?

KK: By the power of Tawsi Melek the universe and the Earth were created. He made the four elements.

Tawsi Melek sent the Seven Angels to create the universe and the Earth.

At first the Earth was completely covered by water. The Seven Angels created the land. Four of the Seven Angels became guardians of Earth's four directions. Each Angel created one of the seven continents and then became its guardian. The original name of each continent came from the Angel that created it.

After the land was created on Earth there were no plants, no grass, no trees. Tawsi Melek came to Earth and gave it vegetation.

MAP: For many years I have been seeing temples in Sedona, Arizona made from the red rock. They exist both on the third and fifth dimensions. Did one of the Seven Angels make these temples?

KK: Yes. There were many missionaries who came from the stars and worked under the command of Tawsi Melek. They built the temples. Tawsi Melek sent them out with the symbol of the peacock. Many of the temples were given the head of a peacock, and many had the image of a dove. Both birds represent safety. The temples were sanctuaries of peace. Similar temples to the ones you found in Arizona can be found on all seven continents.

MAP: Do you recognize Tawsi Melek to be the same as what other religions call God or Allah?

KK: Yes. All the people in the world give their worship to Tawsi Melek but by different names.

MAP: That is what my research reveals. I have found that there are deities all over the world that have the same characteristics as Tawsi Melek but are called a different name. The Sumerians had Enki, the Hindus have Sanat Kumara. So are you now saying that they are all manifestations of Tawsi Melek?

KK: Yes. Tawsi Melek was even the God of the Jews. He was the "Father" of Jesus. Tawsi Melek gave the power to Moses to destroy the Pharaoh and cross the Red Sea. He was the one that gave the secrets to Moses.

MAP: Was he also the Burning Bush?

KK: Yes. He has taken many forms.

MAP: For the past ten years Tawsi Melek has appeared to me in the form of etheric peacocks. Does he also appear to you?

KK: Yes, but I can not tell you the form he takes. There are some things that must remain secret.

MAP: Do other Faqirs get massages from Tawsi Melek like you do?

KK: Not too many, but most have knowledge of Tawsi Melek

MAP: What other ways does he appear?

KK: Many good, pure people can see him in dreams or when they are alone. Sometimes they can hear him as subtle sounds.

MAP: Does he mainly appear in the form of a peacock?

KK: He has 1001 different forms.

MAP: Which form of his is good to worship?

KK: The Sun is Tawsi Melek's light. To worship Tawsi Melek you can pray to the Sun each morning. If you worship the Sun you worship Tawsi Melek.

MAP: Did Tawsi Melek teach his secrets in other parts of the universe?

KK: Yes, Tawsi Melek sent thousands of (extraterrestrial) missionaries to other planets.

MAP: What does Tawsi Melek say about the times were are living in?

KK: There will be disasters. The Earth has been destroyed many times. The first time it was destroyed by water. Another time it was destroyed by wind. Because of the past disasters there are places in the Middle East that are covered with forty meters of sand and soil. This time the world will be destroyed by fire, the fire caused by weapons.

There will be a war in the Middle East. Tawsi Melek will send one of his messengers to Earth to end it. He will stop all the weapons, even the aircraft and satellites will stop. He will stop all the machines.

The big changes will begin in 2014.

To help make the new world Tawsi Melek will send two [extraterrestrial] messengers [the Twins] and there will be 11,000 helpers with each one of them.

MAP: When the wars end and we move into the new world will people be able be able to see Tawsi Melek and know that he is the Lord of the Universe.

KK: Yes. The people will be able to see both Tawsi Melek and his missionaries.

MAP: Why has there been so much suffering among the Yezidis.

KK: The 72 exterminations were tests for the Yezidis to see if they would keep worshipping Tawsi Melek or leave the religion.

MAP: Does Tawsi Melek tell you that things will get better for the Yezidis?

KK: Yes. After the wars people will know of Tawsi Melek and serve him for 3,000 years.

MAP: Did Tawsi Melek have a relationship with Jesus?

KK: Yes. Tawsi Melek created Jesus. He was Jesus' Father in Heaven. Tawsi Melek told the Angel Gabriel to blow on Mary's womb and she became fertilized.

MAP: Was Tawsi Melek a teacher of Jesus?

KK: Yes, and Jesus got his special powers from Tawsi Melek's messenger Melek Sharfadin.

MAP: What happened to the *Black Book* that Tawsi Melek gave the Yezidis?

KK: The *Black Book* was stolen from the Yezidis. But it still exists. They lost it at the end of the Babylon civilization. The *Black Book* is now in the British Museum. The Yezidis tried to get it back but the British would not give it to them.

MAP: What is the best way to help the Yezidis in Iraq now?

KK: We need a radio and television station. That would help us a lot.

We would like people in the world to help all the minorities of Iraq, not just the Yezidis. We would like reporters to come to our land and report back about what they see so the rest of the world can know what is happening. If people can come and bring cameras and write what they see, that will help us very much.

Sadly, Faqir Kamal Kaso passed away on July 14, 2015 just as this book was going to print. Faqir Kamal spent his last days on top of Mt. Sinjar in northern Iraq taking care of his immediate family and all the Yezidi refugees still trapped on the mountain after fleeing from ISIS. He will be remembered both as a man of great wisdom, as well as one of the most dedicated activists who was martyred in the fight for Yezidi human rights. He will be greatly missed by his people and all those who knew him.

The Current Return of the Peacock King

The Peacock King is slowly returning to mass consciousness. He is currently making himself more visable in popular culture through fashion, music and art. He is also manifesting in people's dreams, visions, and meditations, as well as by taking the form of physical peacocks that unexpectedly manifest in front of people in their living environments and while away from home. Here are some examples of the Return of the King of the World.

The Peacock Angel is appearing in the clouds.

And as magnificent creatures on the ground.

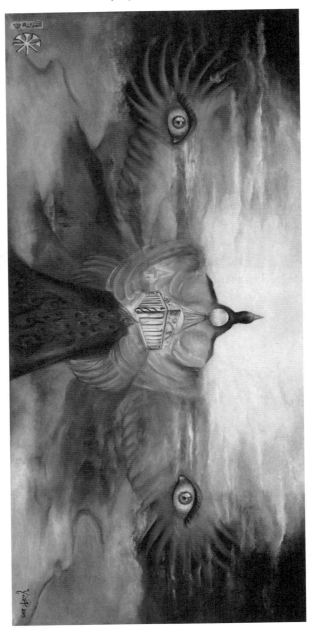

This is an oil painting created by international artist Yara Pirk for the Yezidis. The artist reveals that the Yezidi people and their culture are now globally known. The Peacock Angel is spreading its wings and giving a magical lift to its people who have remained faithful to him and their ancient homeland.

Sedonians Speak

Interviews with Sedonians

Ani Williams..pg 304

Enocha Ranjita Ryan....................................pg 312

Sakina Blue-Star...pg 318

Jesse Kalu..pg 327

Interdimensional/ET Experiences

Peter Sterling..pg 335

Lyssa Royal Holt..pg 339

Devara ThunderBeat.....................................pg 340

Shekina Rose...pg 341

Lane Badger..pg 345

Kurt Bagley..pg 346

Interview with Ani Williams

MAP: When we lived together many years ago you told me about the cosmic way in which you awoke to your destiny as a musician. Unfortunately, I'm not sure I have the details right anymore. Please refresh my memory.

AW: The awakening came about through a series of dreams I had in the 1970s. These were more than dreams however. They were very vivid, very lucid experiences. They seemed more like profound visitations.

In one very vivid dream I found myself in a huge coliseum where a rock band was playing. As I looked around I noticed one person there that appeared to be a guru. He had long hair and a beard and reminded me of the Hatha Yoga guru of India, Swami Satchidananda. All of a sudden he started singing a sweet song, like a sacred chant, and I joined him because it was so beautiful. As we sang together the band stopped and all 10,000 people were listening only to our song. When this guru suddenly stopped singing I loudly objected, saying "Wait a minute, I can't do this alone!" "Oh yes you can!," he replied. "You know the song, sing it!" So that dream was my first inkling that I had something important to do in the world that involved music. This was a shock to me because I never set out to be a musician.

The second major dream I recall occurred around 1976 or 1977, two years that were immensely powerful for many people's spiritual awakening. I was visited in my dream by a group of angels, an angelic host. They all wore long gossamer gowns with a sort of apricot color, and their energy was very clear and illuminating. Speaking to me telepathically, they said that I had forgotten who I really was, so they had come to remind me. I was part of their family and my mission on Earth was to bring harmony and music to the planet. This dream occurred in Sedona two years after an earlier dream I had had in Southern California, during which I was told I would be given a harp. Finally, a year after the second dream I was actually gifted with a harp by a friend of mine. So, for a couple of years a lot of synchronistic things happened between my dream and waking states to let me know I had work to do.

MAP: Did the angels have the appearance of those portrayed by the Catholic Church…or were they different?

AW: They did not have wings, but they were definitely light beings. They had an illuminating presence, a gossamer translucence to them. And they radiated love and understanding.

MAP: Have you felt their presence since, such as those times when you are playing your harp or composing?

AW: I know they are around. Sometimes I hear them playing my harp at night. At those times there is no wind in the house but something intangible stirs the harp strings. This has happened a few times. This is how they let me know they are there and supporting me.

As I have moved along in my musical career I have stopped seeing the angels, but other people continue to see them. Some people see light body presences and angelic beings around me when I am playing.

MAP: Have you learned any more about them, where they came from or your karmic connection to them?

AW: You may know of the Ascended Master El Morya? His name was mentioned by them. They arrived in a light vehicle, although I would not say it was a spaceship, and said they were from El Morya's tribe or clan. They were his celestial family.

MAP: So perhaps you have a connection to El Morya?

AW: Yes, absolutely. I feel that.

MAP: I also remember you recounting an interdimensional temple experience you had in Sedona. Can you tell me about that event again?

AW: In the summer of 1975, right around the time I first arrived in Sedona, I had one of those dreams that are very soul expanding and feel very real. In the dream I was standing next to that mound that you see on your left side of the road just before reaching the Airport Vortex parking lot. Today, I think of this mound as the hub of a wheel that is Sedona.

In the dream an etheric temple hovered right above the mound. It appeared to be a temple made of etheric glass; it wasn't solid. I approached it and on the right side of the temple I saw the name of Serapis written upon it. I had no conception of what Serapis was at the time. So I walked into the temple and found myself in what appeared to be a study center; it was a place of learning with a large library. There were many students there and they were all busy studying. The place kind of reminded me of an ancient scriptorium. As I walked through the temple I recognized everyone there, but at the same time I kept saying to myself "I've done this before. I don't have to stay in this school because I've done this before." So I continued walking out through another door at the opposite end of the temple.

This dream occurred about the time that I moved to the area near Oak Creek that is on the other side of and just below that mound. Since the dream I have learned so many interesting things about Serapis and his connection with Osiris and the temples in Egypt. There was a Serapeum next to the Library of Alexandria. There were Serapis temples everywhere around the Mediterranean. They were places of high learning There is even a Serpaeum in the Greek temple in Spain where I take my groups to now.

MAP: Do you believe that the Serapis Temple is still there hovering over the Airport Vortex?

AW: I don't know if it is still there. I don't see it anymore. In the old days [of Sedona] it was easier to access the higher dimensions. Once the heavy businesses came the higher dimensions became a bit obscured. I believe that the Serapis temple was here to imprint the consciousness of those who arrived early to Sedona. Just like today, people who came to Sedona at the earlier time couldn't eat or sleep because something unusual was happening to them. I believe Sedona is a spiritual school and people are drawn here because they sense that it is. Over time, temples such as the Serapis Temple have imprinted many people with important ideas and images. People come here to get inspiration and wisdom and then they spread it around the world. Spielberg came here to write *Close Encounters of the Third Kind*.

306

MAP: I can relate to what you say. For some time I have felt that the population in Sedona has disconnected with the higher dimensions because of all the commercialism in the city. How do you think we can now reconnect to the other worlds and dimensions?

AW: Good question! We need to make a conscious effort to reconnect. When I first came here I did not have a computer. I did not run a business. I had not produced any cds or dvds. Now my world, our world, is so full of distractions. I think it is important for all of us to get back to nature. Go into the canyons of Sedona, sit on the stones. Be close to the water. Through meditation at those places the visions will return. Getting quiet and disconnecting from all the distractions is the way.

MAP: Do you have any special UFO experiences you would like to share?

AW: Yes, I have had quite a few of them. I will begin with a vision that both myself and my ex-husband had. One day in 1976 we left our home near Oak Creek and climbed upwards towards Airport Vortex. When we were just below the big mound that the tourists now climb to the top of we both noticed a pronounced shift in the energy. My husband was employed by the Forest Service at the time and pretty much a "normal guy," so such experiences were very rare and notable for him. We had stepped across an energetic bearer and everything was completely silent. We could not hear any birds, we could neither hear nor see any bugs. It was like we had stepped into a complete "still zone." Sensing the strangeness of the new area, we both asked psychically if it was okay to keep going, and we got that it was. We then sat down to mediate and soon afterwards opened our wide eyes at the same time. We looked at each other in disbelief and asked: "Did you see that!!??" Whatever it was, both of us saw it with our eyes closed! It was apparently in another dimension. We had both seen this very large disc of light coming towards us and then entering the mound behind us. When we asked those energies that were piloting the light ship what they were doing we intuitively received the answer that they were refueling because the electromagnetic energy was so strong there.

MAP: Judging by the experiences you have had there it certainly appears that the Airport Vortex has been extremely important for you, perhaps even more so than the other vortexes.

AW: Yes. I also have a very strong connection to the area in and around Cornville where there were a number of ancient Anasazi settlements. Pine Valley in the Village of Oak Creek has also been very significant. A series of sightings occurred when I lived out there for a few years. On several occasions I saw a large moon-shaped green object that would hover above the horizon. When I first realized it was not the moon or a planet I stared at it for awhile and then it quickly moved down below the horizon. I had many more sightings of green crafts. One of my encounters was in a vivid dream that revealed to me the owners of the green crafts. I dreamed that I was camping out at a nearby mesa and some little green ships kept dive bombing me, trying to get my attention. I told them to stop bothering me, that I was trying to sleep, but they persisted. I then got up and they came to me and told me to follow them, that they had something important to show me. I followed them into one of the crevasses in Jack's Canyon. And then they said "we want you to see this." They projected a current of sound into the canyon and all of a sudden I saw these huge columns of crystal about 90 feet tall. They had grown these crystals with the sound frequency. Then they told me: "That's one thing you can do with sound. You can create, you can construct, you can heal" Then, with another beam of sound frequency, the columns of crystal cracked and crumbled to the ground. They destroyed them. "You can also do this with sound; you can destroy, liberate, clean and make things disappear," they said. This was quite an important teaching for me given my life's work with sound and healing.

MAP: Do you have a sense of who these aliens were?

AW: I don't know. I didn't have a sense that these were more friends of mine from the past who had a vested interest in breaking open my consciousness and helping me remember something.

   I now call these the green aliens. There were also red ones that I experienced. And then there were a series of close encounters. The first one was in 1981. I was at *A Course in Miracles* class which they used to hold on Brewer Road at the old Sedona Elementary School. David Hawkins (author of *Power vs Force*) was teaching the Course at the time. We had night classes that were very well attended. At the end of one class we all were outside the school building looking up at the stars. A friend and I were looking at the sky over the Airport Mesa and noticed a perfect triangle of stars there. Then we realized they were part of a large spacecraft that was moving towards us. My friend, who was an older and very pragmatic woman, had just moved from New York. When she saw the craft she became very excited. Grabbing my arm she started saying: "They are here! They are here! I want to go!" Then everyone there, about twenty people, all started seeing the same triangle of lights and the huge craft. When they began talking among themselves, trying to identify the craft, I told everyone to be quiet. I said that this was something amazing. Why ruin the moment by filling it with conversation? Let's just experience it and see what it is! Then the craft kept getting closer and closer. When it came near us it completely blacked out the sky above us. We guessed it was about a football field in size but it could have been larger if it was higher in the sky than we estimated. It emanated a very low tone, a low hum. It went slowly over us and then it took off in a whoosh of light and sound towards Schnebly Hill. The message I got at the time was that this was the first of many encounters that Sedona would have. The following week at the same class many students who had seen the craft could not remember it. Their memories had been completely blanked out. But there was five or six of us who clearly remembered what we had seen. An addendum to this story involves Page Bryant, the local psychic who was the first to start talking about the Sedona vortexes. She was a good friend of mine. When a group of us went to study with her the week after the event we all told her about the UFO encounter. She said "Oh my God, that's the one I was told about!" Apparently she had been given guidance that a close encounter would occur. She was told it was going to happen in Northern Arizona; but she wasn't told Sedona. So she thought she would get a better view of the event if she went to the Hopi Reservation, where the sky is clearer and not obstructed by the lights of the city. So she went up to Hopi and missed the entire event. She was very upset about that. Anyway, it was not just me witnessing this UFO event. There was a whole group of people that experienced it, including David Hawkins.

MAP: Did you later see other ships that were part of this series of encounters?

AW: I only saw one more. Other people may have seen the others.

MAP: I wonder if this is connected to the Hopi's sightings. I understand that the Hopis believe a series of sightings that began in the 1970s and 80s are heralding the return of the Star People.

AW: Absolutely! I used to work with Hopi Grandmother Carolyn Telangana, who was part of the Badger Clan. She was one of my teachers in the mid 1980s. I used to go up to Hopi and help her in her kitchen and meet with the other grandmothers. She used to tell me so many stories of the sightings people had at the Hopi Reservation. Then in 1987 I took her to Machu Picchu to be part of an indigenous gathering of 12 tribes from around the world. She was the Hopi representative and there were representatives of the Tibetans, Egyptians, Celts, Australian Aborigines, and Inuit. In fact, there was one representative person from each part of the world. This was May of 1987, just before the Harmonic Convergence.

We had many days of ceremony at Machu Picchu during our gathering, including our final ceremony. At the end of the final ceremony we all said prayers and made our offerings since it was the end of a great cycle of time. Then the entire group witnessed a close encounter. It was a vehicle of light that hovered over Huanya Picchu [a mountain next to the Machu Picchu ruins], but everyone had a different experience of it. One of our guides, who was part of a UFO group from Lima and had met Shirley Maclain when she was in Peru, witnessed the vehicle of light as a space ship in the sky. Grandmother Carolyn Telangana saw it as the vision of a great two-horned priest. The Australian Aborigines also saw something completely different. One man there, Casta Mira Flores from the Island of Taquille in Lake Titicaca, was surprised at our reaction to the craft and laughed that it was such a big event for us. He was used to often seeing ships coming in and out of the lake all the time while fishing for his family. He often saw a huge vehicle of light moving under the water.

I had more close encounters. I had one in 1992 while walking at night with my granddaughter right underneath Airport Mesa at the Grasshopper Flats area. We noticed what looked like a merry-go-round in the sky. It resembled a double decker, two story merry-go-round. Instead of animals there were two decks of colored lights that were circulating around and around. It was moving right over our heads. It was very large, about the size of the UFO I had witnessed at the Sedona Elementary School. My granddaughter asked "Nana, who is that?" I replied "It could be angels." Then she said "I want to fly." For a solid week afterwards she was completely obsessed with flying.

Another close encounter was in Sycamore Canyon in 1989. There was an lunar eclipse that was supposed to occur about 3 am, so about six of us, including Nicholas Mann, Peter Sterling, and some friends from Glastonbury hiked out there with our instruments. We were going to have music, sing around the campfire, and have a meal while waiting for the eclipse. Just before the eclipse happened one of us looked up in the sky and commented that there were ships up there. They were large lights that moved across the sky before suddenly making a 180 degree turn and darting in the opposite direction. It appeared that one ship was playing cat and mouse with another vehicle. We didn't know if we were seeing only UFOs or military vehicles and UFOs flying together. Sycamore is famous for military personnel abruptly showing up in the canyon; in fact I personally know some people who have had such encounters, so it could have been them. Anyway, we all saw the ships. Another time when I was out there with Alan Leon, who is now a guide in the Andes, I had a similar experience. After we set up camp on a mesa out there I tried to sleep but couldn't. I was kept awake by light vehicles that were parading through the canyon. Alan experienced it differently. He saw kingdoms of elemental light beings moving around the landscape. He is very much a nature guy.

MAP: I guess that is how we get our different myths. We all see similar things but through our filters we experience them quite differently.

AW: Yes! I have a friend who calls us the "New Mythmakers."

MAP: Any other experiences you want to share?

AW: There is one more piece to the Serapis thing. When I came to Sedona I did not know what Sedona was, I had not even seen a picture of it. I was simply looking a for a place to live with my new husband and my daughter. But even before we arrived in Sedona, when we drove down Oak Creek Canyon, I went bonkers. Between sobs I cried out "I am home!" So we stayed and never left. That was back in August of 1975. Enocha Ranjita also came here in August of 1975. There was a whole family of us that came that year.

One day soon after I arrived I took my daughter to the grocery store. There was a nice old lady sitting in the front of the store waiting for her husband to finish shopping. I brought my daughter, who was five at the time, and asked the lady if she wouldn't mind watching her for about five minutes while I ran and got something else. This old lady happened to be Evangeline Van Pollen, a famous psychic of the area. My daughter looked at her and said "My, what deep eyes you have!" About a month later I was looking for work and decided to visit a spiritual center called the Rainbow Ray Focus on Airport Road between job interviews. So I went and knocked at the door and this same lady, Evangeline, opened the door. Our eyes got big as we looked at each other, and then she said "There you are again!" She studied me and said "You are thirsty," possibly a spiritual metaphor, and then invited me in. We talked for quite awhile and I told her I had just moved to Sedona and was looking for work. She said "I'm looking for a secretary." So we worked out a deal and I embarked on a two year period transcribing the channelings of Evangeline and her husband, Carmen. One of the Ascended Masters they worked with was Serapis Bey. Eventually I discovered that according to their channeled information their place right below Airport Vortex was dedicated to Serapis Bey. They had received the same information as me!

Ani Williams is world-renowned harpist and singer who has recorded more than two-dozen albums of original sacred music based on ancient spiritual traditions. She has done seminal work in the study of sound healing and the relationship between musical tones, the human voice and healing. She leads pilgrimages to earth's sacred places and her writings have been published in numerous international publications. Her music, writing and sound therapy can be found at www.aniwilliams.com.

Interview with Enocha Ranjita Ryan

Enocha Ranjita and "Canyon Mama" in the background

MAP: Please tell me what originally brought you to Sedona?

ERR: I came to Sedona after first going through a deep spiritual purging at my home in Milwaukee that brought me to a place of surrender. The voice of my soul opened up and began to guide me. I was told that I was to quit my job, quit school, say goodbye to everyone familiar to me, pack up my apartment, and that I would be buying a van. I was told that I was going to have an adventure during which I would be led every step of the way. When I told my sister of my plans she said "You aren't going without me." Within 30 days we had done everything I was told to do, including buying a van, which we called "Van Morrison." We were ready for an epic adventure although we had no idea where we were we going. We just knew we wanted to go all around the entire country and see as many states as we possibly could. And we knew we would be guided.

During our journey we found Sedona. We weren't looking for Sedona. We just came down Oak Creek Canyon while headed for Jerome, where we planned to stay that evening. But we were interrupted by the amazing Sedona

312

energy. So we stopped off at the Slide Rock apple orchard and met a person who invited us to come to their home and take showers, etc. They could tell we were two young girls on the road and needed some assistance. Afterwards, we continued into Sedona and as soon as we reached the area of Indian Gardens I burst into tears. I told my sister "This is my soul's home!" We had already been to so many amazing places, but when I reached here my heart opened up like it had never done before. So we decided to stay in Sedona. It was perfect for us. At that time it was a tiny little town with a small group of metaphysical people who had already gathered here. I joined their group and we gathered each morning at Paula's Gold Dust Café for breakfast and to talk about our dreams and spiritual experiences. Everyone was on fire with this awakening energy. But I was surprised. I couldn't find a permanent place to stay in Sedona. Sedona kicked me out! It kept telling me "You are not ready to settle down yet. You have to keep traveling." So I ended up living on the Monterey Peninsula in California for awhile. Then Sedona sent a messenger to my door and I knew it was time. I came back and everything fell into place.

One morning I was sitting at El Rincon Mexican Restaurant in Telaquepaque that had just opened. I said to myself, "If I am going to stay in Sedona I am going to work here." The next day I went back and the manager put out his arm to welcome me. He said: "You're hired." I hadn't even asked him for a job!

At that time there was no such thing as vortexes that had been officially located and named. But the energy of the vortexes was so strong that every night I would go in my van and spend the night at one of them. Eventually they were named vortexes by Page Bryant and her guide Albion. Seven of them were named by Albion, including Indian Gardens where I live now.

MAP: Were there any vortexes that you were initially drawn to?

ERR: Different ones at different times. I spent a lot of time on Airport Mesa. I called it my bedroom. At that time West Sedona was a little tiny community with a dirt road running through it. It was such a small community that we all recognized each other.

In the early days I had lots of amazing experiences, a lot of Third Eye openings during which I encountered many teachers, many masters. Some would spontaneously appear sitting right next to me. Jesus would sometimes appear and I used to have walks and talks with him. He helped me heal from my Catholic upbringing, which I had vehemently rejected by the time I was thirteen. The Catholic God was not my God. It was not the God that *I* know. So consequently I never had a relationship with Jesus. These walks and talks were profound and instructional. Jesus explained many things to me in a way that made prefect sense. He told me that the prayer pose was not for piety, but by placing the hands together all the nadis and channels in the body would come together to make a perfect circuit to help your body heal and become balanced. So I would walk in this pose while Jesus would give me his true teachings that had been twisted over time by the Church to keep us away from our divine nature. Osho would also show up a lot. This was before Rajneesh was known as Osho. He would float over Oak Creek and give me discourses in his wonderful Hindu accent on subjects he would introduce as Tantra, a term I had never heard before.

I had many UFO experiences at this time. One night I was down at Sedona mobile home park near Oak Creek – which is where I met Ani Williams - when I looked in the sky and saw this huge band. It was like a huge rainbow but it was bright white light. I was awed by it. That's all I remember until about 3am in the morning. I thought no time had passed, so I went running into the house I was living in and told everyone to come out and see the light. Everyone had gone to bed. They awoke and immediately asked what had happened to me. They had been very concerned. I thought I had just been gone for a couple of minutes until I looked at my watch and realized that many hours had passed! I believe that I was taken up during that time. But I also believe it was a very benevolent encounter. It wasn't a forceful abduction.

Then I met my teacher of the Ramana Maharshi tradition and I knew that I did not need to be something or someone else. I did not need to have any more information or special psychic experiences given to me. I just needed to live life in the moment. That led me to where I am now and the relationship I have with Canyon Mama and the earth energies here.

After returning from India, where I had been with my teacher at Ramana Ashram at the foot of Arunachala Mountain in South India, I first walked upon the property I live on now. I came to visit a friend of mine that lived here. As I walked around my inner voice emerged, and clear as a bell it said "Welcome to your new home." I immediately said that I wasn't looking for a new home. I had a healing center in the Village of Oak Creek at the time and was happy there. But my voice said "No. This place wants to be a sanctuary so that people can come and receive the teaching and healing of the land. You are going to be the steward of the land and the priestess of the temple." I was then told that the woman who owned the property would soon be called forth to work in the world in a much greater capacity and not to worry. Everything would work out so I could buy the place. When I told my friend the message she looked at me like I had nine heads; there was no way it was going to happen. But then, within just two days, everything began to unfold. My friend was called to move to Boulder Colorado to work in a spiritual center there. When I returned to the property a day later I found her very confused about what to do with her home. My inner voice spoke through me and

I asked her: "What makes you think that your renter is not right in front of you?" So she began to think about renting it to me. Then we asked for a sign if this should happen and almost immediately a big red-tailed hawk came and circled directly over our heads. When my friend was still not convinced, another red-tailed hawk appeared and then there was two big birds circling directly over our heads. That was enough.

I returned a couple days later and my friend, Diana, and I did a meditation to see if we could receive any more guidance. Within a couple minutes of closing my eyes I heard outside myself a deep female voice saying "this is Canyon Mama, would you please tune in." I asked Diana if she had heard the voice and she had not. I thought for a moment that I must have tuned into a local truck frequency and Canyon Mama was a trucker's code name. Since I didn't know how to "tune in," I asked "Canyon Mama, "Who are you, what are you and where are you??" All she said was "Come to me." Then I felt an energy lift me up from my seat inside and draw me outside onto the front deck. Once there I heard her say, "I am right in front of you." So I looked up and saw a huge heart in the mountain. I asked "Canyon Mama, are you the big heart I see?" "Yes," she replied. But then she said "I might look like a heart to you but what you are seeing are my legs open in a heart shape. You are looking right into my sacred yoni (female genitalia)." She then told me that she was a healer and a teacher of the female principle. She said that she would draw people to the property for healing and teaching and I would know who they were. Once there, she would ignite the female principle within them that we as humans have lost. Then she informed me that Heaven and Earth meet at her feet as two rivers. At her feet Oak Creek from high up in Flagstaff (Heaven) unites with Munds Creek from below (Earth). After they meet the rivers flow as one river directly to her partner, which is a red rock formation in the shape of a huge lingam or phallus that I could see off to my left. His name was "Red Rock Papa." She said there is a continual flow of loving energy that comes out of her womb into the valley, which she called a birth canal, to the Red Rock Papa. Those that would come to the Sanctuary could be given the assistance to let go of their blockages and toxins and become part of this flow. As the river reaches the Papa Rock he propels the energy back to her womb, so there is a circuit of energy. She said she could do this work partly because of the two male mountains on either side of her; they are sentinels that hold the energy. She said that when people come here they will be within this perfect male-female flow and be able to make the same balance within themselves.

Canyon Mama has been true to her word. She has sent people here from all over the world. I never advertise. They all come by word of mouth only. I have now been here 18 years and the Sanctuary has completely supported itself during this time. Thanks to Canyon Mama my inner feminine and masculine have both evolved and work perfectly together whenever I need something to happen.

One day I looked around at all the changes that have been brought about in the Sanctuary and knew they had occurred through the synnastry of the inner feminine who dreams the idea and the inner masculine who then works out the details and makes it happen. As I was acknowledging this synnastry the veils magically came down and in front of me there I was as a little four year old girl. She was jumping up and down saying "I'm your Golden Girl, I'm the one that never got wounded!" "You protected me a long time ago, but then you forgot about me. Now that you have a good mommy and daddy inside of you I can come back now!" She then literally jumped into my heart, and from that day onwards my innocence has returned. Later that day I went on a magical walk with my dogs and found myself singing and dancing. My inner child was having great fun. Then a few days later another miracle happened. Canyon Mama also gave birth to a child! It was a confirmation of what I had experienced within myself. An eight ton boulder broke off and came tumbling down the canyon right towards my house. By inches it missed everything that would have been tragic to lose, and it only hit those things, like the pump house and hot tub, that needed replacing. It was so loud I thought a plane had crashed. I ran outside just in time for the boulder to come soaring over my head and crash into the pump house.

Soon after this I had a couple friends come out here and map out the ley lines of Canyon Mama. They drew out a grid very similar to Stonehenge. They also found that the place where the new boulder-child had landed perfectly enhanced the grid. I have since found that on one of Nicholas Mann's maps there is is a dove or phoenix over Sedona. Canyon Mama sits right in the area of the tail.

Today I help people go through the process I personally underwent, of balancing the male and female and giving birth to the inner child. I call it Coming Home.

Enocha Ranjita Ryan owns and operates **Your Hearts Home Retreat Sanctuary** *in the Center of Oak Creek Canyon, Sedona AZ. Please visit: www.yourheartshome.com*

"Red Rock Papa"

The "Child" of Canyon Mama

Interview with Sakina Blue-Star

MAP: What originally brought you to Sedona?

SBS: After my husband died I sold my big sea captain's house on Cape Cod and set out in my Dodge Van Camper to see where I wanted to live next. I went from Cape Cod to San Deigo, and various places in between, and finally ended up in Sedona.

MAP: Had you heard about Sedona before you moved here?

SBS: Not really. I had only heard some vague things about it. Before discovering Sedona I had gone to Taos, New Mexico and loved the town. I also went to Santa Fe and loved it. But I wasn't meant to live there and kept going. In Taos I picked up a hitch hiker and she started traveling with me. She had just been to the Hopi Reservation and other Native American reservations. So we went together to Phoenix, then up to Prescott and over Jerome to Cottonwood, and finally to Sedona. I remember the first person I met in Sedona. His name was Al Butler. I met him at the Coffee Pot Restaurant, which was across the road from where it is now. I asked him if he knew any good realtors in town. He asked why I wanted to live in Sedona and I told him that I had heard that it had good spiritual energy. He laughed and said "There's a lot of people like you here!" He told me about some realtors and some spiritual events that were happening locally. One was an event on Airport Mesa near the large cross next to the Masonic Lodge. When I arrived there soon afterwards I found a platform set up and Ani Williams playing her harp. Mary Lou Keller next came on the platform with Hirindrah Singh from India. Hirindrah Singh told the gathering "Don't think of the Earth as your mother, think of it as your child. And give love to it like you would a child." He always wore pink because he had made a vow in India to follow a specific spiritual tradition. His ideas of spirituallity were, however, very different than most people's. He had many girlfriends. He would tell them all "You are my princess. You are wonderful. I worship you." He was quite an impressive guy. Sometimes he and Mary Lou would go over to India and take people on tours there. Hirindrah would say that he had lived in an ashram in India about seventeen times. I think he neglected to say that he had been kicked out of the ashram sixteen of those times!

After arriving in Sedona in 1983 I began taking all kinds of workshops and classes. There were so many amazing people who would come here then.

MAP: So there was a lot happening in Sedona at that time?

SBS: Oh yes. Continual events. There was one movie theater in town back then, the Flicker Shack. Everyone would go there on Tuesdays because it was bargain night and you could see all your friends. On Saturday afternoons special speakers would often come there. They gave workshops that you could sign up for. One of the speakers came up from Phoenix and gave a workshop on past life regression. His name was Frank Baranowski, a relatively famous man who had a weekly radio show called *Mysteries Around Us*. He could take a person back to a different time and place. He would record the session, including all the details of when and where they lived, their names etc. And then he would find who they had been according to actual historical records. He found the identity of one man who had been a soldier in the Civil War. Another man had been at Pearl Harbor.

When Frank Baranowski came up to Sedona a second time about 12 of us joined him in a private residence to directly experience personal past life regression. He began the workshop by using me as an example. I was taken back to a Native American life when I was "Girl who loves the forest." I had visions of growing up in the forest, having my own family, and then dying when my village was massacred by the US Calvary. During the attack I fell on my daughter to save her life and she became the only survivor of the village. It was all so real. Sometime after that regression I learned from documents that the daughter I saved was an actual historical figure. She had been a member of the Lakota tribe and called Little Dove. And her mother, the woman I had been in the regression, was known

319

in the records as Turtle Woman. About the same time that I learned the identities of both the mother and daughter I also discovered that they are my direct ancestors on my mother's side. I learned that Little Dove eventually married a Choctaw Cherokee and moved down south, and her daughter, who was my grandmother, graduated from the University of Mississippi in 1897.

MAP: You were not aware of your Native American ancestry before that?

SBS: No, I was never told. During my earlier years if a local family was descended from natives they hid that fact. Natives were still considered savages. If people knew you had native blood you were discriminated against.

MAP: But now you have written an entire book about your ancestor Little Dove, right?

SBS: Yes. I even drew her picture. Following my past life recall I took a course from a well known local spirit artist, Stan Matrunick, on how to draw people as they were in other lifetimes. To start, I did one on my own past lifetime and painted Little Dove. I eventually learned to also draw guardians and spirit guides. And then I began to do drawings professionally for people. I did this for about 30 years.

About a year after taking the course I went out to Boynton Canyon, the canyon known through the ages as "Sacred Canyon," and I went to the top of the hill where Kachina Woman is. Kachina Woman looks like a Hopi maiden holding a child. She has curls like the Hopi maidens do when they are of marriageable age. It is here that for thousands of years that native maidens would come to pray when they wanted to conceive a child. And it works! My daughter wanted to have a child so I went there to pray and soon she gave birth to her first child at the age of 43.

Stan Matrunick's wife, Grandmother Golden Eagle (aka Jacki Matrunick) and I became good friends. She was of Cherokee and German descent, and she possessed the special abilities of the Cherokee that her great grandfather had given her when she was born. She had the gift of being able to see and talk to spirits. We would go out to all the canyons together. I would draw pictures of the spirits and Jackie would see and speak to them directly. We found places where groups of natives had been killed off by the US Calvary and then we would do ceremonies to help their spirits rise into the next world. One time when we were in Long Canyon I was walking along when Grandmother said "Sakina, there is something here." She told me to use my eagle feathers to sweep away the negative energy. I did, and then she received an answer as to why the energy was there.

Apparently some medicine people had put it there. What she saw was that there had been a settlement of Yavapai there in their wickiups [primitive Yavapai houses], and that the US Calvary had shown up and told them that they would have to leave the area and be transplanted to the Apache reservation in the San Carlos area of southern Arizona. The Yavapai said "How can we go now? It's the middle of the winter. The children will die." The Calvary said "Oh, you are worried about the children?" So they killed the children. When the elders of the Yavapai came back and saw this they put an energy drain there so no one could settle there.

The Yavapai have been in Sedona for thousands of years. They are the original guardians of the area. There was a time that they would not let anyone enter the area unless they could tell they had a good heart and had reached a place of evolution conducive to working with the Sedona energies. Otherwise, they were told they would have to wait until they were ready before they could enter.

MAP: What sort of structures did the Yavapai live in?

SBS: They lived in wickiups. That is the Apache name for them. They are cone-shaped structures made of branches and brush.

MAP: Once you were in Sedona did you stay in one place or continue exploring other sacred sites of Arizona and the American Southwest?

SBS: I did a lot of traveling with my husband, Sundance, whom I met about this time. He was 20 years younger than me - a tall, blond and handsome man from Santa Fe. He was of Celtic ancestry but had grown up among the Native Americans and knew their ways. We had a lot of adventures together. We traveled to many places. He knew a lot about the southwest. He was very sensitive, so he could feel the spirits in the canyons we visited. We were together for five years and then he passed over.

At one point Sundance and I moved down to the Phoenix area. There was a man there who had founded the Staircase Project. He had discovered a special cave in the Superstition Mountains that led to a flat topped pyramid that was as big as the one in Giza, Egypt. He called it the Staircase Project because there was a circular stone staircase that led down to it. He felt there was a King's Chamber inside the pyramid and he wanted to go and access the knowledge inside of it. Grandmother Golden Eagle told me she knew that there was a lot of information there and she could even see the starship that had planted some information in the pyramid. So Sundance and I moved down there and got a place close by so we could help with the project. But this man was jealous about anyone trying to steal his project. Even Jacques Cousteau's son showed up hoping to film the pyramid. But the man's anger got the best of him and the project never really got off the ground.

MAP: What do you know about the history of the Sedona vortexes?

SBS: The vortexes were known about before Page Bryant arrived, but she made them famous. When Page Bryant came to Arizona she visited a friend of mine, Alice Bowers, a minister of the University of Light Church in Phoenix. Bryant told Alice Bowers that she had been talking about a lot of esoteric things on her radio show, such as the continent of Atlantis that sunk off Bimini, but people were getting tired of hearing about that. So Bryant asked if there was anything in the Arizona area that was interesting. Alice told her to go up to Sedona and speak to Mary Lou Keller. Keller had lived in Sedona for 25 years and knew it better than most people. She knew many of the energy spots because she had been told them by the natives. She also found many on her own. Sometimes her horse would recoil when she was riding along and moved within the boundaries of a strong energy field.

So Page Bryant came up and talked to Mary Lou Keller. She would then go out to the places that Keller had told her possessed special energy. She would meditate at these places and her spiritual guide Albion would tell her "this is a negative, magnetic vortex, or this is a positive, electric vortex." This was similar to what another man, Pete Sanders, one of the founders of Sedona's Center for the New Age, got regarding the inflow and upflow tendencies of the vortexes. Page Bryant compiled the information she had learned about the Sedona vortexes and then spent years telling people in seminars around the country about them.

MAP: Was Bryant the first to use the term "vortex"?

SBS: I believe that Mary Lou Keller used the term vortex but Bryant made it famous. However, the natives of this area know about hundreds of vortexes and Bryant only spoke about seven of them.

During the 1980s many people were locating and marking many of the other vortexes in Sedona. For a few years there was an older woman who marked many of the vortexes with medicine wheels. She had been on her death bed when a Venusian spirit came to her and asked if it could use her body for three years to mark and activate the vortexes. She agreed. Some vortexes, she would later say, were marked by her to hold in their energy so Venusian ships could enter their field and recharge. This lady always wore white clothing and addressed everyone as "Master."

My connection has been mostly with the Boynton Canyon vortex. It began one day in the canyon while I was on the Kachina Woman Rock mound which I was visiting with another person. I raised my staff to the sky and said in an unknown native language that came through me: "Use me to help as long as it is in the Light." The man who accompanied me told me afterwards that as I spoke hundreds of birds appeared right above us, and when I stopped speaking they all dispersed. That's when I began to be a Spirit Speaker. Different languages began to spontaneously come through me. Sometimes they were in the form of songs. Eventually I knew that it was my ancestors speaking through me, as well as the ancestors that had lived here at the same time I did many lifetimes ago. This was when Sedona was known as the "Crystal City of Light."

MAP: Did you have a pastlife recall of when Sedona was referred to as the Crystal City of Light?

SBS: Yes, but not just me. Many people have remembered that Sedona was once called that.

After being activated at Kachina Woman I started doing ceremonies in Boynton Canyon. At that time we could park down near where Enchantment is now and hike in. The resort wasn't built yet. A stone circle had been constructed in Boynton Canyon for a ceremony to help heal White Bear Fredericks. After that ceremony I used the circle every full moon night to lead a meditation. There would be anywhere from 30-80 participants and I would bring messages to them from the People of the Star Nations.

MAP: Did the Star People come directly to Sedona in ancient times?

SBS: Yes, this is one of the first places they came to because of its power.

MAP: What other information have you received from the Native Americans about Boynton Canyon?

SBS: I have heard that the canyon was sacred to all tribes. They would come here from great distances for their vision quest. The Great Spirit would then tell them what it wanted for their lives. It was easier to do a vision quest here because of the vortexes and the interdimensional columns of light that would unite people with the spirit realms. Some say that canyon also gets its energy from the bones of great chiefs and holy men who were buried out there in Boynton Canyon.

MAP: You mean the graves where Enchantment now sits?

SBS: Not necessarily. I have heard that there are bones buried in the canyon in places other than Enchantment. There are those who would prefer that you did not know where these bones are buried. They don't want them disturbed.

MAP: Do the Yavapai have anything special to say about Boynton Canyon?

SBS: It was a very holy place for them. But there are very few Yavapai left. Most were killed off. So it is hard to get information from them.

SBS: The Hopis also speak about Boynton Canyon. Hopi Grandfather David Monongye loved Boynton Canyon and knew much about it. Before he passed I used to go to Hopi Mesas to visit him. He knew much about Sedona. He told me that Long Canyon was an inter-tribal ceremonial ground. Now they have built a golf course and condominiums there. Enchantment has also been built up in the last few years. If the spirits don't like it they will do something about these places.

The chiropractor David Milgrim would occasionally bring Grandfather David down to Sedona. The only thing he wanted to do while in Sedona was to go into Boynton Canyon. Grandfather David said there are eight places in there that are very sacred to the Hopi. Every year a group of chiefs would go into Boynton Canyon for ritual at one of these spots. It is a cave high up at the far end of the canyon that had a very big crystal in it. The crystal has since been removed by the government. The medicine men would energize their crystals a couple times a year by placing them near or on top of the big crystal.

MAP: You have been in contact with the Hopi for many years. Did you make contact with them soon after arriving in Sedona?

SBS: Before arriving, actually. When I was traveling with the woman I met in Taos we went to Hopi Mesas. We went to First Mesa to the town of Walpi. When we arrived it was just getting dark and there was a ceremony in the plaza there. I brought with me a little Kachina doll I had bought in Taos. It had been made by a Hopi artist named Rohanna. I found out where she lived on the reservation and went to meet her. That is how I met my Hopi daughter. Later, when I returned to Hopi I would always visit her and eventually we became family. She became my adopted daughter. She is unique because she still speaks Hopi and knows many of the old songs.

MAP: Was Sedona originally part of Hopiland?

SBS: Yes, the Hopi were here along with the Yavapai. They lived in the cliff dwellings. Later the Apaches came through and also settled here.

MAP: I am curious to know what the Hopi believe about Sedona. I heard once, I think by you, that Grandfather Martin said that the Kachinas once lived down near Red Rock Crossing. So perhaps the Hopis think of Sedona as a home of the Kachinas?

SBS: Right. Grandfather Martin would stay with a friend each summer down there by Oak Creek. Many of his friends, including chiefs, would come to meet with him there. It is the area that they recently cleared for a big development that Martin said was where the Kachinas would come and do their sacred dances.

MAP: How do the Hopis feel about Sedona these days?

SBS: There aren't many traditional Hopis left. A lot of them are getting converted to Christianity, and many have left the reservation. Some of the modern Hopis say that the old ways are the work of the Devil. It used to be that when I went to the Hopi dances I would see 400 dancers. Now I might see half that number. Many of the Hopis have left for other towns and cities, but they often return for the important Kachina dances.

MAP: Do the Hopi still believe that Pahana will return with a corner of one of the tablets.

SBS: That is their traditional belief, but as I said there are very few that still hold closely to the old beliefs. As you know Grandfather Martin had copies of the Fire Tablets. He was guardian of the original tablets for many years, which he received from his uncle, a man the US government kept imprisoned for many years because he would not agree to live the white man's ways. Martin carried the tablets in a bandana around his waist and went to Santa Fe, which is the oldest of the non-Hopi cities in the southwest, and told some politicians there that they needed to tell the people to treat the Earth better or, according to the tablets, there would be some major Earth disasters. The Hopis got mad at Martin for taking the tablets off the reservation. So Martin was forced to give the tablets to another person of his family for safekeeping. Now he keeps replicas of them.

MAP: Do the Hopi believe we are in the Fifth World yet?

SBS: No, they say we are still in the time of the purification leading up to the Fifth

World. Grandfather Martin said that in the Fifth World there will be harmony and we will all speak the same language again.

MAP: Through your name are you connected to the end-time Hopi prophecy of the Blue Star?

SBS: Yes. Chief Golden Light Eagle of the *Star Knowledge Conferences* once told me that my star ship was the Blue Star ship. I began using the name sometime later.

MAP: So the Blue Star that will herald the Fifth World is a starship?

SBS: It could be. I saw the Blue Star ship once when I was returning from Second Mesa. It was a big disc-shaped ship that moved in front of the Full Moon. I just knew it was my ship. But my name Blue-Star came from the sister of Wallace Black Elk, Grandmother Eloise, who I used to spend a lot of time with. She gave me the name and inducted me into her family, the Wallace Black Elk family.

MAP: Do you have a sense of what Boynton Canyon was back in Lemuria times?

SBS: Yes, it was a sacred, ceremonial place. There were sacred dances. I have seen them. The women would go one way in a circle and in an outer circle the men would move another way to keep the balance. As they danced they would say thank you to the Earth Mother and to the Sky Father while singing sacred songs and sending out a positive vibration into the world.

MAP: Where did you learn the ancient name of Sedona, "Nawanda?"

SBS: In the 1980s there was a group of us that went into the canyons to explore. They helped me build a couple of medicine wheels close to Kachina Woman. One of them was a woman from one of the Oklahoma tribes named Trish. She said she had learned that in ancient times Sedona was known among the North American tribes as Nawanda. So Sedona was anciently Nawanda, the Crystal City of Light.

Sakina Blue-Star is the author of Little Dove, Lakota Ancestor, which is available through www.Amazon.com.

Interview with Jesse Kalu

MAP: What originally brought you to Sedona?

JK: Before Sedona, as a native from the Mariana Islands in the Pacific I was living in Santa Monica, California. In the winter of 1990 I decided to drive to Florida on my favorite route cross country to visit my friends via I-40. On my return trip west I drove past Flagstaff, Arizona and saw an exit sign for Sedona. Up to this point I had not even been aware of Sedona let alone this sign.

MAP: Obviously you weren't supposed to notice that sign until that time.

JK: Right! Normally I would drive past, but this time the sign beckoned me, as if it had a gesturing hand. If it had a heart, it would have welcomed me with joyful heartbeats. I made a mental decision to continue home and explore Sedona later, but I got "Vortexed." The steering wheel turned on its own.

MAP: Do you mean a force or presence actually took over the steering wheel?

JK: Yes. A peaceful presence led the way. I simply surrendered and remembered saying at the time, "Okay, I'm going to Sedona! I drove down into Oak Creek Canyon until the pine trees gave way to the red rock vistas. I pulled over near Slide Rock Park, walked to a red stone formation, placed my bare hands and feet on warm smooth sandstone. With all my senses awakened, I heard a voice say, "You are home." In my response, teary eyed I said, "I'll be back!"

MAP: Interesting! In my other interviews for this book I heard similar stories of people who knew they had come home mid-way down Oak Creek Canyon.

JK: Yes, I felt the embrace and welcome home, as well! That day, before continuing on route to Santa Monica, I drove through Sedona. I found myself connecting not with the town itself, but with its natural wonders and timeless beauty. I felt a divine presence, absolutely still, silent and vast. This led to an awareness of the boundlessness that I am. Infinite stillness, no separation. At that moment Sedona became my love, my teacher. She had revealed my true nature. After returning to Santa Monica, I felt the Spirit of Sedona calling me, as if not to forget. I kept finding myself in environments that would evoke my experience. When I was on the beach of Santa Monica, I saw red sand. On the city sidewalks, I saw red rock trails. In downtown high rises, I saw red sandstone vistas. So after a few months of reminders I knew it was time to return. Without any arrangements for a place to live or a job, I simply drove to Sedona June of 1991.

MAP: That was very courageous of you.

JK: Well, it really wasn't so difficult. Camping was allowed in and around Sedona at the time. I set up my tent on the red rocks in a series of places that were completely off the beaten path, hidden under trees, up against a red cliff, or high above with a view. I was on the back side of Thunder Mountain for awhile, I was also near Cathedral Rock. I wanted to be alone in nature and its wildlife.

MAP: How long did you live in a tent?

JK: Nine months. There were times returning to my tent at night I'd pass near campers while trying not to be seen. I would turn off my flashlight and continue under the light of the moon. Sometimes there would be the rattling sound of snakes, or rustling coming from the surrounding bush. I heard a huge crash near me once that sounded like a bear or mountain lion. I stopped, kept the flashlight off and played a flute until I was certain it had passed. I often felt that the wildlife was watching me and listening. Every night I would scan the night sky, but didn't see anything unusual. When I finally broke camp and moved into town, I was told an entire parade of star ships was seen in the night sky over Secret Canyon, which I had a great view of on the back side of Thunder Mountain. Had I stayed a little longer I would have seen the entire event.

MAP: I think harpists Ani Williams and Peter Sterling were witnesses to that event.

JK: Yes, I was surprised when I heard that I had missed it. But fortunately I was able to find a home in exchange for handy work. Eventually I found a small ranch house on three acres and lived there for the next 15 years.

MAP: Tell me about when you began to play the flute.

JK: My love of the flute began when I was involved with Native American ceremonies and teachings in Sedona. In 1991 I attended many inipis (sweat lodges) and took part in all aspects of them as an assistant, but not as the facilitator. The music of the native flute reminded me of the healing sounds I'd grown up with as a young boy on my island. A bamboo forest only a short distance from my home was my playground and sanctuary. Sometimes I would hang out there all day having no worries or fears. When the hollow bamboo swayed in the breeze the leaves sounded just like rain. I could hear music coming not only from the dry cracked bamboo stands, but from within and all around me. So when I heard the Native American flute I felt that I was home again. The music took me back to the nurturing and comforting sounds I heard in my bamboo forest. Shortly after I was called and led into Boynton Canyon which intimately inspired my first time playing flutes.

MAP: Boynton Canyon has been a teacher for many of us, including myself.

JK: Yes. When I first played in Boynton Canyon I only had a $5.00 souvenir bamboo flute from a tourist shop in Sedona. In spite of the limitations of this off key major scale flute, I was determined to discover for myself how to play it. Without knowing how to read or write music I intended to explore the minor scales of native flutes. I walked half way into the canyon and hid off the trail. For the first two hours I used a strong and fast breath on the flute. I was over zealous, got hyperventilated and very light headed. The annoying sour notes from the flute reverberated in the canyon and the terrible sounds I was producing came right back to me. I was sure that others in the canyon had heard them as well and could have thrown stones in my direction. Because of my failed attempts I surrendered absolutely and declared, "I am not a flute player."

In that moment of silence and stillness I tuned into the canyon for the first time that afternoon. It seemed as though my hearing suddenly became super acute. I could hear the wind through the trees, bird songs, and lady bugs crawling on dry leaves. I could hear my own breath - gentle, loud and clear. As I continued to focus on my breath I was finally at peace and one with the canyon. Then, as if guided by a force other than myself, I blew softly, played a few notes, paused, listened to the echoes, and my breath again, before playing more notes. This continued until I realized what came through was the music I heard in the bamboo forest on my island when I was a child. With tears in my eyes I was home again, but simultaneously in the here and now with great joy.

After two hours of struggling initially, I was now in a state of bliss. Through the next two hours of effortless music I wondered, "Who is playing who?" My eyes remained closed while a consciousness guided my fingers over the holes on the flute. Then for the second time I heard a voice say, "Don't open your eyes or you will disconnect." When I finally opened my eyes I was in a profound state of gratitude for this gift. I felt a divine presence, so I held the flute above my head and said in prayer, "Thank you Great Spirit, Grandfather, Grandmother, Earth and Sky. Thank you for this wonderful gift!" Then I heard a voice for the third time say, "Good. Now take it and share it with the world." I looked around but no one was there. For a moment I had a vision of presenting my flutes before hundreds and thousands of people. If this was my future I wasn't prepared for it. Most of my life to that point I'd kept to to myself.

MAP: So after that experience were you able to play the flute at will?

JK: Yes. My intention then was to acquire a Native American flute so I shopped around for the right one. There were many beautiful and amazing flutes but most were above my price range. Soon after I discovered wild bamboo groves in Sedona and decided I would make my own flutes with local grown bamboo.

At that time there was only one Native American flute maker in town, Hollis Little Creek. He's gone now. I approached him four different times in 1992 and asked him if he would teach me how to make a flute. I remember my first heartfelt request as I stood directly in front of him. He looked up at me for a moment and then returned to his flute crafting. He didn't say a word. Over the next several months it was the same with the second and third time I asked. Finally, on the fourth try I went to Hollis's home with a mutual friend. I sat across from him and said: "Grandfather Hollis, I'm aware that you make ceder, walnut and pine flutes for a living. My wish is to make bamboo flutes and not compete with you. I am from the Pacific islands and I would like to learn from your art how to make bamboo flutes for myself. I feel strongly guided by Spirit to do this." He looked as if right through me for awhile. Then he reached for a small rectangular piece of wood he had for carving an animal fetish on the whistle. With his left hand under my right, he gently placed the wood into my hand. Looking into my eyes he said, "You will never learn unless you do it yourself." In that moment I realized the gift in his words and thought, who taught the first flute maker?! With great affection I placed my hand over his and said, "Thank you, grandfather, thank you."

It wasn't long before I gathered some local bamboo to cut into small pieces that I would later craft into flutes. On July 25th 1992, at 8:00 AM I sat down on a bench in my living room facing the rising sun. I was so excited to begin my first flute crafting venture that hours went by without me noticing. I did not want to stop even for meals until I had created a flute. At 12 midnight, 16 hours later, I was exhausted and defeated. In front of me were three cracked pieces of bamboo. In my failed attempts I had drilled holes too large or in wrong angles. Again, as in the canyon, I totally surrendered to discouragement and declared, "I am not a flute maker so I will focus on being a flute player." I rolled onto the futon behind me and slept soundly for eight hours. At 8:00 AM the next morning it felt like the night had passed within five minutes. I woke completely renewed and energized. Then I heard the fourth voice say, "Get up. You now know what to do."

I returned to my work bench and reached for a piece of bamboo, but realized I had not asked for guidance the day before. So this day I began with a prayer. I raised the bamboo as an offering and said, "Oh Great Spirit, Grandfather, Grandmother guide me and help me transform this dying piece of wood into a magical musical instrument that will touch the hearts of many." I put the bamboo down for a moment and immediately felt a guiding presence. When I picked it up again I knew just what to do. After thirty minutes I had made the clear sound of the flute whistle. In gratitude I did another prayer to honor the east of four directions before drilling my first hole. It came out clean. I enlarged it until the right note emerged. I continued through all the other directions until I had seven unique holes. Eight hours passed this way until my first flute was completed on July 26th 1992. With my new flute in hand I stood out on the patio, faced the setting sun, raised the flute above my head and said, "Thank you Great Spirit for this wonderful gift and in honor of your guidance I name this first flute "Spirit."

In order to honor the guiding presence I'd felt while making my next flutes, "Divine" and "Grace" came forth as the names for them. The voice I'd heard in the canyon, "Now take it and share it with the world," played regularly in my head, so a few days later I invited some friends over to experience my flutes. I played a little on each and welcomed their sincere response. To amplify the flutes and make them echo as they had in Boynton Canyon I used a special effects foot pedal.

When I finally opened my teary eyes after playing the last flute I looked into the eyes of the woman in front of me and noticed that not only she, but all my other friends had tears in their eyes, as well. She embraced the experience and with praise said to me, "Oh Jesse, this is good. Now take it and share it with the world!" Surprised, I quickly responded, "What did you say?!" Amazingly, there it was again! So I said to Spirit, "I got it. I will take it and share it with the world! Please show me the way."

By 1993 I began presenting free flute concerts in a gallery, bookstore and quiet places in town. Later I moved on to resorts where I present now.

MAP: Why do you start and end your concerts with Amazing Grace?

JK: To honor and give back to the Omnipresence. Music and nature relax the body, quiet the mind and inspire. Singing in my island language touches softly on the common and neutral, so for just a moment regardless of religion or ideology, there is no separation from this living and loving Grace. All one.

MAP: Tell me how you met the musician you eventually performed with, John Dumas.

JK: I met John in Boynton Canyon about 1995. I was playing my flute in an ancient ruin high above the trail, which created beautiful resonating echoes. As I was playing I heard someone below thrashing through the brush apparently in a great hurry to get to me. I called out to the person that there was a clear path, but it did not seem to matter.

Although short-winded, John Dumas excitedly introduced himself. He was from the east coast with an educational background in the fine arts, psychology, and study of indigenous cultures and was on a personal quest to experience ancient cliff dwellings. On his visit to Sedona, Boynton Canyon mystically summoned him. Although one hundred ruins have been logged and recorded there, he had traversed almost three miles to the end of the canyon and not seen any. Suddenly, hearing the flute reverberating throughout the canyon, John thought he would at last find one! He just needed to get to the source of the music. He was ecstatic to discover a native ruin behind me! He shared how the music, as it echoed through the canyons, drew him in. Feeling a kindred connection, I gave him my schedule of concerts in town and he came to one. Like a kid in a candy store, he was impressed by anyone who could play and make instruments without having studied music. At the end of the concert I gave him my calling card and offered to teach him the art of flute crafting. I felt guided to share this gift with him. John was amazed and very excited. I spent the next week sharing how to handcraft his own bamboo flute. During this time he had also met another musician, who taught him how to make didgeridoos from dried stalks of aged Century Plants. Later he was able to make beautiful, fine quality, cedar, walnut and pine flutes. He even created a four barreled flute. He called it the "four chambered heart flute." John now lives on Hawaii and I've not seen him since.

MAP: But you performed publicly with him before he left?

JK: Several times. John is a great craftsman, a gifted musician, and a sound healer on multiple instruments. There was also a third musician, ThunderBeat, who completed our band. Together we produced a CD. Because we were three hearts creating music in the moment, we called the recording of the improvisations from our live concert in Sedona, "One Heart."

MAP: So bringing this back to Boynton Canyon, apparently the vortex assisted both you and John in beginning your flute careers.

JK: Absolutely! I've met other musicians who have found their calling in Boynton Canyon. Peter Sterling with his harp is another.

MAP: I believe that many of us have past karmic connections with Boynton Canyon, as well as Mu or Lemuria.

JK: Yes, Boynton Canyon presented me with a vision of myself in Lemuria, similar to your own experience with the temples of Boynton Canyon.

In my vision I saw myself at four years of age as an androgynous being. My golden body was covered in a long white robe with gold embroidered trim. My head was shaved. I was flying through the air in a ship. Not a space ship, but a silent sea-like going vessel with sails. I looked behind me to see my tall mother and father, who were standing confidently. They also had golden skin and wore white robes with the same trim. I held something in my hand, which I could not see, but I knew it was a flute. Somehow the flute had an essential and magical influence on not only the flight of this vessel, but upon all the things around us and within us. I've had a sense of other experiences on Mu, but that is the only actual vision I have had.

MAP: Have you had any UFO experiences in Sedona you would like to share?

JK: There was one about 1998. I was sitting alone on my cabin porch one night facing east towards the right side of Schnebly Hill and the Mogollon Rim. I saw the underside of an object that was composed of three tiers of radiant asterisk-like shapes emitting rays within a pyramid-shape of light, similar in size and brightness to a full Moon. It approached me in complete silence, stillness and serenity over the ridge before effortlessly turning around to follow the same course it had just flown in on. Suddenly there was a big whoosh and the thunderous sound of two Air Force fighter jets with flashing red and green lights in pursuit. They were not able to make a quiet easy turn like the silent luminous ship just had. Their efforts were much wider and noisier as they continued their chase. In spite of all the jet's commotion I was still left in a worry-free state, "at ease."

MAP: Thank you for sharing and best of luck with your music.

Jesse Kalu has shared his flutes with people from all over the world. He currently crafts bamboo flutes by special order and weekly performs in some of Sedona's resorts.

For Jesse's weekly performance schedule please visit: http://www.gatewaytosedona.com/sedona-calendar-of-events/eventdetail/ 9565/-/jesse-kalu-heartfelt-presentations

To email Jesse: kalu@sedona.net.

**The Profile of a Lemurian Guardian behind
Kachina Woman in Boynton Canyon
Photo by Michael Patton**

Peter Sterling

It was just before my 32nd birthday on 7 October in 1992. I had my new harp for a few weeks and could already feel the presence of the angels guiding me as my improvised strumming and plucking turned lovely sounds into distinct melodies. Still, I had a gut feeling that I needed to make a stronger connection and commitment to the Angels, who seemed to be surrounding me more and more frequently with each passing day.* I decided to take a hike with my harp back into the sacred vortex area of Boynton Canyon

It was a crisp fall day in northern Arizona. White, puffy cumulous clouds slowly floated through a bright blue sky. The temperature was perfect for hiking – not too warm and not too cold. I was joined by my new friend, whom I will call Julia, a sweet, brown haired, fairy-like woman whom I had met the week before at the Mount Shasta Ascension celebration. Julia had decided to ride back to Sedona with me from Mount Shasta so that she too could check out the mystical energy of the vortexes.

The two of us hiked for an hour or so back into the heart of the canyon with my magical harp slung over my shoulder. We decided to walk barefoot on the soft, sandy trail so that we could feel the energy of mother Earth rise up through our feet. After a short time, we found a secluded place in the shade of some pine trees where we could sit and enjoy the view of the canyon.

Julia began to play the harp as I lay on my back and watched the clouds float by like big balls of cotton candy. She was a singer and guitarist in her own right and this was her first time playing the harp. At times, she appeared to fall into

*The Angels had been assisting Peter in learning to play the harp.

a trance and allow the harp to work its magic with her; she played so beautifully that we were both astonished. It was like a scene emerging right out of the song "Lucy in the Sky with Diamonds." As I lay there, looking up at the sky, being serenaded by a gorgeous woman playing the harp, I thought to myself, "what more could a guy want?"

All of a sudden, I felt inspired to take my harp up on the ridge overlooking the valley. Climbing some 500 feet above the valley floor, I was able to look down at Julia, who seemed tiny to me from my perch on the cliff. As I surveyed the commanding view that stretched out before me, I began to tune into the angels, who I knew were around me. The feeling of being so blessed by the music that was beginning to come through me in beautiful melodies assured me that this was what I was meant to do. So I wanted to make a statement about that to the universe in someway.

I raised the harp over my head and toward the sky, the angels, and the heavens. I felt my connection to the greater cosmos and my place within it. As I held the harp high, I asked the angels and God that I might be used as a vessel to bring forth God's heavenly music. In that moment, I went beyond merely being in agreement with the Angels request; I was finally ready to dedicate myself in humble service to this mission, which I felt had been preordained in some far gone time.

Lowering the harp, I then sat on the cliff and began to play a song inspired by the power of the moment. I felt a great surge of energy move through my body and spirit as my hands moved on the strings with a power and confidence that I had not known before. My hands trembled on the strings, and my eyes poured out tears of joy. Beads of sweat began to form on my forehead as my body temperature rose in response to the intense and powerful energy surge. "Trust... Surrender...and let go," I heard the angel say to me once again as my hands moved on the strings by themselves. I knew that if I could let go completely, a force would move through me and my hands that would enable me to play on the strings like a seasoned harpist.

One angel in particular [had been] chosen to become my personal harp teacher. Although I never heard or sensed a name, this angel always felt like a feminine energy to me. As I played, she would hover above me and, as it is called in esoteric circles, overshadow me. She would merge with my energy field and send fourth palpable energetic impulses that would somehow be translated through my nervous system to my fingers as they danced by themselves on the strings. As my vibration was lifted to match that of the angel, I would experience the bliss and ecstasy of the higher dimensions.

I often say that this experience was similar to what was portrayed in the movie Ghost. Do you remember the scene when Patrick Swayze's character comes into the body of Whoopi Goldberg so that he can be with his wife, played by Demi

Moore, one last time before walking into the light forever? This is similar to what happened to me. But it was not a human spirit that entered my body; it was the spirit of an angel.

Aligning my vibration with that of a higher dimensional angelic lightbeing required much preparation. That is why I had been guided to do extensive healing work on my body and nervous system. Without that preparation, I could have burned out my electrical system by connecting with such a high-frequency energy and that was something the angels wanted to avoid at all costs.

I have heard many stories of people who have connected with powerful spiritual forces before they were physically, emotionally, and spiritually ready, and they paid a heavy price. I believe that many of the mental institutions in the world have people like this in their care. These unfortunate souls have had a rapid spiritual opening but no support system to help them understand what has happened to them. In many instances, their rantings are merely conversations between them and spirits on the other side of the veil.

After my birthday prayer on the clifftop, things started to move into higher gear. I was told by the angels that they were waiting for me to give my full permission for them to merge at even deeper levels with me that I had up to that point so that we could work in full union as a team. Generally speaking, angels will never override our personal will in order to effect change in our lives; they do not act unless they are given permission. To do otherwise would break a universal law of the sovereignty of personal will.

But there are occasions when the angels will step in without our conscious knowledge – primarily when our lives are threatened by dangerous circumstances beyond our control. Stories and reports abound of angelic intervention when people's lives are endangered – for instance, because of car accidents, physical abuse, near drowning, and other dramatic events.

It is said that everyone of us has at least one guardian angel who watches over us at all times to make sure that we are kept out of harms way. And though the Angels love for us might tempt them to intervene in every unfortunate circumstance, they must restrain themselves. When our karma and soul agreements have created what seems like unfortunate events for our own growth and learning, it is necessary for the angels to step back and watch – though always with tremendous compassion.

Certain events and circumstances may seem cruel and unfair and may even make some people lose faith in God and the inherent goodness of the universe. Sometimes it may be years before we understand why an event occurred that left us or a friend or loved one seriously injured – or worse. But even tragedy and death can have a positive effect on all involved when seen through the lens of the higher self.

We must keep in mind that the Angels perceive from a perspective that allows them to see further along the timeline to discern possible future outcomes and potentials for our soul growth. This is also the view of our own higher selves. We have been designed to link with the higher self so that we can have that broader and wiser viewpoint to guide us along our earth journeys. If and when we make contact with the higher self, or soul, then the angel's job is mostly done, and we can progress more smoothly along the ascending path of enlightenment and soul illumination.

I believe that it will benefit all of us to make conscious contact with our guardian angels, especially during this time of uncertainty on planet earth. To have our angel's guidance and love is a blessing that has come to us from the creator. Your angels are here to protect and assist you in living a magical, inspired, and synchronistic life full of possibilities! Choose to make conscious contact with them, initiate a conversation with them, and watch with amazement as your life begins to take on added richness and depth. A new feeling tone of joy and wonder will permeate your being as Miracles begin to be every day occurrences that continually encourage and inspire everyone around you to live guided by higher spiritual principles.

As Julia and I made our way out of the forest and back to our car, we reflected on the beauty and magic of our day in Boynton Canyon. This ancient canyon, one of Sedona's major vortex sites, holds a special energy that unites earth and sky and allows the spirit to soar while feeling securely anchored to mother earth. It is the energy of this mystical and powerful place that lifted me aloft, allowing me to kiss the sky and bring back the gifts of heaven to share with the people of the world through my harp music. And for this I am grateful!

Excerpted from the book *Hearing the Angels Sing* by Peter Sterling, Light Technology Publishing

*Peter Sterling is an award winning self- taught harpist who began to play after a series of life changing angelic encounters in the canyons of Sedona in the early 1990's. His book **Hearing the Angels Sing** published by Light Technology Publishing chronicles his 20 year journey as one of the angels" harpists, bringing the heavenly harmonics to earth during this time of rapid planetary transformation. www.harpmagic.com*

Lyssa Royal Holt

In 1990, I was living with one other person on a remote 1-acre forest property off of Upper Red Rock Loop Rd in Sedona. There was a 500-ft red rock hill in our back yard. One night, we had an overnight guest. In the middle of the night, we were all awakened by a very eerie, thick blue light that was swirling in our home through the windows. It looked like what is depicted in movies. The light was so thick and blue that it illuminated the inside of the home completely. Stunned (and in a kind of sleepy fog), the three of us went out the back door. We could see that the light was emanating from behind the red rock hill in our back yard. This was a very remote area and we knew there were no homes or even roads in that area. It felt as if time had stopped.

I've seen Northern Lights before, but those lights appear at a distance. They do not engulf you, at least not in my experience. We watched as this strange swirling light engulfed us even more until the entire landscape was glowing blue.

At this point I am very confused about what happened. Despite this stunning display and our interest in UFOs and unexplained phenomena (I was already channeling my ET contacts and had published books), we all decided to go back to bed. We went back to bed and fell asleep while the blue light was still illuminating the land and the inside of our home. The next morning, we barely remembered it - as if it was a distant dream.

I had all but forgotten about this experience until, a few years later, someone who lived in Cottonwood told us about a strange blue light he saw emanating from Sedona. I asked for the location and sure enough, the person saw it coming from the Upper Red Rock Loop Rd area of West Sedona. This is now more than 25 years ago and I have not heard of another experience like this. To this day, I so wish that I had investigated more thoroughly and not succumbed to the typical "contact fog" that compelled us to return to our beds!

Lyssa Royal Holt has been an author, channel, seminar leader and contact researcher since 1985. www.lyssaroyal.net

Devara ThunderBeat

When I was four years old I was taken up in a spaceship while playing in my driveway in upstate NY. As they pulled me up into the craft my mother ran out of the house and tried to catch me and they took her up too. These benevolent star beings have been in contact with me and my mother throughout our whole life.

In the year 2000 I moved to Sedona. One day while driving from the Village of Oak Creek in Sedona I saw a yellow craft fly out from the middle of the red rocks. I grabbed my cell phone and took a picture of it (see color plate).

That evening I was looking up at the stars and noticed a glowing yellow object that was low in the sky. It was in the area I saw the yellow craft earlier that day. I felt it was the same spaceship. I decided to drive closer to it. I parked alone on one of the viewing areas overlooking the red rocks and watched the glowing object in the eastern hemisphere. It was not a star because it was oblong shaped, and it was much larger, and brighter than any stars I had seen. When I looked towards the west, from the light of the moon I could see the red rocks clearly. As I was looking at all the rock formations I suddenly saw a large white glowing light about fifteen feet wide coming out of the mountain near the top of a rock formation. I said to myself, "That cannot be anyone hiking up there it's too steep and extremely dangerous." After watching the light for a few minutes three glowing balls of light also came out of the mountain. Two of the balls of light were green and one was red. They hovered above the white light for a minute and then shot up towards the sky. All three colored balls of light then changed to white. They moved up higher, circled around each other, and then positioned themselves in the sky. They blended in perfectly with the stars. You could not tell the difference between them and the stars. After half an hour, both the yellow glowing object to the east and the white balls of light in the sky did not move. The large white light in the mountain slowly faded out.

Devara ThunderBeat is an International, Multi – Award winning, Musician / Composer, Author, Teacher, Speaker, and a Pioneer in Sound Healing. You can view her new book about her ET and Angel encounters at: www.ETSandAngels.com

340

Shekina Rose

It was late afternoon on 11/11 2013 at Cathedral Rock Vortex in Sedona when the Pleiadians of Peace first made their presence known to myself and one other person. We saw them in their silver cigar-shaped ship on a totally clear blue sky day with not a plane or cloud in sight. (Other times when I saw their ship it was also in a clear sky. It would always vanish quickly into thin air, leaving no question that it was something other than a plane.)

This initial sighting was startling at first. I had never seen a UFO before, and this one was very close as I was high on a mountain top. The ship was moving rather slow and in an unusual way. When I asked who they were I heard telepathically: "We are here for Peace." It took some time before I realized who they were.

After this initial contact, a developing relationship with the Pleiadians of Peace ensued, which created gateways to the higher realms and a re-opening of one of the Stargate Light Portals. This Stargate Light Portal connects Earth to Source.

As a result, downloads of enormous amounts of Ancient Sacred Technologies from the higher realms came through to me for months. I began creating Ancient Sacred Technologies, Stargate Time Travel pieces, Light Frequency Generator Pendants and Copper Crystal Crowns. I saw these designs very clearly as the higher realms would literally open for me. I just knew without question or doubt how to make them, the specific correlations for the movement of energy and how to balance the field of the auric energetic system to the higher realm connections.

Also, at this time a Pleiadian ET woman showed up in my room in the middle of the night. She was standing where I had been making a Blue Ray Crown. She appeared to be very young, maybe 23 years of age, though I somehow knew she was a lot older and wiser. Her skin was very white, her hair platinum blond. She was wearing a long white dress. She then projected a light show of pictures into the air that went very fast, yet the focus kept coming back to one picture in particular. Though I was unsettled, I calmed down a bit after I realized these were the very photos I had taken of myself at the Pleiadian of Peace Light Portal at the Cathedral Rock Vortex. She telepathed to me that the crown I was making was a Pleiadian Blue Ray Crown.

The next day I relayed the story of this extraordinary visitation to Mary Angelico, my dearest friend and the graphic artist who collaborates with me on all my visual activators. She sensed that we needed to use the specific picture highlighted by the Pleiadian women on the Star Gate Language of Light Portal Activator that we were working on. Mary, being extremely intuitive and spiritually gifted, also felt that I needed to get the Language of Light codes for the Activator. Although I had channeled the Language of Light as a Harmonic Vocalist singer of the Ancient Solfeggio Frequencies, now it was time to take a step beyond sound to see if I could obtain the Language of Light codes in visual form.

I found it was not always easy going into the Sedona Vortex Portals alone, as one can get disorientated, especially with the extreme heat of the summer. Still I knew it was time to go into the Light Portal at Cathedral Rock Vortex. I took special paper and a gold pen with me, said my intentions and prayers and poured ice cold water over my head and neck before going into the portal.

I was given to know that the Languages of Light codes that resulted are a vibrational frequency of protection to enter the higher realm to activate more of our Divine DNA resonances. The picture of the Pleadian ship and Language of Light codes transcripts are now embedded in the Star Gate Language of Light Portal Activator.

Culminating at this time, an amazing gift came to me when three Pleiadians unexpectedly came to me at Cathedral Rock Vortex a few days before Easter. They told me that I was one of them. I was so surprised; I said "No, I am from Sirius!" But they proceeded to say that I was from the Galactic Brotherhood. I had to agree that I could feel a kinship with them. They asked me to hold out my hand. They said they had a gift for me. As soon as I did a beautiful egg of shimmering Light appeared in my hand. I instinctively brought it to my heart. As I did an amazing Light flooded through my body and I felt incredible Divinity and Peace.

The Pleiadians then showed me a Stargate Pendant to make with three stones and copper that would symbolize our sacred connection in the Galactic Brotherhood. I was able to find the perfect round clear crystal and after it was created, the Pleaidians came that night and encoded it with Light. It was amazing to see these Light Encodements like Morse Codes of Light coming from the other dimensions to the Stargate Pendant.

**Shekina moving into the Light Portal
at Cathedral Rock**

Shekina immersed in the Light Portal

Pleiadean Stargate Pendant

Shekina's Mother Mary Visitations in Sedona

The first Mother Mary visitation occurred on Christmas Eve 2011, when a friend and I sat down to mediate together on the Christ Spirit before going to a festival party. We started by listening to a new song called "Invocation" by Mary Angelico. This song was given to Mary from Mother Mary to help in invoking the Divine Feminine energies. I had never had a connection to Mother Mary, though when she appeared simultaneously to me and my friend we found ourselves transported and transfigured in Holy Heart Bliss for two hours. We did not speak or move. After two hours Mother Mary left and all we could do was open our bright and tear-filled eyes and look at each other. Not knowing if the other had experienced the same thing, we both said at the exact same moment- "MOTHER MARY!"

This phenomenal experience occurred for months as my friend and I continued to meet together, opening ourselves for Mother Mary to come to us. And she did! She came with the Rose Ray and brought amazing healing, insights, blessings for our whole bodies and being. We were immersed in profound heart joy communion with Mother Mary and the Rose Ray. To spread her Divine Love, I continued to place the Rose Ray Miracle Water at the Mother Mary altars to purify the Earth and heart of humanity at the Cathedral Rock Vortex.

These experiences, I now understand, unfolded to anchor the Rose Ray of the Sacred Heart through the Holy Spirit of Shekinah. This is to bring the Mother of the World's heart to transform the sadness of human suffering and awaken the essence of God in human form within the Angelic Human DNA and Christ embodiment.

On one of the visits to the Mother Mary altar at the Cathedral Rock Vortex she asked for pictures to be taken. These would be transmissions and testaments of the Rose Ray Heart. A sacred gathering took place in March at Cathedral Rock and the Sedona Creative Life Center, drawing people from all over the US and around the globe that fully anchored the Rose Ray of Creation back on the planet. The Mother Mary Rose Activator was created from images of her light apparitions and appearances.

Shekina Rose, a Blue Ray Starseed, is a Priestess of Light, Messenger of Mother Goddess SHEKINAH, Channel of the Blue Ray Transmissions, and is the Language of Light Harmonic Vocalist for the Sedona Cosmic Choir and Creator of Stargate Pendants and Wands. She sings, tones, chants and speaks in the 528 Hz Ancient Solfeggio Frequencies in the Language of Light, the Language of the Angels that activate the Divine Original Blueprint and Travel Stargates. www.shekinaspeaks.com

Desert Eyes
by Lane Badger

Dusk in the high desert. The wind hushed in the fading light, a moment paused in reverence. I closed my eyes and whispered a prayer to the Sun Spirit, the flowing waters of Oak Creek and the verdant green valley below. Surrounded by rock towers in ombré shades of red; I was perched atop Cathedral Rock, near the great limestone temple of old. Its name forgotten; its power not.

Everything slowed into that perfect balance between worlds of light and dark—the twilight. Thought flickered in and out. There was just breath to guide me on a silent journey— peacefully underway—until the flutter of wings sent quivers of air touching my skin. The 'bird tribe' was making a final patrol; beautiful beings from a world past, within a parallel existence, active in this ancient portal where interweaves of time and space effortlessly fade in and out. Sacred space.

The wind whipped up a bit as the light became an aurum glow, stretching itself across the horizon of the western front.

The perfect moment—again—embracing me, the aeon stretched out before me, drawing me deeper and further into holy union.

Suddenly, I felt watched—watched! Presence intruded into my reverie. Pulling myself from that distant place, I opened my eyes in a start.

Big eyes were looking at me from all sides of the rock cliffs. Rock eyes, shaped like ellipsoids in stone. Large, alive, with the fierce intensity of the Rock people!

Oh no! What next, I wondered?

Then I softened into the warm perfection of the Creation; the rock eyes receded into their timelessness, and I treaded a careful path down the mountain trail in the afterglow.

Lane Badger is a publisher, editor and journalist and a passionate advocate of sacred sites around the world. She is director of Cities of Light Media and Next in the West Magazine in Sedona, Arizona.

At the Court of the King
by Kurt Bagley

I have been going to the Court of the King in Boynton Canyon for years with my friend and colleague, Mark Amaru Pinkham, who introduced me to the place. Beginning with my first trip there I have enjoyed the gift of being able to see ancient architecture superimposed upon the canyon's natural red rock formations. In the Court I have found my interdimensional sight vivified and enhanced. Some of the more accessible, grounded visions that I and others have witnessed include: the inter-dimensional architecture of the Court that is still active and very close to the physical red-rock structures of the Court; multidimensional peacocks that are alive and moving in the canyon; and other peacocks embedded in the stone as canyon guardians. Also looming about have been large guardian, God-like temple statues of various shapes and sizes watching and protecting the sacred energies of the canyon, as well as Sphinxes and pyramids and ornately carved obelisks. In addition to the visionary openings granted me, the greatest experiences I've had at the Court have been life-changing Gnostic revelations, such as the awareness of being one with the Peacock Angel. At one time I became an open eye amongst the many eyes in the Peacock Angel's tail. At another time there was an ineffable feeling in my heart. It was something similar to a growing, joyful optimism, but deeper. There was a feeling of loving gentleness for everyone and everything. This opening of my heart chakra and connecting with the canyon further expanded my awareness to visions and experiences too numerous to elucidate. These are just the tip of what I and others have perceived in the Boynton Canyon vortex and its Court of the King in Sedona. I would encourage anyone who has a sincere and open heart to embark on a holy vision-quest to this sacred place. They will perceive similar interdimensional sights (and insights), as well as have their own special individualized experiences.

Kurt Bagley is a knight of the The International Order of Gnostic Templars, whose world headquarters is in Sedona.

Footnotes

Chapter 1

1. *Echoes of Sedona Past* 1990 Light Technology Publishing, Sedona, AZ
2. Ibid
3. *SEDONA VORTEX GUIDE BOOK* 1991 Light Technology Publishing, Sedona,
4. Ibid
5. Ibid

Chapter 2

1. *Past Lives, Future Loves* Dick Sutphen 1978 Pocket Books, NYC
2. *EDGAR CAYCE ON ATLANTIS* Edgar Evans Cayce 1968 Warner Books NYC
3. Ibid
4. *SECRET PLACES OF THE LION* George Hunt Williamson 1996 Destiny Books, Rochester, Vermont
5. *THE ALIEN TIDE* Tom Dongo 1990 Hummingbird Publishing Sedona AZ
6. *Past Lives, Future Loves* Dick Sutphen 1978 Pocket Books, NYC
7. *SEDONA PSYCHIC ENERGY VORTEXES* Dick Sutphen 1985 Valley of the Sun Publishing Malibu, CA
8. *SEDONA VORTEX GUIDE BOOK* 1991 Light Technology Publishing, Sedona, AZ
9. Ibid
10. *THE LOST CONTINENT OF MU* James Churchward 1987 BE Books, Albuquerque, NM
11. Ibid
12. Ibid
13. *EDEN IN THE EAST* Stephen Oppenheimer 1999 Phoenix, a division of Orion Books Ltd, London
14. *SEDONA, POWER SPOT, VORTEX, AND MEDICINE WHEEL GUIDE.* Richard Dannelley 1992 Vortex Society
15. *SEDONA: SACRED EARTH* Nicholas R Mann 1989 Zivah Publishers Prescott, AZ
16. *GENISIS: The First Book of Revelations* David Wood 1985 The Baton Press, UK

Chapter 3

1. *The Orion Zone: Ancient Star Cities of the American Southwest* Gary David 2006 Adventures Unlimited Press Kempton, IL

2. *Jesus: Last of the Pharaohs*, Ralph Ellis 1999 Edfu Books, Dorset, UK

Chapter 4
1. *BEASTS, MEN AND GODS* Ferdinand Ossendowski 2004 1st World - Literary Society Fairfield, IO
2. *DARKNESS OVER TIBET* T.Illion 1997 Adventures Unlimited Press Kempton, Illinois
3. *ShaMBhala* Nicholas Roerich 1985 Nicholas Roerich Museum NYC
4. *Ponder on This* Alice A. Bailey 1971 Lucis Publishing Co. NYC
5. *PUEBLO GODS AND MYTHS* Hamilton A. Tyler 1964 University of Oklahoma Press
6. Ibid
7. Ibid
8. *The Kivas of Heaven: Ancient Hopi Starlore* Gary A David 2002 Adventures Unlimited Press Kempton, IL
9. *Kataragama: The Mystery Shrine* Patrick Harrigan 1998 Institute of Asian Studies, Chinnai, India
10. Ibid

Chapter 5
1. *The Fourth World of the Hopis* Harold Courlander 1971 University of New Mexico Press, Albuquerque, NM
2. *The Orion Zone: Ancient Star Cities of the American Southwest* Gary David 2006 Adventures Unlimited Press Kempton, IL
3. . Brinton's "Myths of the New World," p. 247.
4. *AMERICAN INDIAN MYTHS & MYSTERIES* Vincent H. Gaddis 1977 Indian Head Books NYC
5. Ibid

Chapter 6
1. *BOOK OF THE HOPI* Frank Waters 1977 Penguin Books NYC
2. Interview with Clifford Mahooty. See Chapter 11
3. *STAR ANCESTORS* Nancy Red Star 2000 Destiny Books Rochester, VT
4. *Sipapuni: Space, Time, Spirit and Ceremonial Architecture in Indigenous America* Allan MacGillvray 2005 AuthorHouse
5. *The Traditions of the Hopi* H.R. Voth 1905
6. *BOOK OF THE HOPI* Frank Waters 1977 Penguin Books NYC
7. *The Traditions of the Hopi,* H.R. Voth 1905

8. *The Fourth World of the Hopis* Harold Courlander 1971 University of New Mexico Albuquerque, NM

9. *BOOK OF THE HOPI* Frank Waters 1977 Penguin Books NYC
10. Ibid
11. *PUEBLO GODS AND MYTHS* Hamilton A. Tyler 1964 University of Oklahoma Press
12. *THE DESTRUCTION OF PALATKWAPI* Field Columbia Museum of Natural History Chicago 1905

Chapter 8
1. *SEDONA, POWER SPOT, VORTEX, AND MEDICINE WHEEL GUIDE.* Richard Dannelley 1992 Vortex Society

Chapter 9
1. *PUEBLO GODS AND MYTHS* Hamilton A. Tyler 1964 University of Oklahoma Press
2. *BOOK OF THE HOPI* Frank Waters 1977 Penguin Books NYC
3. Ibid
4. *BEASTS, MEN AND GODS* Ferdinand Ossendowski 2004 1st World - Literary Society Fairfield, IO

Chapter 10
1. *EDEN IN THE EAST* Stephen Oppenheimer 1999 Phoenix, a division of Orion Books Ltd, London

Chapter 11
1. *BOOK OF THE HOPI* Frank Waters 1977 Penguin Books NYC
2. *BEASTS, MEN AND GODS* Ferdinand Ossendowski 2004 1st World - Literary Society Fairfield, IO
3. *The Kingdom of Agartha: A Journey into the Hollow Earth* Marquis Alexandre Saint-Yves 2008 Inner Traditions 1st US Edition

The Author

Mark Amaru Pinkham is an author, mystic and futurist. He lives in Sedona, Arizona with his wife, Andrea, where he serves as Grand Prior of *The International Order of Gnostic Templars* and Commander of *The Djedhi Templar Corps*. As Co-Founder of *Sacred Sites Journeys*, Mark leads vortex tours around Palatkwapi (Sedona) and to the other power spots and temples throughout the world. Mark is the Director of *The Seven Rays of Healing School,* and an Astrologer of both the Western and Vedic (Hindu) Systems. Please visit www.GnosticTemplars.org to learn more.

Mark also serves on the Advisory Council of *Global Genius Trust*, an organization dedicated to developing alternative technologies and designing cities of the future that are in complete harmony with the Earth. www.GGTrust.com.

The Djedhi Templar Corps trains spiritual warriors to meet all their challenges in life. They become adept at wielding both the inner and outer weapons they need to meet any encounter on their path.

The Djedhi Templar Corps is a revival of the Djedhi Knights of Egypt, which the Jedi Knights of Star Wars are based upon. Like a mythical Jedi Knight, when a person becomes a Djedhi Knight he or she is a Master of the Force and a Gnostic Mystic whose answers come intuitively from within.

Djedhi Templar Training occurs in Sedona near the Court of the King and in other countries worldwide. All ages and both sexes are welcome. Please visit our website for further information and our upcoming schedule.

www.djedhitemplarcorps.wix.com/djedhitemplarcorps

The International Order of Gnostic Templars

A Johannite Mystery School
Dedicated to the Revival of Gnostic Wisdom &
the Goddess Tradition of the Original Knight Templars

The International Order of Gnostic Templars (IOGT) is a diverse group of men and women who are committed to assisting in the revival of both the Goddess Tradition (The Path of the Divine Feminine) and the Gnostic Path of knowing one's inner self fully through the development of Gnostic Wisdom.

The male and female members of the IOGT are Johannite Gnostics who follow the Gnostic Path once adhered to by the orignal Johannite Knights Templar. This path is descended from John the Baptist, Jesus, Mary Magdalene, John the Apostle and the grandmasters of the Knights Templar. Levels include Squire, Lady in Waiting, Knight and Lady Knight.

www.GnosticTemplars.org

351

Learn the Most Ancient Mysteries!

Become a Knight of Tawsi Melek!

The most ancient mysteries on Earth arrived on our planet with Tawsi Melek, the Peacock Angel, who is also known as Sanat Kumara by the Hindus and Masau'u by the Hopis. This Star Person became the King of the World and founded the Gnostic-Alchemical Path that leads to Self-Knowledge and full enlightenment. His precious wisdom is taught in Sedona within *The Most Ancient Order of the Peacock Angel.* To learn more, visit www.YezidiTruth.org.

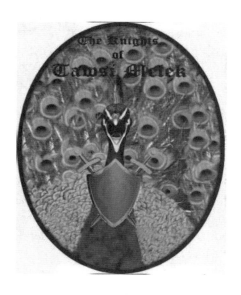

Since 1994...Spiritual Pilgrimages to the World's Sacred Sites

Egypt, England, France, Greece, Ireland, Malta, Peru, Scotland, & Turkey
with
Andrea Mikana-Pinkham & Mark Amaru Pinkham
Shamanic Practitioners, Researchers & Teachers of the Ancient Mysteries, the Goddess Tradition & Ancient Megalithic History

**Tours of Palatkwapi and the Sedona Grid
with Mark Amaru Pinkham
author of *Sedona: City of the Star People***

**www.SacredSitesJourneys.com
info@SacredSitesJourneys.com
888 501-3853 (Toll Free in the US & Canada)
928 284-2384**

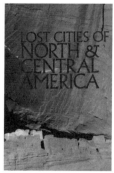

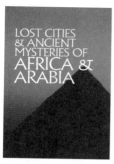

LOST CITIES & ANCIENT MYSTERIES OF AFRICA & ARABIA
by David Hatcher Childress

Childress continues his world-wide quest for lost cities and ancient mysteries. Join him as he discovers forbidden cities in the Empty Quarter of Arabia; "Atlantean" ruins in Egypt and the Kalahari desert; a mysterious, ancient empire in the Sahara; and more. This is the tale of an extraordinary life on the road: across war-torn countries, Childress searches for King Solomon's Mines, living dinosaurs, the Ark of the Covenant and the solutions to some of the fantastic mysteries of the past.

423 PAGES. 6x9 PAPERBACK. ILLUSTRATED. $14.95. CODE: AFA

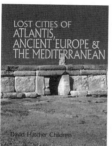

LOST CITIES OF ATLANTIS, ANCIENT EUROPE & THE MEDITERRANEAN
by David Hatcher Childress

Childress takes the reader in search of sunken cities in the Mediterranean; across the Atlas Mountains in search of Atlantean ruins; to remote islands in search of megalithic ruins; to meet living legends and secret societies. From Ireland to Turkey, Morocco to Eastern Europe, and around the remote islands of the Mediterranean and Atlantic, Childress takes the reader on an astonishing quest for mankind's past. Ancient technology, cataclysms, megalithic construction, lost civilizations and devastating wars of the past are all explored in this book.

524 PAGES. 6x9 PAPERBACK. ILLUSTRATED. $16.95. CODE: MED

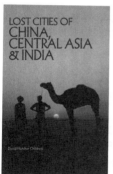

LOST CITIES OF CHINA, CENTRAL ASIA & INDIA
by David Hatcher Childress

Like a real life "Indiana Jones," maverick archaeologist David Childress takes the reader on an incredible adventure across some of the world's oldest and most remote countries in search of lost cities and ancient mysteries. Discover ancient cities in the Gobi Desert; hear fantastic tales of lost continents, vanished civilizations and secret societies bent on ruling the world; visit forgotten monasteries in forbidding snow-capped mountains with strange tunnels to mysterious subterranean cities! A unique combination of far-out exploration and practical travel advice, it will astound and delight the experienced traveler or the armchair voyager.

429 PAGES. 6x9 PAPERBACK. ILLUSTRATED. FOOTNOTES & BIBLIOGRAPHY. $14.95. CODE: CHI

LOST CITIES OF ANCIENT LEMURIA & THE PACIFIC
by David Hatcher Childress

Was there once a continent in the Pacific? Called Lemuria or Pacifica by geologists, Mu or Pan by the mystics, there is now ample mythological, geological and archaeological evidence to "prove" that an advanced and ancient civilization once lived in the central Pacific. Maverick archaeologist and explorer David Hatcher Childress combs the Indian Ocean, Australia and the Pacific in search of the surprising truth about mankind's past. Contains photos of the underwater city on Pohnpei; explanations on how the statues were levitated around Easter Island in a clockwise vortex movement; tales of disappearing islands; Egyptians in Australia; and more.

379 PAGES. 6x9 PAPERBACK. ILLUSTRATED. FOOTNOTES & BIBLIOGRAPHY. $14.95. CODE: LEM

TECHNOLOGY OF THE GODS
The Incredible Sciences of the Ancients
by David Hatcher Childress

Childress looks at the technology that was allegedly used in Atlantis and the theory that the Great Pyramid of Egypt was originally a gigantic power station. He examines tales of ancient flight and the technology that it involved; how the ancients used electricity; megalithic building techniques; the use of crystal lenses and the fire from the gods; evidence of various high tech weapons in the past, including atomic weapons; ancient metallurgy and heavy machinery; the role of modern inventors such as Nikola Tesla in bringing ancient technology back into modern use; impossible artifacts; and more.
356 PAGES. 6x9 PAPERBACK. ILLUSTRATED. BIBLIOGRAPHY. $16.95. CODE: TGOD

PIRATES & THE LOST TEMPLAR FLEET
The Secret Naval War Between the Templars & the Vatican
by David Hatcher Childress

Childress takes us into the fascinating world of maverick sea captains who were Knights Templar (and later Scottish Rite Free Masons) who battled the ships that sailed for the Pope. The lost Templar fleet was originally based at La Rochelle in southern France, but fled to the deep fiords of Scotland upon the dissolution of the Order by King Phillip. This banned fleet of ships was later commanded by the St. Clair family of Rosslyn Chapel (birthplace of Free Masonry). St. Clair and his Templars made a voyage to Canada in the year 1298 AD, nearly 100 years before Columbus! Later, this fleet of ships and new ones to come, flew the Skull and Crossbones, the symbol of the Knights Templar.
320 PAGES. 6x9 PAPERBACK. ILLUSTRATED. BIBLIOGRAPHY. $16.95. CODE: PLTF

THE HISTORY OF THE KNIGHTS TEMPLARS
by Charles G. Addison, introduction by David Hatcher Childress

Chapters on the origin of the Templars, their popularity in Europe and their rivalry with the Knights of St. John, later to be known as the Knights of Malta. Detailed information on the activities of the Templars in the Holy Land, and the 1312 AD suppression of the Templars in France and other countries, which culminated in the execution of Jacques de Molay and the continuation of the Knights Templars in England and Scotland; the formation of the society of Knights Templars in London; and the rebuilding of the Temple in 1816. Plus a lengthy intro about the lost Templar fleet and its North American sea routes.
395 PAGES. 6x9 PAPERBACK. ILLUSTRATED. $16.95. CODE: HKT

OTTO RAHN AND THE QUEST FOR THE HOLY GRAIL
The Amazing Life of the Real "Indiana Jones"
by Nigel Graddon

Otto Rahn led a life of incredible adventure in southern France in the early 1930s. The Hessian language scholar is said to have found runic Grail tablets in the Pyrenean grottoes, and decoded hidden messages within the medieval Grail masterwork *Parsifal*. The fabulous artifacts identified by Rahn were believed by Himmler to include the Grail Cup, the Spear of Destiny, the Tablets of Moses, the Ark of the Covenant, the Sword and Harp of David, the Sacred Candelabra and the Golden Urn of Manna. Some believe that Rahn was a Nazi guru who wielded immense influence on his elders and "betters" within the Hitler regime, persuading them that the Grail was the Sacred Book of the Aryans, which, once obtained, would justify their extreme political theories and revivify the ancient Germanic myths. But things are never as they seem, and as new facts emerge about Otto Rahn a far more extraordinary story unfolds.
450 pages. 6x9 Paperback. Illustrated. Appendix. Index. $18.95. Code: ORQG

GUARDIANS OF THE HOLY GRAIL
by Mark Amaru Pinkham
This book presents this extremely ancient Holy Grail lineage from Asia and how the Knights Templar were initiated into it. It also reveals how the ancient Asian wisdom regarding the Holy Grail became the foundation for the Holy Grail legends of the west while also serving as the bedrock of the European Secret Societies, which included the Freemasons, Rosicrucians, and the Illuminati. Also: The Fisher Kings; The Middle Eastern mystery schools, such as the Assassins and Yezidhi; The ancient Holy Grail lineage from Sri Lanka and the Templar Knights' initiation into it; The head of John the Baptist and its importance to the Templars; The secret Templar initiation with grotesque Baphomet, the infamous Head of Wisdom; more.
248 PAGES. 6x9 PAPERBACK. ILLUSTRATED. $16.95. CODE: GOHG

THE CRYSTAL SKULLS
Astonishing Portals to Man's Past
by David Hatcher Childress and Stephen S. Mehler
Childress introduces the technology and lore of crystals, and then plunges into the turbulent times of the Mexican Revolution form the backdrop for the rollicking adventures of Ambrose Bierce, the renowned journalist who went missing in the jungles in 1913, and F.A. Mitchell-Hedges, the notorious adventurer who emerged from the jungles with the most famous of the crystal skulls. Mehler shares his extensive knowledge of and experience with crystal skulls. Having been involved in the field since the 1980s, he has personally examined many of the most influential skulls, and has worked with the leaders in crystal skull research, including the inimitable Nick Nocerino, who developed a meticulous methodology for the purpose of examining the skulls.
294 pages. 6x9 Paperback. Illustrated. Bibliography. $18.95. Code: CRSK

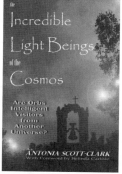

THE INCREDIBLE LIGHT BEINGS OF THE COSMOS
Are Orbs Intelligent Light Beings from the Cosmos?
by Antonia Scott-Clark
Scott-Clark has experienced orbs for many years, but started photographing them in earnest in the year 2000 when the "Light Beings" entered her life. She took these very seriously and set about privately researching orb occurrences. The incredible results of her findings are presented here, along with many of her spectacular photographs. With her friend, GoGos lead singer Belinda Carlisle, Antonia tells of her many adventures with orbs. Find the answers to questions such as: Can you see orbs with the naked eye?; Are orbs intelligent?; What are the Black Villages?; What is the connection between orbs and crop circles? Antonia gives detailed instruction on how to photograph orbs, and how to communicate with these Light Beings of the Cosmos.
334 pages. 6x9 Paperback. Illustrated. References. $19.95. Code: ILBC

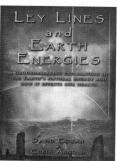

LEY LINE & EARTH ENERGIES
An Extraordinary Journey into the Earth's Natural Energy System
by David Cowan & Chris Arnold
The mysterious standing stones, burial grounds and stone circles that lace Europe, the British Isles and other areas have intrigued scientists, writers, artists and travellers through the centuries. How do ley lines work? How did our ancestors use Earth energy to map their sacred sites and burial grounds? How do ghosts and poltergeists interact with Earth energy? How can Earth spirals and black spots affect our health? This exploration shows how natural forces affect our behavior, how they can be used to enhance our health and well being.
368 PAGES. 6x9 PAPERBACK. ILLUSTRATED. $18.95. CODE: LLEE

ORDER FORM

10% Discount When You Order 3 or More Items!

One Adventure Place
P.O. Box 74
Kempton, Illinois 60946
United States of America
Tel.: 815-253-6390 • Fax: 815-253-6300
Email: auphq@frontiernet.net
http://www.adventuresunlimitedpress.com

ORDERING INSTRUCTIONS

✓ Remit by USD$ Check, Money Order or Credit Card
✓ Visa, Master Card, Discover & AmEx Accepted
✓ Paypal Payments Can Be Made To:
    info@wexclub.com
✓ Prices May Change Without Notice
✓ 10% Discount for 3 or More Items

SHIPPING CHARGES

United States

✓ Postal Book Rate { $4.50 First Item
                     50¢ Each Additional Item
✓ POSTAL BOOK RATE Cannot Be Tracked!
    Not responsible for non-delivery.
✓ Priority Mail { $6.00 First Item
                  $2.00 Each Additional Item
✓ UPS { $7.00 First Item
        $1.50 Each Additional Item
    NOTE: UPS Delivery Available to Mainland USA Only

Canada

✓ Postal Air Mail { $15.00 First Item
                    $3.00 Each Additional Item
✓ Personal Checks or Bank Drafts MUST BE
    US$ and Drawn on a US Bank
✓ Canadian Postal Money Orders OK
✓ Payment MUST BE US$

All Other Countries

✓ Sorry, No Surface Delivery!
✓ Postal Air Mail { $19.00 First Item
                    $7.00 Each Additional Item
✓ Checks and Money Orders MUST BE US$
    and Drawn on a US Bank or branch.
✓ Paypal Payments Can Be Made in US$ To:
    info@wexclub.com

SPECIAL NOTES

✓ RETAILERS: Standard Discounts Available
✓ BACKORDERS: We Backorder all Out-of-
    Stock Items Unless Otherwise Requested
✓ PRO FORMA INVOICES: Available on Request
✓ DVD Return Policy: Replace defective DVDs only
ORDER ONLINE AT: www.adventuresunlimitedpress.com

10% Discount When You Order 3 or More Items!

Please check: ✓

☐ This is my first order   ☐ I have ordered before

Name			
Address			
City			
State/Province		Postal Code	
Country			
Phone: Day		Evening	
Fax		Email	

Item Code	Item Description	Qty	Total

Please check: ✓

☐ Postal-Surface
☐ Postal-Air Mail (Priority in USA)
☐ UPS (Mainland USA only)

Subtotal ▶	
Less Discount-10% for 3 or more items ▶	
Balance ▶	
Illinois Residents 6.25% Sales Tax ▶	
Previous Credit ▶	
Shipping ▶	
Total (check/MO in USD$ only) ▶	

☐ Visa/MasterCard/Discover/American Express

Card Number:

Expiration Date: Security Code:

✓ SEND A CATALOG TO A FRIEND: